# CHINESE
# COMMUNITY
# LEADERSHIP
## Case Study of Victoria in Canada

# CHINESE COMMUNITY LEADERSHIP

## Case Study of Victoria in Canada

## David Chuenyan Lai
University of Victoria, Canada

**World Scientific**

NEW JERSEY · LONDON · SINGAPORE · BEIJING · SHANGHAI · HONG KONG · TAIPEI · CHENNAI

*Published by*

World Scientific Publishing Co. Pte. Ltd.

5 Toh Tuck Link, Singapore 596224

*USA office:* 27 Warren Street, Suite 401-402, Hackensack, NJ 07601

*UK office:* 57 Shelton Street, Covent Garden, London WC2H 9HE

**British Library Cataloguing-in-Publication Data**
A catalogue record for this book is available from the British Library.

ISBN-13 978-981-4295-17-8
ISBN-10 981-4295-17-5

Printed in Singapore by World Scientific Printers.

# 唐人街權力核心

## 域多利中華會館之今昔

### 黎全恩

 **World Scientific**

NEW JERSEY · LONDON · SINGAPORE · BEIJING · SHANGHAI · HONG KONG · TAIPEI · CHENNAI

To Roberta Manyuk, my beloved wife,

For her understanding, encouragement and assistance

**Dr. David Chuenyan Lai** received his B.A (First Class Hons.) and M.A. in Geography at University of Hong Kong, and Ph.D. in Geography at London School of Economics and Political Science, University of London. He has taught at the University of Hong Kong for five years and University of Victoria, Canada, for 35 years. After his retirement in 2003, he was named Professor Emeritus of Geography, and appointed as a Research Affiliate at the Centre of Aging, and Adjunct Professor of Department of Pacific and Asian Studies.

In Canada, Dr. Lai's research interests concentrated on Urban Development of Chinatowns and History of Chinese Canadians. Above half of his 300 publications were related to these two areas. Dr. Lai has surveyed over 30 Chinatowns across North America and has been a honorary consultant to the Chinatown gateway projects of Victoria, Edmonton, Vancouver, Toronto, Ottawa, and Portland. He has received 30 awards in recognition of his scholarship and community service. Notable academic awards are *Applied Geography Citation Award* by Association of American Geography; *Award of Merit* by American Association for State and Local History, *Award of Merit* by Education Foundation of Chinese Canadian Professionals (Ontario), and *Legacy Award for Excellence in Teaching* by University of Victoria Alumni. Significant non-academic awards are *Member of the Order of Canada* by Government of Canada, *Honorary Citizen* by City of Victoria, *Gabrielle Legar Award* by Heritage Canada Foundation, and *Heritage Award* by British Columbia Government.

# Contents

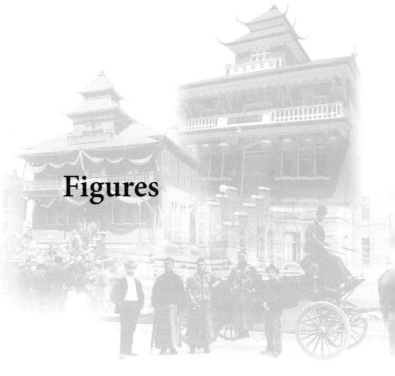

# Figures

# Tables

# Plates

## Credits

# Preface

# Preface

I came to Canada from Hong Kong as a landed immigrant in the summer of 1968. By chance I came across Alan Phillips' article "The Criminal Society that Dominates the Chinese in Canada," published on 7 April 1962 in *Maclean's*, a popular Canadian magazine. Phillips wrote that

> Canada's Chinese are controlled by a group which by our standards is criminal ... Chinatown is not merely a tourist trap baited with Canton's exotic food. It's a genuine fragment of pre-Communist China, a China that will never be again. Behind the bamboo screen of our Chinese ghettos, behind the bland closed faces and the incomprehensible language, the clannish culture of ancient China persist ... They (the Chinese) have their own civil service, foreign office, spies, and axes and, most important, their own law ... They pay lip service to our government but it is their own they obey, their local Chinese government, the Chinese Benevolent Association (CBA)...The law of the CBA takes precedence over Canada's courts ... The power of CBA spokesmen is well known to police ... They (the CBA leaders) subvert our legal system... bribe our politicians. The CBA will continue its underground war against the government.

This article was the first piece I read about Chinatowns and Chinese Benevolent Associations (CBAs). I soon discovered that what I experienced in Chinatowns and CBAs was different from what had been portrayed by

Phillips and other writers, especially the journalists of the late nineteenth and early twentieth centuries. Western society did not understand how CBAs were structured and operated and so judged them inaccurately. Most newspaper reports about the Chinese communities and Chinatowns were either biased or distorted. In many cases, there was no truth in reports about how CBAs functioned. That might partly have been due to racial prejudice and partly misunderstanding or ignorance about Chinese culture and society in Canada. Because of their reticence, Chinatowns and their institutions were vaguely known or unknown not only to Westerners in the past but also to post-1960s Chinese immigrants. For example, many Hong Kong and Taiwan immigrants are still bewildered by Chinatowns and their organizations. Because of this situation, I wanted to rewrite the history of Chinatowns from an impartial perspective, dispel myths about them, and integrate them into the urban fabric of Canadian cities. To achieve these objectives, pure academic research seemed insufficient because insights into the inner dynamic of a Chinatown cannot be gained without active participation in its activities. Hence the seeds of my involvement in community work and research into Chinatown organizations and activities were sown three years after I landed in Victoria.

During the twenty years since my arrival, I have intermittently surveyed more than thirty Chinatowns across North America and interviewed many Chinese community leaders. My laborious study of Canadian Chinatowns resulted in the publication of *Chinatowns: Towns within Cities in Canada* in 1988 and *The Forbidden City within Victoria: Myth, Symbol and Streetscape of Canada's Earliest Chinatown* in 1991. Both volumes emphasize the origins, functions, townscapes, internal structures, and urban problems of Canadian Chinatowns at different stages of development. The present book complements the previous publications. It presents in-depth research on the CBA in the City of Victoria as a case study of the Chinese community leadership in Chinatown, and the operation of a Chinatown government within a municipal government in Canada. Readers should not be misled by the title of the book. It not only examines the evolution of a Chinese association leadership in a Canadian Chinatown but also reflects the history of the socio-economic and political activities of Chinese in Canada before the turn of the twentieth century.

In the past, a CBA in a Chinatown was an overall organization of Chinese social and economic associations. It was at the top of the Chinatown power structure and exercised power over its Chinese residents; the president was occasionally nicknamed the "mayor of Chinatown." Before the 1950s, city and provincial governments had little or no interest in what was going on inside Chinatown, and what the CBA was doing so long as the decision of this "Chinatown government" did not affect the city and the community. Hence, the CBA was virtually an *imperium in imperia*. In some Chinatowns today, the CBA still represents the Chinese community. Knowledge of its organization, functions, and leadership patterns is essential to the study of the Chinatown power structure. Such a study will not only help municipal governments understand Chinatown problems, but also will help town planners adopt appropriate approaches to community planning.

The CBA in Victoria, established in 1884, is called the Chinese Consolidated Benevolent Association (CCBA). I chose it for a detailed study for five reasons. First, CCBA was an official voice for all Chinese across Canada for twenty-five years (1884–1909) before the Chinese Consulate-General was established in Ottawa in 1909. A study of the work of CCBA reflects the early history of Chinese in Canada.

Second, CCBA is the only CBA in Canada that preserves records of its constitutions, routine meetings, circulars, notices, donation receipts, correspondences, newspaper clippings, posters, old photographs, and a great variety of other historical documents. In September 1970, I discovered cardboard boxes of these archival materials in the association's unheated and dusty basement. I was permitted by Sam Lum, CCBA President, to browse through the materials. Some go back to the 1880s. Indeed, no other CBAs in Canada has maintained their vitality and kept records of its work for more than a century as has Victoria's CCBA. The archival materials are indispensable in the study of the association's development and the early history of Chinese in Canada. To do this work, I received a grant from the Social Science Research Centre of the University of Victoria from 1970 to 1972, and was given permission by Augustine Low, CCBA President in 1971, to do a preliminary catalogue of the archival materials. Study of CCBA archives will not only lead to an insight into the operation of Victoria's CCBA but also lead to the discovery of many events in other Chinatowns which have been unknown to the public. This book taps a rich vein of data in a selection of hitherto unpublished records held by CCBA. It includes, for the first time, a pristine reproduction of the most important documents from the association's archives. I have selected some important documents and translated the text into English. I vacillated between a word-by-word translation and the translation of only the main idea of the text. I decided on the latter.

Third, Augustine Low invited me in 1972 to be an Honorary Advisor of CCBA and assist the association in looking after the archives and organizing the transfer of them to the university library for preservation. Most are preserved in the library of the University of Victoria; some have been digitized for public use. As CCBA's Honorary Advisor, I am trusted as an insider. I attend its meetings and participate in discussion on important issues, and can plough through documents in the association's archives. Historical research into CCBA's minutes and other documents has caused a substantial revision about its internal structure, and the image of reticence and appeasement that had generally been accepted by Western society. CCBA's activities and personalities still echo in the present in haunting ways. I am a good friend of many CCBA directors who represent various Chinese social and economic associations. With their help, I have been able to study their archives and find additional information on Chinatown's leadership pattern and power structure.

Fourth, in terms of the size of the Chinese population and its businesses, Victoria's Chinatown was unequivocally the largest in Canada for fifty years before it was overtaken by Vancouver's in the 1910s. It held second place for thirty years before dropping to third place after Vancouver's and Toronto's Chinatown in the 1940s. In the past three decades, Victoria, unlike other metropolitan cities, did not have a great influx of new Chinese immigrants. The 2006 census reveals that Canada had a Chinese population of 1,346,510: Metropolitan Areas of Toronto (537,060), Vancouver (402,000), Montreal (82,665), Calgary (75,410), Edmonton (53,670), Ottawa-Hull (36,605), Winnipeg (16,695), Hamilton (13,600), Victoria (13,550), Kitchener (10,970), Windsor (8,830), and other cities and towns (95,455). In term of population size, Metropolitan Victoria was in the ninth place, but it has the oldest surviving Chinatown in Canada which still retains its nineteenth-century townscape. It is the only Chinatown in Canada that has a complete history of a functioning Chinatown dating back from the first Chinese arrival in Canada in 1858 to the present. It was designated in December 1995 as a National Historic District by the Government of Canada. For nearly thirty years before the trans-continental Canadian Pacific Railway was completed, Victoria was the first port of entry of nearly all Chinese immigrants from China to Canada. No one can study the history of Chinese in Canada without reference to Victoria, and no descendants of Chinese immigrants entering Canada before the 1890s can trace their roots without returning to Victoria's Chinatown.

Finally, Victoria has been my home since I landed in Canada. I know the Chinese community and its history very well. I have become a collector of Chinese archival materials about Chinese voluntary associations across Canada. In this book I have utilized all the available Chinese documents extensively as a way to analyze CCBA's leadership and many historic events.

There are different methods of transliterating for Chinese names: the traditional postal office Romanization, the Wade-Giles system, and the Hanyu Pinyin System. In addition, many transliterations are based on Cantonese, Taishan, or other dialects. A Chinese surname can be transliterated into different English spellings. For example, the surname Mar, Mah, and Marr are different spellings of the surname Ma, which is a Hanyu Pinyin System. For consistency, if people, associations, and historical names are already well known in their dialect-based forms, and have been made popular by general usage in Canada, these forms are used because changes to the Pinyin system in spelling may cause confusion. For example, Lee Mong Kow is used instead of Li Mengjiu, Hakka instead of Kejia, Chee Kung Tong instead of Zhigongtang, and Hook Sin Tong instead of Fushantang. However, except for established spellings of Chinese place names such as Hong Kong, spellings of place names will follow the Pinyin system, such as Taishan instead of Hoy Sun or Toi Shan. I also use the Pinyin system when the names of persons and associations do not have a conventional English name, or a generally accepted local spelling. In Appendix A, the English names of important persons, companies, associations, and others are listed with their Chinese names. In Appendix B, CCBA presidents are listed both in Chinese and English, and years of their service.

# Acknowledgments

# Acknowledgments

I have incurred countless debts of gratitude in the past three decades in doing research for this book. My deepest thanks go to the presidents and directors of the Chinese Consolidated Benevolent Association (CCBA) in Victoria for permission to read the meeting minutes and other archival materials. I am particularly grateful to former presidents Yu Chaoping, Jack Lee, Sam Lum, Augustine Low, Ken Chee, Ben Lowe, Peter Lou-Poy, John Joe, Joe Leung, Paul Chan. and Paul Chow, and the present President Dr. Kit Wong, for sharing inside information about CCBA. I also thank its secretaries such as Lee Tung Hai, Chan Chee, Anderson Ku, John Nip, and Kileasa Wong. I benefited from conversations and interviews with many old-timers in Victoria about the early history of the association; it is nearly impossible to list everyone, but I particularly wish to thank Harry Lou Poy, Fred Chow, Ben Mar, Nelson Lee, Frank Wong, Jack Tang, and many other community leaders in Victoria for clarifying historical events.

I interviewed many current or former executives of CBAs across Canada. I am deeply grateful to them for being interviewed and sharing the history of their associations. In addition, I deeply appreciate the help of many Chinese community leaders in Chinatowns in other cities. Their memories, insights, and reflections are the invaluable meat of my research. If an interviewee wishes to remain anonymous, I do not give his or her name or quote him or her as John Doe in references. In over two decades,

I might have forgotten or missed some people who have helped me and whom I fail to acknowledge. I apologize deeply for any such oversights.

I would like to thank the hard-working staff members of the library of the University of Victoria, the Provincial Archives of British Columbia (now known as British Columbia Archives and Record Service), the City of Victoria archives, the Heritage Conservation Branch of British Columbia, and the Heritage Trust. They have provided me with research materials and facilities. Staff members of university libraries, city archives, and public libraries in other Canadian cities have assisted me in various ways. I offer my sincere thanks.

Special mention should also be made of the advice and help of colleagues at the University of Victoria. Thanks are extended to Ole J. Heggen, Ken G. Josephson, and Anita Jessop for their cartographic and graphic work; Richard Sykes, Smile Xiaomei Liang, and Tom Ackerley for computer technique advice; Lois Edgar, Anita Jessop, Lindsay Cassie, Diane E. Braithwaite, and Marta Ausio-Esteve for printing advice. I would also like to thank John Nip and Shannon Tao for typing the Chinese characters. I am deeply indebted to my wife, Roberta Manyuk, for doing nearly all the domestic chores so that I could have time for research. Furthermore, as a geographer, teacher and librarian, she has read draft sections of the manuscript and given me her thoughts for improvement. Last but not least, I thank Jean Wilson for providing editorial advice and Smile Xiaomei Leung for proof-reading.

Finally, I wish to acknowledge the Social Sciences Research Centre of the University of Victoria for the financial support in my research on the CCBA archives in 1970–72.

1

# Introduction

# Introduction

The infrastructure of overseas Chinese society is a system of voluntary associations, which organize the political and socio-economic activities of Chinese communities in the host society. Maurice Freedman's study of the Chinese community in Singapore suggested that population size and heterogeneity were critical in explaining the growth and diversity of overseas Chinese associations.[1] However, W. E. Willmott found that the simplicity of Chinese organization in Phnom-Penh during the French occupation was due to the *congregation* system rather than the small demographic size, and the rise of many associations after the Second World War represented responses to the growth of Chinese nationalism and the influence of Western organizational concepts.[2] Edgar Wickberg suggested that discrimination by the host society and continuing cultural influences from China played a major role in shaping Chinese organizational development in Canada.[3] These studies revealed that overseas Chinese communities in the world are fragmented societies of many associations. Each association or society tends to have its own leaders and functions autonomously. Differences in politics, personal conflicts, and group consolidation have been sources of tensions in inter-association relationships. In the past, *Zhonghua Huiguan* (commonly known in English as the Chinese Benevolent Association or CBA) was a community-wide organization in most large Chinatowns in North America. Its objective was to unite different Chinese associations and interest groups inside Chinatown and provide leadership in articulating community concerns to Western society. In the past, CBA claimed to be the supreme ruling body of the Chinese people in its respective city and presumed to represent them to deal with the host society. Today its authority is rejected and its leadership challenged by many other Chinese organizations, especially those formed after the Second World War. This book uses the Chinese Consolidated Benevolent Association (CCBA) in Victoria as a case study of Chinatown leadership, and organizational development in Canada.

## Ethnic Leadership and Power

Studies on ethnic leadership, especially the elites in an ethnic group, are few in Canada. Kurt Lewin, a social psychologist, points out that an underprivileged group is likely to choose leaders whose economic success or professional attainments make them relatively acceptable outside the group.[4] These ethnic leaders usually have little loyalty and may be eager to leave the group. Hence, Lewin is skeptical about their leadership because he feels that they may be "marginal" to their own groups and unreliable as strategists and spokespersons. However, Lewin's hypothesis is inapplicable to Chinese leadership patterns in Canada because even peripheral leaders still rely on Chinatown and the Chinese community to sustain their representative role in the host society. Willmott has suggested that the more positions a community leader occupies, the greater his influence and power.[5] This proposition does not hold if a Chinatown has been depopulated and its traditional associations are declining. If these associations no longer exert their power on the Chinese populace, the power and influence of their elite will wane. Fewer people will want to run in association elections. Hence, a particular leader ceases to be influential although he may hold several association positions. Robert Schulze, investigating the power structure of an American community, put forward the hypothesis that in a self-contained community, those persons who exercised major control over the community's economic system would tend to be the same persons who exercised preponderant control over its socio-political system.[6] With increasing urbanization, the local power structure would bifurcate — with those who exercised primary direction over its socio-political system no longer being the same set of persons who exercised primarily control over its economic system.

In this book I attempt to test whether the bifurcation hypothesis is applicable to the CCBA leadership pattern in Victoria. The association was initially under the oligarchic control of a few wealthy merchants who were the "centre" of the Chinese community in Victoria and managed its socio-economic and political system. Gradually CCBA became more pluralistic and was later run by representatives of county associations, then by many other types of organizations. In other words, the decision-making structure of Chinatown has changed from a monolithic to a polylithic model. In the monolithic decision-making structure, a small number of merchants at the top of the hierarchy have greater influence than those at middle or lower levels. They are influential in all issue areas. However, in a polylithic decision-making structure, no single power elite has a dominant influence in all issue areas such as education, hospital and housing. Each issue area is characterized by a more democratic decision-making structure. I use this monolithic-polylithic model to study the leadership pattern and power structure of Victoria CCBA.

The phenomenon of power cannot be understood without reference to the political and cultural context within which it exists. Unlike other Chinatowns in Canada, the salient characteristics of the Chinatown power structure in Victoria has been its long-standing dominance by CCBA, which functioned like a "central government" for over two decades before establishment of the Chinese Consulate General in Canada in 1909. Since then, both the political and socio-economic development of Chinatown has shaped the style and character of CCBA leaderships. I examine the leadership patterns in the association during its 125-year history, assess the impact of leaders at the centre and those beyond the periphery of the Chinese community, study the association's principal power or decision-making roles, and explain the power conflicts within the community.

## Names of Zhonghua Huiguan

This "umbrella" organization has different names in different Chinatowns, and sometimes at different times. For example, it is known as *Zhonghua Huiguan* in Victoria, Vancouver, Montreal, Winnipeg, San Francisco, Portland, and many other North American cities, but *Zhonghua Gongsuo* in Halifax, Moose Jaw, and London, Ontario, and *Huaqiao Zonghui* in Lima. In Edmonton, it was called *Huaqiao Gongsuo* before 1957 and *Zhonghua Huiguan* after that. The English translation of the association also differs.

For example, CBA is the English corporate name in Vancouver, Edmonton, and Portland. It is called the Chinese Community Centre in Hamilton, Toronto, and Ottawa, and the United Chinese Society in Honolulu. Both in Victoria and San Francisco, the association is called CCBA but San Francisco CCBA is more popularly known to the Western community as the Six Companies. Calgary's Chinatown did not have a CBA although the *Kacheng Zhonghua Xiehui* (the United Calgary Chinese Association) was organized like a CBA in 1969, and represented 24 Chinese associations in Calgary.[7]

## Origins of CBAs in Canada

In the early 1950s, many CBAs in Chinatowns across Canada were defunct mainly because they had lost their importance in providing social and economic services to Chinese residents. They no longer protect them against Western discrimination for several reasons: depopulation of Chinese residents in Chinatown, diminishing discrimination of Chinese by the host society, greater integration of local-born Chinese into Western society, and disunity in Chinese community because of there being two governments in China (on Taiwan and mainland China). Lee Tung Hoi, secretary of Victoria CCBA, listed 27 CBAs in Canada in 1967.[8] He obtained the list from the CBA (National Headquarters) in Vancouver and did not contact these associations personally. He estimated that over half CBAs were not functioning.

From 1990 to 1994, I visited over 20 cities outside Victoria and found that 17 CBAs in 16 cities across Canada were still in operation (Vancouver's Chinatown has two CBAs) (Table 1). I interviewed former and current officials and found that there was a dearth of written materials about the history of their associations. Information about their origins and structures are frequently vague and incomplete. Some CBAs in Canada have not kept old records. Some CBAs destroyed their records before or after May 1960 when the Royal Canadian Mounted Police raided the associations to gather evidence against Chinese immigration racketeers. Some CBAs do keep old records but they have been misplaced and cannot be located. One or two CBAs still preserve their archives but their officials are unwilling to let outsiders to read them. I have also relied on reminiscences of Chinese old-timers who remember what the founders of the CBAs had told them. Some community leaders did not respond to my questions, and claimed that they did not know or could not remember certain events, especially those related to internal dissension or inter-association rivalry.

Suspicion of outsiders is a recognized cultural feature of the closed society of overseas Chinese. If a researcher wants to do an in-depth

Table 1   Chinese Benevolent Associations in Canada in the early 1990s

| Location | Name Of Association | Year Of Establishment |
|---|---|---|
| Victoria | Victoria Zhonghua Huiguan (CCBA) | 1884 |
| Vancouver | Vancouver Zhonghua Huiguan (CBA) Known as Vancouver Zhonghua Zonghuiguan [CBA (National Headquarters)], 1949–1978 | 1906 |
| Montreal | Mandike Zhonghua Huiguan (L'Association Chinoise de Montreal Inc.) | 1912 |
| Winnipeg | Mainsheng Zhonghua Huiguan (CBA of Manitoba) | 1919 |
| Regina | Shasheng Leizhenda Zhonghua Gongsuo (CBA of Regina in Saskatchewan Province) | c1920s |
| Edmonton | Huaqiao Gongsuo (Chinese Public Benevolent Association) | 1929 |
| Halifax | Xiacheng Zhonghua Gongsuo (CBA of Halifax) | 1934 |
| Saskatoon | CBA of Saskatoon | c1940s |
| Toronto | Ansheng Zhonghua Zonghuiguan (Chinese Community Centre of Ontario) | 1945 |
| Prince George | Zhonghua Huiguan (CBA) | 1946 |
| Moose Jaw | Wucheng Zhonghua Gongsuo (CBA of Moose Jaw) | 1946 |
| Ottawa | Jiajing Zhonghua Huiguan (Chinese Community Association of Ottawa) | 1946 |
| Hamilton | Kanwendun Zhonghua Huiguan (Chinese Community Centre Association of Hamilton-Wentworth) | 1946 |
| Kingston | Jingshidunbu Zhonghua Huiguan (CBA of Kingston) | 1946 |
| London | Zhonghua Gongsuo (CBA of London) | 1946 |
| Quebec City | Gubibu Zhonghua Huiguan (Asociación de Bienfaisance Chinoise de Quebec Inc.) | 1946 |
| Duncan | Dangjin Huaqiao Gongsuo (Duncan Chinese Community Association) | 1961 |
| Vancouver | Quanjia Zhonghua Zonghuiguan (Chinese Benevolent Association of Canada) | 1978 |

study of a city's CBA, he or she has to live there for a long time, become acquainted with a wide circle in the Chinese community, and develop close rapport with CBA officials and other community leaders. Having gained their trust, a researcher may obtain the available archival materials and inside information about the community and its organizations. The origins and functions of CBAs vary a great deal from one Chinatown to another. Their organizational history and structure are even more complicated and diversified. Because of time constraint and insufficient research funds, I stayed only briefly in each Chinatown across Canada. Based on scattered references and intermittent interviews over five years, I gleaned bits of information about the origins of 17 CBAs in cities outside Victoria.

Victoria CCBA, established in 1884, is the first Chinese community-wide organization in Canada. Vancouver CBA was established in 1896 but was in embryo for a decade until it was officially established in 1906 by Yip Sang (Yip Chun Tin), Lee Sai Fan, Wong Yuk Shan, Loo Yang Kiu and a few other prominent merchants.[9] Without drawing up a constitution, it followed the constitution of Victoria CCBA in election, organization, and welfare activities.

The Canadian government still enforced a discriminatory policy on Chinese immigration even after it abolished the Chinese Exclusion Act on 14 May 1947. Foon Sien (alias Wong Mun Po), president of Vancouver CBA, took up the fight against these regulations. In 1949, the name of Vancouver CBA was changed to *Quanjia Zhonghua Zonghuiguan* (meaning Pan-Canada Chinese Benevolent Association Headquarters); its English name is the Chinese Benevolent Association (National Headquarters).[10] This name enabled Foon Sien to claim in Ottawa that "CBA(NH) is a representative body of Chinese across Canada."[11] In fact, the board of the directors of CBA(NH) was not elected by CBAs in other cities. It was not a legal national organization since it was not registered with the Registrar of Companies. Nevertheless, Chinese people in Canada accepted CBA(NH) as their representative mainly because of Wong's dedication in fighting against discriminatory regulations. CBA(NH) executive committee had three co-chairmen: one from Kuomintang (KMT), one from the Chinese Freemasons and a third from either the Chinese Workers Association or the Hoy Sun Association. As Wong was a prominent leader both in the Chinese Workers Association and in Hoy Sun Association, he played an important role in minimizing the conflicts between the pro-Taiwan KMT and the pro-China Freemason members.

Throughout the late 1960s, CBA(NH) was increasingly dominated by KMT members and concerned more with the anti-Beijing movement than with local issues that affected Chinatown and the welfare of the Chinese community in Vancouver. After Canada recognized the People's Republic of China in 1970, CBA(NH) held a national conference in June 1971 and changed its constitution. Before 1971, 41 of the 61 CBA(NH) directors were appointed by Chinese organizations in Vancouver and the remaining 20 directors were elected by members at the annual national convention.[12] At the 1971 national conference it was decided that (a) Chinese organizations in Vancouver could send only non-voting observers to the convention; (b) voting privileges were reserved for delegates from Vancouver CBA and CBAs in other cities in Canada; (c) delegates to the convention must support and recognize the Taiwan government as the sole legal government of China; (d) CBA(NH) would permanently fly the flag of Taiwan; and (e) the national convention would be held once every three years instead of annually.[13] Many young directors who were educated in Canada did not approve the conference's decision and resigned from CBA(NH).[14] Many Chinese associations in Vancouver and other cities also did not recognize CBA(NH) as the official voice of Chinese in Canada, and considered it a national vehicle for anti-Beijing propaganda in Canada. In spite of protests in Vancouver against CBA (NH), many CBAs in other cities which were controlled by KMT members, still considered it as the Head of CBAs in Canada.

According to Vancouver CBA's constitution which was registered with the provincial government in 1933, any Chinese aged over 18 could pay a member fee of $1 and become a member. (Vancouver CBA was renamed CBA(NH) unofficially in 1949 but its official constitution remained unchanged). As CBA(NH) prepared to hold its election in January 1978, many Chinese applied for membership in order to challenge its revised constitution which was illegally created in 1971.[15] When their applications were rejected by CBA(NH) executives, 35 Chinese organizations and 1,000 Chinese individuals in Vancouver formed a Committee to Democratize the CBA on 4 December 1977.[16] The Committee, headed by Victor Li as president, and Bill Yee as vice-president, took CBA(NH) executives to court for planning to hold a general election in January 1978 without following the registered constitution. After the court case was won, thousands of Chinese in Canada applied for membership in CBA(NH). On 29 October

1978, an election was held and a new group of young people were elected as board directors. The organization's name was then changed back to Vancouver CBA.

Defeated CBA (NH) executives moved out of the association building at 108 East Pender Street. In December 1978, they established another association, namely, the Chinese Benevolent Association of Canada (CBAC) at 537 Main Street which was recognized by a few CBAs in other cities. Hence, there are two CBAs in Vancouver: the Vancouver CBA, which recognizes the People's Republic of China, and the CBAC, which recognizes the Republic of China in Taiwan.

In other Canadian cities, several CBAs grew out of *Huaqiao Juri Jiuguohui* (meaning, Overseas Chinese Resisting Japan and Saving the Nation Association). In English, it was known as the Chinese National Salvation Bureau which was formed after the Japanese invaded Manchuria in 1931. For instance, the Chinese community in Toronto organized *Kangri Jiuguohui* (Resisting Japan and Saving the Nation Association) in 1931. Soon after it was formed, similar associations were set up in Windsor and Sudbury which asked the Toronto association to coordinate all the fund-raising and resistance to Japan campaigns in Ontario.[17] Accordingly, the Toronto association was renamed *Ansheng Huaqiao Tongyi Kangri Jiuguohui* (Ontario Overseas Chinese United Association to Resist Japan and Save the Nation). This umbrella organization was reorganized on 29 November 1945 as *Ansheng Zhonghua Zonghuiguan* (Chinese Community Centre of Ontario Incorporation).[18] Similarly, *Kangri Jiuguohui* was formed in Moose Jaw during the war and renamed *Wucheng Zhonghua Gongsuo* (CBA of Moose Jaw) in 1946.[19] In the 1930s, an Anti-Japanese Association was formed in Ottawa and was renamed *Jiajing Zhonghua Huiguan* (Chinese Community Association of Ottawa) after the war was over.[20] In Prince George, the Chinese National Salvation Bureau was formed in 1937 and renamed CBA in 1946.[21] In the early days, KMT members were responsible for the organization of several *Zhonghua Huiguan* (CBA) in small Chinatowns where Chinese were few in number and most were KMT adherents. For example, the KMT branch in Winnipeg established *Zhonghua Huiguan* in 1919. The KMT and CBA there had always been run by interlocking directorships.[22] In Kingston, KMT members organized the Anti-Japanese Association in the late 1930s, renamed as *Jingshidunbu Zhonghua Huiguan* (CBA of Kingston) after the war and run by KMT members.[23] Similarly, both the KMT branch in Hamilton and Quebec City established an Anti-Japanese Association in the 1930s. After the war, the association in Hamilton was renamed *Kanwendun Zhonghua Huiguan* (Chinese Community Centre Association of Hamilton-Wentworth) in Hamilton,[24] and the association in Quebec City was renamed *Gubibu Zhonghua Huiguan* (Association de Bienfaisance Chinoise de Quebec Inc. or CBA of Quebec).[25] Similarly, KMT members in London organized the Anti-Japanese Association during the early 1940s and renamed it *Zhonghua Gongsuo* (CBA of London) after the war.[26]

At least two CBAs were formed initially with the objective of uniting the divided Chinese community in Chinatown. In the 1900s, about 90% of the Chinese in Montreal were surnamed Tam, Wong, and Lee and inter-clan conflicts were frequent. Soon after the Republic of China was formed in 1912, the Chinese consul in Ottawa visited Montreal's Chinatown and helped the Chinese form a CBA.[27] Six directors, two from each clan, ran the association. When a dispute between two clans happened, it would be taken to CBA where the two directors from the third clan would resolve the conflict. Many Chinese in Montreal were not pleased that CBA directors were elected by only three clans. Hence, in February 1915, the Chinese consul suggested that the board of directors would have one member from each of the five clans (Tam, Wong, Lee, Chan, Woo, and Ng), one member of an association such as the Chee Kung Tong and Constitution Party, and any Chinese who made an annual donation of $2 to the association.[28]

Similarly, the divided Chinese community in Edmonton led to formation of a CBA. The KMT branch there was divided into left-wing and right-wing KMT factions in 1927, both of which claimed for the branch's funds.[29] As many members of the Chinese Dramatic Club, the Mah Society, Wong's Benevolent Association, and the Gee Poy Kuo Tong in Edmonton's Chinatown were also KMT members, the entire community split into two factions. Some community-minded KMT members such as Charlie Yat Wah, Lim Hing Yee, Henry Mah, and Gordon Chan tried to reunite the divided community by forming *Huaqiao Gongsuo* (Chinese Public Benevolence Association) in 1929 and extended its service to the Chinese people in northern Alberta, Yukon, and the Northwest Territories, where no Chinese organizations existed. This new organization was run by representatives from all Chinese organizations in Edmonton. It had been active in raising funds to help the poor and unemployed in Chinatown and to help China to fight the Japanese. In the 1950s it worked closely with CBAs in other Chinatowns to fight for equal treatment of Chinese immigrants. In September 1957, *Huaqiao Gongsuo* was reorganized, and renamed *Dianwendun Zhonghua Huiguan* (CBA of Edmonton).[30]

Two CBAs were formed with the primary objective of helping the poor and unemployed. In Regina, many Chinese were unemployed during the late 1920s and had nowhere to go. Accordingly *Zhonghua Huiguan* was established and rented a hut on Broad Street so that unemployed Chinese had a social gathering place.[31] Similarly, many elderly Chinese in Halifax were single and poor during the economic depression of the 1930s. When they died, there was no one to look after their burials. Hence the Chinese community established *Xiacheng Zhonghua Gongsuo* (CBA of Halifax) in February 1934 to collect donations and purchase burial plots in the city's cemetery for deceased Chinese.[32]

In Duncan, the Duncan Chinese Language School was destroyed by a fire in 1947. A group of conscientious native-born youths and new immigrants re-established the Chinese Language School in 1961. At the same time, they formed *Dangjin Huaqiao Gongsuo* (Duncan Chinese Community Association) to serve the community.[33] In Saskatoon, it is unknown when CBA in Saskatoon was established. In August 1990, I interviewed Fay Foo, CBA vice-president. He did not know the history and referred me to Chuck Chuen Seto, a former official of CBA in the 1960s. He said that CBA was organized probably by KMT people during the Second World War.[34] However, Daniel C.M. Mack, a former CBA president, said that someone from Vancouver moved to Saskatoon and found that there was not a single association to represent the Chinese in the city. So, he started CBA to speak for the Chinese community.[35] In 1963, CBA bought a lot on the 19th Street at F Avenue and bought an adjoining lot in 1984. The two lots were later merged, and CBA ran a Chinese school there.[36]

## Endnotes

1   Maurice Freedman, "Immigrants and Associations: Chinese in Nineteenth-Century Singapore," *Comparative Study in Society and History*, III ( 1960), 47–48.

2   W.E. Willmott, "Congregations and Associations: the Political Structure of the Chinese Community in Phnom-Penh, Cambodia," *Comparative Studies in Society and History*, 11, (1969), 297.

3   Edgar Wickberg, "Some Problems in Chinese Organizational Development in Canada, 1923–1937," *Canadian Ethnic Studies*, XI, 1 (1979), 97.

4   Kurt Lewin, *Resolving Social Conflict: Selected Papers on Group Dynamism* (New York: Harper & Row 1948), 57.

5   W.E. Willmott, op. cit., 299.

6   Robert O. Schulze, "The Role of Economic Dominants in Community Power Structure," *American Sociological Review*, 23, (1958), 3–9.

7   David Chuenyan Lai, *Chinatowns: Towns Within Cities in Canada* (Vancouver: UBC Press 1988), 135.

8   David H.T. Lee, *Overseas Chinese History in Canada* (Vancouver: Canadian Freedom Publisher 1967) 198–202 (in Chinese script).

9   Dai Yun, "Investigation of the date of the establishment of CBA in Vancouver," *Special Issue to Commemorate Victoria's Chinese Consolidated Benevolent Association, 1884–1859 and Chinese Public School, 1899–1959* (Victoria: Chinese Consolidated Benevolent Association 1959) V, pages unnumbered (in Chinese script).

10  David H.T. Lee, op. cit., 196.

11  Foon Sien Wong "A Brief for Presentation to the Prime 24, 1950," 1 (unpublished mimeograph).

12  De Chuen Lee, ed., *Inside the Chinese Benevolent Association: A Report of Some Activities of the Highest Governing Body of the Chinese in Canada.* (Vancouver: CBA(NH) 1969), 102 (in Chinese script).

13  Committee to Democratize the CBA, *CBA Issue*, Vancouver, 1978, 5.

14  *The 100th Anniversary, 1906–2006, of Chinese Benevolent Association of Vancouver* (Vancouver: Chinese Benevolent Association of Vancouver 2006), 56.

15  *Ibid.*, 50.

16  *The Times*, Victoria, 17 November 1978.

17  Earnest Mark Scrap Book No. 1: Minutes of Anti-Japanese Association, 170 (Ottawa: Public Archives of Canada).

18  Xinghui Zhang "A Brief History of the Establishment of Canada's Chinese Community Center of Ontario." *The Annual Issue of Canada's Chinese Community Center Ontario* (Toronto: Canada's Chinese Community Center of Ontario, 1972), 2 (in Chinese script).

19  Tap Quan, President, CBA, Moose Jaw, personal interview, August 1990.

20  Jiuhu Dong, "A Letter to the Editor," *The Seventies* (December 1977), 82.

21  Roy Yip, President, and Lily Chow, Vice-President, CBA, personal interview, October 1991.

22  "A Brief Introduction to the CBA of Manitoba in Canada," *Special Issue of the Annual Meeting of Pan-American CBAs*, Vancouver, June 1994, pages unnumbered (in Chinese script).

23  Henry Lee, Treasurer, CBA of Kingston and District, personal interview, May 1991.

24  Jason Wong, old-timer in Hamilton, personal interview, August 1993.

25  Ben Woo, and his mother, active members of the CBA of Quebec City, personal interview, June 1989.

26  Gene Lem, Kuomintang member, personal interview, August 1994.

27  Manley Tam, chairman of Montreal's Hum's Family Association (Hum Kong Yu Chung Tong), personal interview, May 1991.

28  *Chinese Times*, Vancouver, 7 February 1915.

29  *Edmonton Journal*, Edmonton, 17 January 1929.

30  *The Constitution of the Chinese Benevolent Association of Edmonton, 26 September 1957*, certified on 3 April 1978 by Harold J. Thomas, Registrar of Companies for the Province of Alberta (ref. No. 2844).

31  "A Brief Introduction of the CBA of Regina, Saskatchewan," *Special Issue of the Annual Meeting of Pan-American CBAs* (Vancouver: Chinese Benevolent Association of Canada June 1994), pages unnumbered (in Chinese script).

32  Jack Suen, Director, Chinese Benevolent Association in Halifax, personal interview, June 1991.

33  Letter, Ming Lowe, manager of Wing On Food Market Ltd. to David Chuenyan Lai, 30 March 1992.

34  Chuck Chuen Seto, former Official of CBA, personal interview, February 2007.

35  Daniel C.M. Mack, former President of CBA, personal interview, February 2007.

36  Fay Woo, Vice-President of CBA, personal interview, August 1990.

# 2

# Establishment of CCBA, 1884–1885

# Establishment of CCBA, 1884–1885

The Manchu government did not establish an embassy or a consulate in Ottawa until 1909. Before that, all Chinese affairs in Canada were dealt with through the Chinese consulate-general in San Francisco or the legation in London. Chinese people in British Columbia found it very inconvenient to communicate with a distant consulate when they were harassed by Western people and discriminated by municipal and provincial governments. They wanted the Manchu government to help them set up a CCBA which would represent them to deal with the host society and resolve Chinese socio-economic problems in British Columbia.

## Chinese Population in BC

The anti-Chinese movement started in British Columbia and persisted there because it had nearly all the Chinese in Canada for more than four decades from 1858 to the 1890s. For example, according to the 1881 census, the total Chinese population was 4,383, of whom 4,350 were in British Columbia; the remaining 33 resided in three other provinces (Table 2).

After the gold rushes ended in the mid-1860s, economic recession set in and Chinese labourers were made the scapegoat for unemployment. Western workers blamed them for accepting longer hours of work at lower wages, thereby taking jobs from the Westerners. An anti-Chinese movement began to boil, and demands for restricting their immigration to grow.

Table 2  Distribution of Chinese in Canada, 1881

| Location | No. of persons | |
|---|---|---|
| BRITISH COLUMBIA | 4,350 | |
| City of Victoria | | 592 |
| Victoria District | | 73 |
| Esquimalt & Metchosin | | 25 |
| N. & S. Saanich | | 3 |
| | | |
| New Westminster | | 485 |
| Keithley | | 413 |
| Quesnellemouth | | 402 |
| Yale & Hop | | 535 |
| Lytton, Cache Creek, etc | | 495 |
| Nanaimo | | 287 |
| Cassiar | | 284 |
| Barkerville & Richfield | | 260 |
| Clinton & Lillooet | | 161 |
| Mainland Coast | | 101 |
| Williams Lake and Canoe Creek | | 80 |
| Kootenai | | 70 |
| Osoyoos | | 36 |
| Omineca | | 28 |
| Nicola, Okanagan | | 20 |
| | | |
| ONTARIO | 22 | |
| Toronto | | 10 |
| Barrie | | 8 |
| Hamilton | | 2 |
| Pilkington | | 1 |
| Renfrew | | 1 |
| | | |
| QUEBEC | 7 | |
| Montreal | | 7 |
| | | |
| MANITOBA | 4 | |
| Winnipeg | | 4 |
| | | |
| Total | 4,383 | |

Source: Census of Canada, 1880–81, Vol. 1, Ottawa, 1882, 206–300.

## Anti-Chinese Movement and Regulations

As early as 1872, the BC legislative assembly passed an act to disenfranchise both Chinese and native Indians.[1] The act received royal assent on 22 April 1875.[2] The following year, the City of Victoria also passed an act to prohibit Chinese or native Indians from voting.[3] Disenfranchisement proved later to be a particularly virulent form of racism and discrimination because the three levels of government and Western institutions used voters' lists to carry out discrimination legally. For example, Chinese were not entitled to a hand-logger's licence or a liquor licence because licences were issued only to voters. For the same reason, they could not be lawyers, physicians, or pharmacists because anyone not on the voting list was ineligible to become a student or apprentice in those fields.

In May 1873 an Anti-Chinese Society in Victoria demanded a revision of the Sino-British Treaty of 1860, which permitted Chinese immigration to Canada, and asked the provincial government to introduce a law to prohibit men from working more than eight hours a day.[4] On 14 August 1875, Victoria passed a by-law excluding Chinese people from municipal work.[5] On 31 July 1878, the provincial government excluded the Chinese from provincial work as well.[6] In the same year the Workingmen's Protective Association was formed in Victoria for "the mutual protection of the working classes of British against the influx of Chinese, and the use of legitimate means for the suppression of their immigration."[7] Every member of the association had to solemnly pledge not to aid, abet, or patronize the Chinese or those employing them, and to use all legitimate means to prevent their patronage. Noah Shakespeare, a Victoria councillor, was the driving force behind formation of the association and later elected its president.

On 2 September 1878, the legislative assembly passed an act by which "every Chinese person over twelve years of age shall take out a license every three months, for which he shall pay the sum of ten dollars."[8] This act, later known as the Chinese Tax Act, imposed an annual head tax of $40 on every Chinese in the province. Merchants in Victoria sent petitions to Guo Songtao, the high commissioner of the Chinese Legation in London, England, and begged him to protest to the British government and fight for disallowance of the Chinese Tax Act.

Meanwhile, the City of Victoria appointed Noah Shakespeare the tax collector soon after the act was passed. On 11 September 1878, accompanied by a policeman and a dray, he tramped through Chinatown to hunt for Chinese workers and merchants. If they refused to pay the tax, Shakespeare forced levies on their belongings or goods.[9] On 17 September, stores throughout Chinatown were closed, and all Chinese cooks, wood-cutters, factory workers, and domestic servants stayed home.[10] Because of the strike, the Belmont Boot and Shoe factory, which usually employed over 50 Chinese workers, had to close; several hotels were short of clean napkins and had difficulty in their kitchens; and some White housewives were inconvenienced for the want of servants. Noah Shakespeare resigned silently and replaced by John Maguire, "an irresponsible party — a perfect stranger too."[11] The city-wide strike was not organized by Chinese merchants, who did not have the means or the radical attitude to initiate such a boycott. It was probably the result of a panic caused by the seizure of Chinese goods. On 22 September, the government returned the goods seized on security being furnished, and then the Chinese labourers returned to work. The Kwong Lee, Tai Soong, Tai Chong, Tai Yune, Wing Chong and other Chinese companies sent a joint letter to the editor of the *Colonist*, stating that "many persons think that we, the Chinese merchants of Victoria, have made the servants, cooks, and others give up their places in consequence of Mr. Walkem wanting some of their money to go to the foot of the Throne. Now, Mr. Editor, we beg to assure you that we have not had anything to do with this matter, and all persons who wish to resume their work can do so as far as we are concerned. The question of the tax will be before the court soon."[12] Meanwhile, Mar Sau of Tai Chong Co. and Wong Soy Chew of Tai Soong & Co. engaged Messrs. Drake and Jackson, and A. Rocke Robertson, QC, to serve an injunction on Shakespeare and Maguire, restraining them from further levying tax on Chinese merchandise, or disposing merchandise already seized. Disregarding the injunction, Maguire proceeded with the sale of the goods. On 26 October 1878, Justice John Hamilton Gray found Maguire guilty of disobeying the court's order and fined him $40. The judge also requested Maguire's lawyer to deposit $950, the value of the goods seized under the Chinese Tax Act, subject to further orders of the court.[13] On 27 September 1879 the Supreme Court declared the Chinese Tax Act of 1878 unconstitutional and void because it "interferes with the authority reserved to the Dominion Government as to the regulation of trade and commerce, the rights of aliens and the treaties of the empire, and because it interferes with the foreign as well as the internal trade of the country."[14] Because of this event, Chinese merchants in Victoria felt the need for an organization empowered to collect money from every Chinese in the province and to use it to fight against discriminatory acts in courts.

In 1880 Andrew Onderdonk, who got most of the contracts to build various sections of the Canadian Pacific Railway (CPR) in British Columbia, asked Lee Tin Poy, a Chinese contractor in Portland, to recruit 1,500 Chinese labourers from the United States who had worked on railway construction in California and Oregon. Soon after construction of the CPR began, Onderdonk asked Lee Tin Poy to bring more Chinese labourers from Hong Kong and China to work on the line. Accordingly, Lee Tin Poy moved to Victoria where he set up the Lee Chuck Co (Lianchang Co.) with Lee Yau Kain of Kwong On Lung Co. and Lee Yick Tack of Tai Yune Co. as partners.[15] The company started recruiting Chinese labourers from China. However, they were not welcome by White labourers and usually harassed upon their arrival. For example, on 11 July 1880 the *Colonist* reported that

> *Yesterday afternoon the British bark Strathearn ... arrived from Hong Kong with 473 Chinamen on board ... was towed alongside Messrs. Janion & Co.'s Wharf ... When the first detachment left the wharf for their quarters, a number of young men availed themselves of what they deemed a rare opportunity to 'have some fun' and commenced to throw stones at the Celestials and otherwise annoy them ... Out of the 473 arrivals there are 333 for the province, and 140 for Portland.*

The arrival of Chinese railway labourers provided the opportunity for racists like Noah Shakespeare to intensify resentment against Chinese immigration. Exceeding his authority as a councillor, he even tried to collect the school tax from new arrivals. For example, on 2 July 1881, the China steamship Quinta brought "514 Chinese, all healthy-looking, well-behaved men who were specially selected for the railway work on the Onderdonk contract."[16] Shakespeare met them when they landed, and demanded the payment of the school tax. Meeting refusal, he took possession of some goods and chattel, and placed them in charge of a bailiff. When local Chinese and new arrivals protested about of his insolence, he arrested them. Shakespeare, a demagogue, was elected mayor of Victoria the following year because his brazen anti-Chinese attitude and activities pleased the racist voters.

On 8 May 1882, the American government passed the Chinese Exclusion Act, which suspended the admission of Chinese labourers into the United States for ten years; Chinese residing in the United States had to obtain an identification certification before 5 August.[17] As a result, many Chinese labourers who had come from the United States to work on the CPR but did not have American identity certificates, could not return to the States after the railway was completed. The Victoria lodge of the Knights of Labour formed in 1883 and rallied other White workers to parade in protest about the stranded Chinese labourers and the continual influx of Chinese immigrants. Their petition, headed by Noah Shakespeare, was based on the following reasons:

> *That they (the Chinese) do not come to make a home or settle in the country, or to add to the country's wealth; but to prey upon our natural resources, and take what they earn out of the country. That they are leprous in blood and unclean in habits. That they are destructive of the means by which the white mechanical and labouring classes earn a living wage. That there are immoral practices, debasing habits, and contagious diseases, peculiar to these people, which they have already introduced to an alarming extent upon the continent, and against which have a right to defend ourselves and our children. We therefore humbly pray for the enactment of such laws as with prohibit any further introduction of this undesirable class of people into any part of the Dominion of Canada.[18]*

On 18 February 1884, the legislative assembly passed three acts: one preventing Chinese from acquiring Crown lands; one prohibiting Chinese immigrants to land in British Columbia; and one requiring every Chinese in the province over 14 years to pay an annual tax of 10 dollars on the first of June each year.[19] Concerned Chinese merchants in Victoria thought that if these three acts were not disallowed by the dominion or British governments, Chinese already in Canada would suffer financially, and Chinese in China would be unable to come to Canada. Therefore, Chinese merchants thought that they should collect money from all Chinese in British Columbia and use it to fight for abolition of these acts. They also thought that a CCBA, like that in San Francisco, would be a suitable body to coordinate the work.

In addition to official discrimination, Western society's hostility was an incentive for the formation of CCBA. Chinese were killed by unprovoked attacks by Western people on several occasions, or by native Indians. For example, on 2 November 1883, a White schoolboy threw a piece of brick at a Chinese from behind and knocked him senseless; he later died.[20] The following day another White boy assaulted a Chinese on Fort Street with the butt of a whip for no obvious reason. One late evening in January 1884 Loo See was struck on the head by an Indian with a rock, and died two hours later.[21] These attacks were unprovoked, and the assailants not charged. If there had been a representative body such as a CCBA, it could have helped Chinese victims fight for justice in the courts, and protect the interests of Chinese in other legal matters.

### Growth of Chinatowns

In 1871 the small Chinatown in Victoria had only 211 Chinese residents, of whom 181 were male and 30 female.[22] The Chinese population increased slowly although hundreds of Chinese immigrants continued to arrive; most went to the gold fields on the mainland. By 1881, Chinatown's population was 592 in Victoria, and 101 in surrounding districts (see Table 2). When construction of the Canadian Pacific Railway began in 1881, hundreds of Chinese labourers entered Victoria and stayed temporarily in preparation for the trip to the mainland. On 24 June 1882, for example, *the Daily British Colonist* reported that

> *about 750 Mongolians landed yesterday on Janion's wharf from the barques Martha and Agate. From dewy morn to dusky eve they filed off the wharf until Cormorant Street clear up to Douglas, Store and Herald streets was swarming with them. At one time there must have been 200 in the yard attached to the old barracks, formerly known as the New Orleans Hotel, on Cormorant Street, seeking quarters.*

By 1884, virtually all Chinatowns in Canada, large and small, were in British Columbia but no significant Chinatowns were in other provinces. Victoria's Chinatown was the largest in the country, having a Chinese population of 1,767, more than three times its Chinese population in 1881.[23] The second largest Chinatown was in New Westminster with 1,680 Chinese, and the third in Wellington with 685. About 20 small Chinatowns were located in Nanaimo, Yale, Hope, and other British Columbia towns. Despite so many Chinese communities, there was no single body representing them and coordinating their activities.

The booming Chinatown in Victoria in 1884 covered three blocks on the northern edge of Victoria. Of its 1,767 Chinese residents, 1,661 were males and only 106 females (41 married women, 34 prostitutes, and 31 girls).[24] The only amenities available for the forlorn male labourers were three Chinese theatres, and several brothels, gambling dens, and opium joints. Prostitution flourished in Chinatown not only because over 94% of the Chinese population were males but also because most of the male immigrants were young. In Victoria, they were free from the strong social controls in their home villages and did not have to restrain their behaviour so much as they did at home. Brothels were run by gangsters who kidnapped or purchased young girls in China and then shipped them to Victoria. These young prostitutes were often abused and had no protection from the host authority. Furthermore, violence in Chinatown over prostitutes and gambling disputes was not uncommon. For example, Ah Kow was stabbed to death outside a brothel on Fisgard Street in the evening of 5 February 1882. Chinese merchants offered a reward of $600 for the discovery of the murderer.[25] On 23 November, Ah Sie was killed in her house on Herald Street, the fifth or sixth Chinese murder in the last five or six years.[26] A few prominent Chinese merchants became concerned about the increase in social vices in Chinatown, especially prostitution, gambling, violence, and murders. They thought that if they were empowered by the Manchu government to form a CCBA to govern Chinatown, they might be able to enforce a sort of approved mode of behaviour in Chinatown and maintain its stability and peace.

## Misery of Railway Labourers

Chinese merchants in Victoria were also concerned about the misery and poverty of Chinese railway labourers in the province. Many had died not only because of accidents but also because of being unable to acclimatize to the cold climate. They were not paid when the construction of railway was suspended during the snowy winter. Without wages, and sufficient food and clothing, they suffered from hunger and cold. When they were ill, they received no medical assistance either from the contractor or from the railway company. Most were seriously undernourished, and many died of beriberi due to lack of thiamine (Vitamin B1). In February 1883, for example, 10 out of a gang of 28 Chinese railway workers died of beriberi or scurvy for the lack of vegetables in their diet.[27] Workers who were laid off and found their way back to Victoria's Chinatown desperately looked for help from their fellow countrymen and waited for vessels to return to China.

Chinatown did not have social welfare services except those provided by the Methodist Church, which had run a Chinese Mission School on Government Street since 1876; services were meagre. Local Chinese merchants began to worry about the stability of Chinatown should it be flooded with a large number of poor and hungry labourers. On 8 June 1883, they held a meeting at which it was resolved to send a dispatch to labour recruiting companies in China, stating that about 2,000 Chinese had died in 1882 on the railway, and that many others had been left helpless and sick, and pleading with contractors not to recruit Chinese for British Columbia.[28] This request probably fell on deaf ears. New immigrants from China continued to arrive. In June 1884, for example, another boatload of 300 more Chinese labourers arrived at Victoria although there seemed to be no particular demand for them.[29]

Meanwhile news about the dreadful plight of Chinese railway workers continued to arrive in Victoria. In the severe winter of January 1884, for example, the depth of snow was 10 inches from Okanagan to Yale and 24 inches at 37 Mile Post. Railway work was suspended and Chinese labourers laid off without pay.[30] Many of them had left the railway before work was stopped, and thus lost their share of the 90 bags of rice which each gang was given. Hence about 500 hungry, unemployed Chinese were stranded near Savona, and at least 2,000 at Spence's Bridge without ostensible means of existence.

After completion of the railway, British Columbia was hit by an economic depression. The Chinese suffered most as hundreds of railway workers faced sudden unemployment. Chinese merchants in Victoria felt that sooner or later they would drift back to Victoria. Who would be empowered to deal with this problem? Would the Manchu government be concerned with it? Without a consulate in Canada, how could the Manchu government help these people? All these questions became a seed-bed for establishment of CCBA.

### Fangkou and Shantang

As the Chinese population increased, two rudimentary organizations emerged: *fangkou* (meaning literally Rooming Mouth), and *shantang*

(Charity Society). Nearly all early Chinese immigrants had come from villages where residents bore the same surname, or only two or three surnames. In Panyu County, for example, the villagers of Nancun were mostly surnamed Zhou; those of Beicun were Xu or Dong; those of Yahu were Cao or Shen; and those of Bengbu were Yang or Su.[31] As nearly all were "bachelor" migrants, they lived communally in Chinatown for security, companionship, and economic reasons, hence maintaining a lineage group. In Victoria, for example, new immigrants tended to lodge with people who bore the same surname or came from the same county. With the same surname, they considered themselves descendants of a common remote male ancestor, hence belonging to the same clan. They spoke the same dialect if they came from the same county. "Bachelor" immigrants pooled their money together to rent a floor or a hut in Chinatown, where they ate and slept together, sharing all monthly or yearly expenses. By living together, they could reduce expenses and help each other. This cooperative boarding floor or hut was called a *fangkou*. Usually lodgers in the same room coined a name for their *fangkou* and wrote it on the door of their lodging. In Victoria's Chinatown, for example, several men surnamed Wu lived together in one room and called it Ding On Fang, and several natives of Zengcheng County shared another room and called it Kun Ying Fang. The name of a *fangkou* was used as an address which was given to the lodgers' families in China, and to a store in Chinatown which dealt with mail. When letters from China were sent to the store, they would be sorted according to *fangkou* and picked up by their respective lodgers. In time, some *fangkou* banded together to form a larger and better organized unit as a clan or county association. Unlike clans in their home villages, which were based on direct lineage, clans in Victoria included all those who shared the same surname; a person was born into a clan rather than joining it.

Before 1885, at least 15 rudimentary clan associations were established in Victoria.[32] They did not have an office nor hold meetings regularly and keep records. When they needed to meet for special business, they did it in a merchant's store. The five largest clan associations included Lee Long Sai Tong, Wong Kong Har Tong, Chan Wing Chun Tong, Chow Oylin Kung Shaw, and Lum Sai Ho Tong. These associations accepted for membership all those bearing the same surname of different counties through the catalyst of a supposed common ancestry. In 1880, for example, Lee Long

Sai Tong was formed by a group of merchants surnamed Lee, namely, Lee Yau Kain of Kwong On Lung Co., Lee Tin Poy of Lee Chuck Co., Lee Yick Tack and Lee Yick Wei of Tai Yune Co., Lee Ying San and Lee Min Sun of Boon Yuen Co. and Ying Chong Lung Co. , Lee Hong Yuen of Hong Yuen Co., and some other prominent merchants.[33] The rudimentary *fangkou* did not have an office and meetings were usually held in Tai Yune Co. Its membership cut across county origins. By 1884, over 40% of Lee members were from Taishan County, 10% from Xinhui, 5% from Enping, 5% from Panyu, and 40% from other counties.[34]

*Shantang* is the predecessor of county associations. Its initial function was to collect bones of deceased members in British Columbia and ship them back to Hong Kong, from where bones would be picked up by people of the same county and delivered to their home village. In the old days, Chinese believed that after a person's death, his soul still existed and hovered over his tomb.[35] If he died in foreign country, his soul would be homeless and unable to rest until his body or bones were shipped back to China and buried in his home village. In the early days, after a Chinese person in British Columbia died and had been buried for seven years, his grave would be dug up and bones exhumed, cleaned, and dried under the sun before being packed into a wooden crate with a label bearing the name of the deceased, date of birth and death, and name of the home village in China. The crates of bones were stored in a brick house in the Chinese Cemetery in Victoria until the number of crates was large enough to charter a vessel for shipping in bulk to Hong Kong. There the bones were stored in the mortuary of Tung Wah Hospital until delivered. Usually people of the same county formed a *shantang* and pooled resources to ship crates of bones. According to a CCBA record dated 12 December 1887, 11 *shantang* already existed in Victoria, namely *Yee Hing Tong* of Taishan County, *Fook Hing Tong* of Xinhui County, *Kwong Fook Tong* of Kaiping County, *Hong Fook Tong* of Enping County, *Hook Sin Tong* of Zhongshan County, *Chong How Tong* of Panyu County, *Yan On Tong* of Zengcheng County; *Fook Yum Tong* of Nanhai County, *Hang On Tong* of Shunde County, *Po On Tong* of Dongguan County, and *Yen Wo* Company of Hakka people (Figure 1). No archives are available about the activities of these *Shantang* because they had no headquarters or records. They usually used merchants' stores for meetings. For example, in the 1880s, a few prominent merchants in Victoria had come from Panyu county, e.g. Wong Soy Chew of Tai Soong

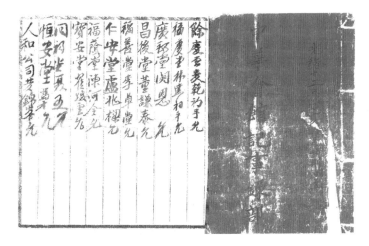

Figure 1　Eleven Shantang, Victoria, 12 December 1887

Co. and King Tyre Co., Xu Weijing and Xu Gongbao of Wing Chong Co., Lee Mong Kow of Seun Yuen Co., Zhou Ruiqi of Fook On Wing Co. and Kwong Tai Chong Co. In 1885, they established a *shantang* known as Chong How Tong to do charity work for Panyu natives.[36] The society had no office and its meetings were held in different stores owned by Panyu merchants such as Tai Soong & Co. or Wing Chong & Co.[37]

## Internal Conflicts

In the early days, Chinatown was quite disunited. Clan or county feuds over *fengshui* (Chinese geomancy) or river water supply in China might be passed down from generation to generation. Feelings of hostility and traditional antagonism between clans or counties might be carried with immigrants to Canada. Clashes between clans or counties occasionally occurred in Chinatown when a clan or county people stood together to defend its common interests against other clans or counties.[38] For example, if a business in Victoria had initially been started by people of a clan or a county, it might be run and dominated by the same clan or county because jobs were not offered to people of other clans or counties. It was not uncommon that customers of a store, and vendors of products purchased by the store belonged to the same clan or county as the store's owner. In the early days, for instance, most cooks or restaurant owners in Victoria were surnamed Lee of Taishan County. All large import and export companies, such as Kwong On Lung, Tai Yune, Boo Yuen, Hoon Yuen, and Lee Chuck, were operated by the Lees.[39] Occasionally, a dispute between two persons of different clans or counties might lead to confrontation because of clan or county solidarity.

Another common internal conflict was found among members of the Hongmen society, a secret society established during the 1760s in South China. With its brotherhood ideology and sacred blood oaths, the society's purpose was to overthrow the Manchu government and restore the Ming Dynasty. Many Chinese immigrants to the United States in the late 1840s were Hongmen members. Upon their arrival in California, they set up branches in various Chinese gold-mining settlements. Most miners joined the Hongmen society because it provided an organized group to which they could be loyal and find a place for themselves in the absence of traditional family, kin and clan relationship.[40] If a Chinese miner was not a Hongmen member, he would be isolated. In San Francisco's Chinatown, three lodges of the Hongmen society were established in the early 1850s — Kwong Duck Tong, Hip Yee Tong, and On Sun Tong.[41] In the 1870s, Kwong Duck Tong was split into three lodges known as Hip Sing Tong, Suey Sing Tong, and Bing Kung Tong. Other lodges such as Chee Kung Tong, On Leung Tong, and On Yick Tong also emerged.[42] The origins and dates of their establishment are difficult to determine partly because they were secret societies and partly because they frequently disappeared, merged with others, or subdivided and then changed their names. Unlike clan and county associations, these tongs transcended spatial boundaries and lineal differences, and set themselves up as a sort of *sub-rosa* government and secret tribunal over their members. They were financially strong, deriving income from gambling dens, brothels, and opium joints in Chinatowns. Rivalry for control of these lucrative businesses often led to the notorious "tong wars" in the United States.

The Chee Kung Tong (meaning "Justice to All" Society) in Victoria was established in 1876 by Lim Lihuang, Zhao Xi, Ye Huibo (alias Yip On), Li Youyao, and other Hongmen members from Seattle.[43] According to a reporter of the *Daily British Colonist*, a secret society in Chinatown had about 30 members in 1877.[44] Two years later, the *Daily British Colonist* reported that the secret society named Freemasons had 300 to 400 members.[45] The real name of the society was Chee Kung Tong (CKT), which was unfamiliar to the Western community. In the summer of 1886,

CKT built a two-storey frame-house opposite the Chinese Theatre in Theatre Alley at 22–24 Cormorant Street (now 528–32 Pandora Avenue). The building was officially opened on 25 September 1886. CKT was known to the public after the *Daily Colonist* reported in 1898 that a society known as CKT was headed by Lim Sam and Yip Wing.[46]

In the early 1880s, another group of Hongmen members from San Francisco came to Victoria and established Hip Sing Tong. It competed with CKT in gambling and prostitution in Chinatown. This new lodge was unknown to Westerners until the *Daily British Colonist* reported in November 1884 that a Chinese had been charged with stealing a carpenter's tools while he was making a Hip Sing Tong flagstaff.[47] Westerners began to be aware of conflicts between Hip Sing Tong and CKT after three Hip Sing Tong leaders were sent to prison by Judge Crease in November 1886.[48]

Chinese merchants in Victoria also understood the rising threat of these tongs to security in Chinatown, and feared that tong wars, like those in San Francisco, might break out in Chinatown between these gangs and between various clans or counties. Some merchants thought that there was an urgent need for a single organization such as CCBA to mediate disputes, stop violence, and defuse warfare. Empowered by the Manchu government, it would function as a kind of law-enforcing body which every Chinese in Canada had to obey.

## Appeal to The Chinese Consul-General

In early March 1884 a group of Chinese merchants in Victoria sent a letter to Huang Tsim Hsim, consul-general in San Francisco, requesting establishment of a consulate in Canada and a Zhonghua Huiguan (CCBA).[49] The draft letter is translated as follows:

> *There were over a hundred Chinese business concerns in Victoria and about 17,000 labourers in British Columbia … This year the Legislative Assembly passed an act to prohibit Chinese immigrants from entering British Columbia, an act to impose a tax of $10 per Chinese resident, and other discriminatory acts. These are external threats. Internally, criminal or immoral behaviour was more commonly seen as Chinatown's population increased. Local residents were bullied by Chinese gangs of ruffians and White scum. The weak and unemployed elderly people suffered from hunger and illness, and died in streets without help. Furthermore, brawls were on*

*the increase because gangsters were fighting for the control of prostitution*
*and gambling dens. These were our internal worries. All of us felt that (a)*
*to fight against the discriminatory acts would eliminate imminent external*
*threats; (b) to terminate prostitution would eliminate internal worries;*
*(c) if we wanted to eliminate both external threats and internal worries,*
*we must establish Zhonghua Huiguan; and (d) if we want to promote*
*fellowship and solidarity, we must have a consulate in Canada. Because*
*of these four objectives, we elected Wong Yim Ho, Chue Lai, Kum Shoong,*
*and Mar Sum Ming to represent us to go to San Francisco and ask for your*
*advice and directive.*

The consul-general of San Francisco was very supportive of the
merchants' proposal. He saw the establishment of CCBA not only as an
example of commendable benevolence on the merchants' part but also
an attempt to maintain Chinese modes of behaviour and customs within
Chinatown which had no basis in English law. He immediately instructed
his *zhushi* (second class secretary), Huang Sic Chen, to assist the Victoria
merchants to establish CCBA.[50] It thus obtained the power and authority to
"govern" Chinatown and Manchu subjects in Canada.

### Circular to form CCBA, April 1884

A provisional board of directors comprising 20 Chinese merchants in
Victoria was formed in April 1884 and sent out a circular for a fund-raising
campaign to all Chinatowns or Chinese settlements in British Columbia.[51]
The circular listed the discriminatory regulations against the Chinese people
in the province, such as the imposition of a $10 tax on every Chinese over
14 years of age; the $15 tax on Chinese gold-miners; the requirement for
a minimum residential density of 380 square feet per person in a Chinese
residence; and other discriminatory rules and regulations (Figure 2). The
circular then stated that Huang Tsim Hsim, consul-general in San Francisco,
had approved the fund-raising campaign for the dual purposes of fighting
against the provincial head tax and forming CCBA. The Chinese populace
was told that their donations could be made to designated companies or
stores in Chinatowns in British Columbia. The circular also outlined rules
for donations:

1.    *Each Chinese should donate two dollars. If a person donates more*
      *than three dollars, his name and county origin will be engraved on*
      *a board to be hung in the association's hall.*

光緒十年三月十五日

公舉總理

副總理

值事

域多利艮鋪戶等公啟

Figure 2  Circular on the Establishment of CCBA, 9 April 1884

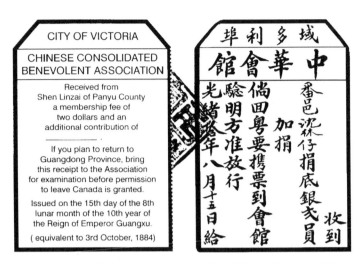

Figure 3   Stub of donation receipt issued by CCBA, 3 October 1884

2. *Every donor should list his age, home village and county, and his address and occupation in Canada.*

3. *Contributions from each Chinatown should be sent to _____ Co. in Victoria before the 15th lunar day of 8th lunar month (3 October 1884). A receipt would be issued by that company.*

4. *A register of names of donors, home county origin, and amount of donations will be made and sent to Consul General Huang.*

5. *If any miser does not make a donation, his name will not be recorded in the association's register. When he plans to leave Canada for China in the future, he will not be permitted to depart until he pays $100 to the association as a contribution to its operating expenses.*

The circular was sent out in the summer of 1884 by a provisional board of 20 directors, with Lee Yau Kain of the Kwong On Lung Co. and Wong Yim Ho of Tai Soong Co. as co-presidents of the proposed CCBA. A few hundred copies of the circular together with donation books were distributed to designated stores or reputable individuals throughout British Columbia. Each donor would be a CCBA member and given a donation receipt. The receipt could be used as a departure permit in future (Figure 3). Meanwhile, the provisional board of directors drafted the CCBA constitution.

## Constitution, 1884

On 28 July 1884, the Zhonghua Huiguan Constitution was published in Chinese. An English copy of its rules and bylaws were sent to the Registrar of Companies, Victoria, and the association was incorporated on 18 August 1884 under its English name, the Chinese Consolidated Benevolent Association.[52] According to the English version, a member of the association would "pay an entrance fee (membership fee) of $2.00, and departure fee of $4.00 when leaving Canada for China." The objectives of the association were

1. *The translation into Chinese language and advertisement of the Laws of the Country which most nearly concern them of which they are ignorant.*
2. *Affording assistance to the officers of the Government in detecting crime.*
3. *Assisting members of the Association who may be in distressed circumstances through sickness, old age or otherwise.*
4. *And for the purpose of the last clause the paying the passage of any sick, infirm, or poor Chinese to return to China.*
5. *The settling of disputes between members of the said Association by arbitration where both or all of the parties shall so agree.*
6. *Members of the said Association shall inform the Committee from time to time of any crime or misdemeanor that shall come to their knowledge, who shall forthwith transmit such information to the proper officers for the purpose of enabling them to detect such crime or misdemeanor.*

The Chinese version of the association's constitution was different from the English version. It was written in greater detail and outlined more clearly the organization, authority, and functions of the association.[53] The constitution was divided into two sections. The first consisted of four rules which defined the overall objectives and functions of the association:

## The Rules of CCBA

1. *With the approval of the Consul-General in San Francisco, Chinatown merchants established Zhonghua Huiguan in Victoria in 1884. It is an organization for the Chinese gentry, merchants*

*and labourers in all towns and cities in British Columbia. It is called "Zhonghua Ren Ai Zhouji Huiguan" (Chinese Benevolent and Charitable Association) which has been approved by the High Commissioner of the Chinese Legation in London, England, and incorporated with the Registrar of Companies in British Columbia. In order to avoid conflict, no one in Victoria is permitted to establish similar types of associations without the approval of the Chinese government.*

2.   *A plot of land will be purchased for the construction of an association building. The top floor will be used as a temple for Guandi (the God of the Righteousness), Tianhou (the Queen of the Heaven), and Caibo (the God of Wealth). The middle floor is for the headquarters of the association, and the ground floor for renting; the rents will be used to pay for the association's expenses. A wooden hut will be built as Taipingfang (Peaceful Room) for the sick and poor.*

3.   *The objectives and the tasks of the association are to promote social interrelationship, carry out charity, arbitrate in disputes, care for the sick and poor, stamp out internal vices, and fight against foreign oppression.*

4.   *The successful operation of the association depends on dedicated people, sufficient funds, and upright and fair play. The rules are itemized as follows and may be changed in due course if necessary.*

The second section included 37 articles. Articles 1 to 7 are regulations for election of the board of directors, and bidding for the post of the temple's custodian:

1.   *Honest, upright and scrupulous persons are qualified to be elected to the Board of Directors which will comprise two Co-Presidents, Six Vice-presidents, one Honorary Secretary, 10 Directors, and 80 Deputy Directors. The names of directors, their county origin, and business concerns will be recorded in a registry, displayed publicly in the hall of the association, and sent to three places: the Chinese Consulate-General, Chinese Legation in London, and the Registrar of Company of British Columbia.*

2.   *The terms of office shall be one year for Co-Presidents and secretary and end in December. On 1 December, Co-Presidents and the Honorary Secretary shall post a resignation notice in the association.*

*The Board of Directors shall meet in mid-December, and re-elect the past Co-Presidents and Honorary Secretary for another term, or elect new persons for these positions from the Vice-Presidents and Directors.*

3.　*The Co-Presidents shall keep the safe's key and be in charge of the association's affairs. The Vice-Presidents shall check the incomes and expenses, and deal with the association's affairs. The Honorary Secretary shall be responsible for Accounting, correspondence, writing minutes, and doing other chores. Directors shall help carry out the association's affairs and attend all meetings. Vice-Directors shall be invited to attend meetings for important issues.*

4.　*There will be no remuneration for Co-Presidents, Vice-Presidents, Directors and Vice-Directors. The Honorary Secretary shall receive an honorarium of $120 a year. When funds are available, a secretary shall be engaged and the salary be decided after a public discussion.*

5.　*If any member of the Board is biased and unfair, handles the association's account dubiously, always makes trouble, and is rebuked by the community, a request will be sent to the High Commissioner in London and the Chinese Consul-General for expelling him from the association. If he has any problem in the future, the association will disregard him.*

6.　*The one-year term of the temple's custodian shall end in December. The bidding for this position shall be held one month before the expiry of the term of office. The custodian shall also look after the association building, dusting, cleaning, washing, and other chores.*

7.　*When funds are available, a public relations officer will be engaged to check departing passengers for their donation receipts, and dealing with Chinese disputes with western people. The salary will be determined after a public discussion.*

Articles 8 to 27 list the tasks and functions of CCBA:

8.　*If important public issues in Victoria or other cities have to be dealt with, the President or the secretary should be informed so that he will call a Board of Directors meeting to decide how to handle them.*

9. *If great expenses are required for the fight to abolish any ill-treating Chinese regulations or policies, the board will carry out fund-raising campaigns for it.*

10. *If a Chinese is bullied, assaulted, or robbed by a Western, or cannot collect his debts, and he himself is incapable of getting a fair settlement, and if he lodges a complaint to the association in person or by mail, the secretary should call a Board of Directors meeting to assist the complainant. If he has not donated $2 towards the foundation fee, he will be ignored.*

11. *If a Chinese is killed by a Western who is still at large, and if his relatives or friends inform the association, the association will immediately give them a subsidy of $25 to institute a suit against the killer, and offer a reward of $200 for information leading to the arrest and conviction of the killer. If the deceased has not donated $2 towards the foundation fee, the association will not deal with this case.*

12. *The Board of Directors will mediate in monetary disputes between the Chinese if the parties involved come to ask for the association's arbitration. The association will disregard the request if the parties involved have not made the $2 donation.*

13. *If a Chinese is killed or murdered by another Chinese who is still at large, and if his relatives or friends inform the association, the association will look into the case. If the victim is proved to have suffered from the wrongs, the association will offer a reward of $200 for information leading to the arrest and conviction of the murderer, and give the victim's family a subsidy of $25. The association will ignore this matter if the $2 donation has not been paid.*

14. *If a Chinese has been wrongly accused by a Westerner and is held in custody, the association will ask a company to go bail for the Chinese victim, and recommend him a lawyer. The association will ignore this matter if the $2 donation has not been paid.*

15. *If a Chinese has been wrongly sued by another Chinese and is held in custody, and if the case is reported to the association, the association will immediately investigate this matter. If the Chinese is wrongly accused, the association will try to settle the case by arbitration. If arbitration is denied, the association will ask a company to go bail for the Chinese victim, and assist him to right the wrongs in court.*

*The association will ignore this case if the $2 donation has not been paid.*

16. *If a Chinese who is always villainous and detested by the community is arrested and jailed, and if the association has decided not to free him on bail, no directors or firms should go bail for him. Anybody who stands bail for the villain will be expelled from the association, and ignored by the association when he himself is in trouble.*

17. *If a Chinese is arrested for swindle, robbery, ganging up, or intimidation, no directors or firms should go bail for him. Anyone who acts against the board's decision will face the same consequence as that outlined in Article 16.*

18. *If a Chinese teams up with Westerners in extortion, robbery or bullying his fellow-countrymen, the association will report him for his crime to the local authority, and the Board of Directors will witness against him in court.*

19. *If a Chinese gangster has a grudge against the directors' fight against crimes and work for justice, and avenges himself on them, the community should work together to report him to the Chinese Consul-General, the High Commissioner in London, the British officials, and local officials in China so that he will be arrested for trial.*

20. *If directors have been notified to attend a meeting, they must come on time. Anyone who is late or absent without reason will be fined one dollar as a contribution to the association's fund.*

21. *If the association is asked to mediate in a conflict between two Chinese or two groups of people, each side should bring their witnesses and no more than three persons to the meeting. The hall will be too crowded if too many people come to the hearing. No one is permitted to bring weapons into the association. No shouting or brawling is permitted while the Board of Directors is conducting the hearing. If anyone does not observe these regulations, he may leave the meeting, but he is not permitted to bluster, yell and scold, making a scene inside or outside the association. Otherwise, he will be expelled from the association or taken to the police. The association will ignore him if he is in trouble in the future.*

22. *If a Chinese of over 60 in age cannot work any more and does not have the money to return to China, the directors will organize a*

*fund-raising campaign for his boat fare, and the association will give him a subsidy of $3. Aid will be denied to him if he has not made the $2 contribution.*

23. *The association is building a Taipingfang. Any Chinese in Victoria or other cities who are sick and have no place to stay will be admitted to the Taipingfang free of charge, provided that he had paid the $2 donation. However, this requirement does not apply to the newly arrived Chinese who is sick and cannot work immediately.*

24. *Any patient in Taipingfang will pay for his own food and medicine. However, if he is proved to be very poor and lacks help from relatives or friends, the directors will organize a fund-raising campaign for him.*

25. *If any patient has no savings and relatives' or friends' help after death, the directors will organize a fund-raising campaign for his funeral expenses. In addition, the association shall give a subsidy of $3. If there is a surplus from the donation, it will be entrusted to his trustworthy relatives or friends and later remitted to his family in China.*

26. *If a patient has recovered from illness, he should not remain in Taipingfang whether he has a job or not. If he refuses to leave, someone will come to drive him out.*

27. *If a young girl has been kidnapped and brought to Canada, she must be surrendered to the association. The association will pay for her fare back to Tung Wah Hospital in Hong Kong and notify her relatives to take her home. If she does not have relatives, the Tung Wah Hospital will arrange the adoption.*

Articles 28 to 37 deal with the revenues of the association, methods of collection, accounting, and auditing. For example, Article No. 28 states that "every merchant, worker etc. had to donate $2 as a foundation fee to help establish the association. The contribution should be received by the eighth lunar month. Anyone who had not paid the foundation fee would receive no benefits and any help from the association." Article No. 30 states that "any Chinese from China or the United States who arrived at Victoria for the first time should report to the association within five days of his arrival ... "

According to the 1884 constitution, CCBA was virtually a *de facto* Chinese government in Canada, making legislation, exercising jurisdiction, and enforcing regulations and orders. Its objectives were not only to carry out charity and look after the sick and poor, but also to arbitrate in disputes, stamp out social vices in Chinatown, and fight against foreign oppression. Articles 10 through 19 were particularly significant because they dealt with conflicts among Chinese themselves, and between Chinese and Western people. These articles also showed that CCBA could wield considerable power to deal with its recalcitrant members. Furthermore, the consul-general in San Francisco had empowered Chinese merchants to form CCBA, and made it the *de jure* representative of the Manchu government in Canada. Hence, CCBA, functioning like a consulate, was the formal mechanism of access to both the Manchu government and the three levels of governments in Canada.

CCBA would not look after any Chinese who had not paid the $2 foundation fee before 17 October 1884. This contribution was a life subscription and not an annual fee. It was voluntary in name only. Board directors could enforce the contribution because some were shipping agents or labour contractors. Chinese agents would not sell tickets to those who had not made the donation, and Chinese contractors would deduct $2 from workers' wages. Furthermore, the association would send inspectors to the wharf to check whether any departing Chinese had made the donation, and prohibit him or her from boarding the vessel if he or she did not have the association's donation receipt. The local authority did not interfere, thinking that the Chinese inspectors at the pier were checking their own people, and preventing debt-dodgers from leaving Canada for China.

## Board of Directors

The first board of directors was elected on 3 August 1884, comprising 2 co-presidents, 6 vice-presidents, 20 directors and 1 secretary. The two co-presidents were Lee Yau Kain of the Kwong On Lung & Co. and Wong Yim Ho of the Tai Soong & Co. (Figure 4). The six vice-presidents were Lee in Poy of the Lee Chuck Co., Lee Yick Tack of the Tai Yune Co., Loo Chock Fan of the Kwong Lee & Co., Mar Sau of the Tai Chong Co., Chue Chuen Lai of the Wing Chong & Co., and Fung Kum Shoong of the Siu Chong. The 20 directors represented other companies or stores such as Kwong On Tai, Sam Kee, Kwong Chong, Fook Yuen, Boon Yuen, King Tyre, Hoon Yuen, Bow Chee Tong (an herbalist store), Yuen Chong, Wing Chong Loong, Yueh Chong Lau (a restaurant), Shing Lee, Yee Chong Tai,

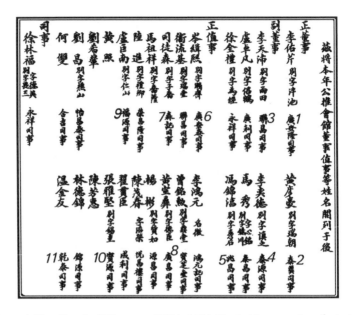

Figure 4 First Board of Directors, CCBA, 1884. No. 1–11 were opium factories

Kam Yuen, and Hop Gut. The secretary was Chue Lum Fook of the Wing Cheong & Co. Eleven directors were either owners or partners of 11 opium factories which were numbered in Figure 4 as: 1 Kwong On Lung, 2 Tai Soong, 3 Lee Chuck, 4 Tai Yune, 5 Siu Chong, 6 Kwong On Tai, 7 Sam Kee, 8 Kwong Chong, 9 Fook Yuen, 10 Boon Yuen, 11 King Tyre.[54] In the 1870s and 1880s, nearly all wealthy merchants in Victoria operated opium factories, which had made a great contribution not only to the economy of Chinatown but also to the revenues of the three levels of governments. In the 1870s, for example, opium was British Columbia's third largest export after coal and fur to the United States.[55] Victoria's Chinatown was the most important opium manufacturing in Canada, having 13 opium factories in 1888 (Figure 5).

When CCBA held its second election of board of directors in 1885, virtually all the 1884 board directors were re-elected for another term. As some directors had never attended meetings regularly, the board decided to reduce its size. From 1886 to 1904, it usually had from 10 to 13 members and only 1 president and 1 vice-president.[56]

CCBA general election was held once a year. At the meeting, the retiring board of directors would present a financial report of the preceding

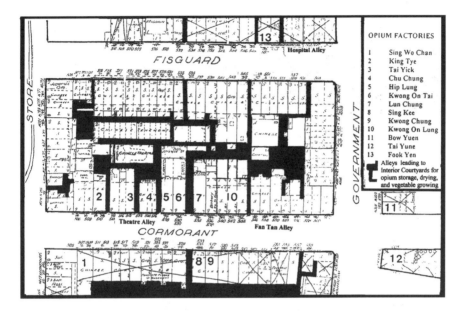

Figure 5 Opium Factories, Victoria's Chinatown, 1888

year and a new board would be elected. The election was usually stage-managed, since names were canvassed well in advance of the election and outgoing directors had worked out well in advance who should be incoming directors. Most were wealthy merchants, social notables, and other prominent individuals, who were both prestigious and authoritative. The candidates with the most votes would be elected. Until 1912 there was an unwritten law that no CCBA directors should be members of secret societies or operators of gambling dens or brothels. CCBA meetings were conducted mainly in Siyi dialect although other dialects were occasionally used. Hence, in the early years, non-Siyi speaking people were at a disadvantage in meeting discussions in comparison with Siyi speakers.

## Association Building

On 17 March 1885, CCBA purchased a 60 × 120 foot lot at 554–60 Fisgard Street (Lot 458 in Block F) from Thomas D. Lindsay for $4,500.[57] The building was designed by John Teague and its woodwork done by S. Gray. It was a three-storey brick structure, decorated with an Italianate cornice, window, and door frames (Plate 1). The street facade displayed a double-

Plate 1   Chinese Consolidated Benevolent Association building, 554–560 Fisgard Street, 1885

tiered projecting balcony with wooden supporting posts, decorative corner brackets, fretwork and turned balusters, dividing screens, and decorative canopies.[58] The back of the building had projecting verandahs. The ground floor of the building consisted of three commodious compartments for commercial use, and a narrow passageway extending from Fisgard Street to the rear. The second floor was used as the association's office, and the third floor housed a temple. The site excavation, carried out by a number of White labourers, began on 27 May 1885 and the building was completed in August.[59] Construction cost $9,475.66.[60]

## Palace of Sages

Soon after completion of the association building, CCBA board directors erected a temple called the Palace of Sages (Lie Sheng Gong) in the middle room on the top floor as a source of income. Based on a geomancer's advice, the Palace of Sages was installed on 27 December 1885 between 11.00 a. m. and 1.00 p.m.[61] Merchants contributed $625.50 for the installation ceremony. The list of expenses revealed that in those days CCBA had to give "a gift" of $300 to the Fire Department and two gold slabs of $57.50 to the fire chief before it could burn incense sticks and light firecrackers (Figure 6). The two gifts accounted for half the total ceremony expenses in the installation ceremony (Table 3).

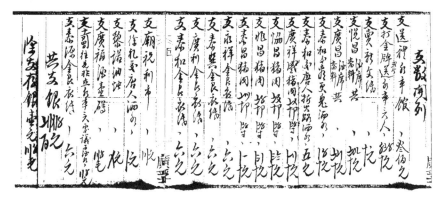

Figure 6  Expenses on the installation of the Palace of Sages, December 1885

Table 3  Expenses on Temple Installation Ceremony, 1885

| Items of Expenses | Amount |
| --- | --- |
| Gift to the Fire Department | $300.00 |
| Vegetarian ingredients and banquet | 146.70 |
| Gold medal to Fire Chief | 57.50 |
| Pork | 49.10 |
| Gold and silver paper | 30.00 |
| Miscellaneous | 40.85 |
| Total | $624.15 |

Source: CCBA archives.

Known to the Western public as the "joss house," the Palace contained a large, gilded shrine which housed statuettes of three sages: the God of Wealth, the God of Righteousness, the Queen of Heaven (The God of Medicine and Confucius statue were added to the Palace after a Chinese school was set up on the same floor in 1899). On both sides of the shrine were a large drum, a huge iron bell, canopies of colourful embroidery, and spears, battleaxes, and other types of Chinese weapons in brass and wood. In front of the shrine was a huge altar on which pewter drinking vessels, incense burners, and candlesticks were placed. The frontal piece of the altar was elaborately carved and gilded. On the walls of the temple were hung many elaborately carved and gilded wooden boards with Chinese inscriptions. These boards were donated by various clan associations, of which seven were identified, namely, Lee Long Sai Tong, Ming Yee Tong, Tong Yan Chung Shan Tong, Wong Kong Har Tong, Chan Wing Chun Tong, Mah Gim Gee Tong, and Xie Yushu Tang. No boards were donated by county associations. It can therefore be deduced that by 1885, several clan associations had already been established in Victoria, whereas rudimentary county associations were insignificant in society. Chinese people tended to pay more attention to the solidarity of their own clans than their own counties.[62] For this reason, county associations were established later than clan associations.[63]

CCBA had regulations for bidding for custody of the Palace of Sages and its management.[64] On 22 December 1885, for example, Li Mingwan made a bid of $1,317 to obtain the contract as temple custodian until 24 March 1887. According to a regulation of the temple, every worshipper had to purchase incense sticks and paper money from the custodian. Another regulation read that the custodian was permitted to keep all annual donations of worshippers but he would have to pay for the lamp oils, incense sticks and other offerings in the temple. He was also permitted to keep all donations during the Qing Ming Festival, Chong Yang Festival, and festivals of other gods on condition that he would give half a pound of barbecue pork and one bun to the donor for a donation of every 50 cents. The temple custodian was also to look after the association building and hospital and keep them clean and tidy. In other words, the temple custodian was also the association's janitor.

## Taipingfang

Another important task of CCBA was to provide accommodation for the very sick, poor, and uncared-for elderly Chinese men. In 1885, it built a small wooden hut on Herald Street behind the association's building, and called it *Taipingfang* (Peaceful Room). One of its regulations stipulated that patients should provide their own food and medicine.[65] However, if a patient did not have relatives or friends to supply provisions, and if two merchants would be guarantors and confirm that he was genuinely poor, CCBA would pay his medical expenses and provide two meals at 20 cents per day.

## Sources of Income

CCBA's regular incomes came from three sources: rental income of the ground floor of the association building; annual bidding for the job as the temple's custodian; the foundation fee of $2. In 1884 and 1885, CCBA sent notices to over 30 localities in British Columbia and asked Chinese to join the association. Although it is unknown how many people had paid the $2 foundation fee, CCBA's archives still have 220 booklets of receipt stubs for 5,056 donors, which probably represented a significant portion of the Chinese population in British Columbia.[66] The total foundation fees from these donors amounted to $10,112. This was a large amount of money in those days and sufficient to purchase a property and build the association building. After nearly all Chinese had joined the association, income from foundation fees was greatly reduced. Incomes from rent and the temple custodian's bidding were insufficient to run the association, its Taipingfang, and other charitable work. Often CCBA had to rely on fund-raising campaigns for special events such as welcoming dignitaries from China, paying legal fees for fighting against discriminatory regulations, assisting poor and sick and elderly people to return home and paying the funeral expenses for the dead in the hospital. For example, when Zhang Yinhuan, Manchu Qinchai Dachen (Imperial Commissioner of the Manchu government) stopped in Victoria on his way to the United States in 1886, CCBA had to rely on merchants' donation of $106 for a banquet to welcome him.[67] As a result, wealthy Chinese merchants who were usually the major donors for any special events were asked to be CCBA directors.

## Endnotes

1  SBC, 1872, 121, and 1876, 3.
2  *Ibid.*, 1876, 13.
3  Consolidated SBC, 1877, 567.
4  *Daily British Colonist*, 16 May 1873.
5  *Ibid.*, 14 August 1875.
6  SPLABC, 2nd Session, 4th parliament, 1883, 229, and Col. 27, October 1878.
7  PABA, *A Constitution of the Workingman's Protective Association.*
8  SBC, *An Act to Provide for the Better Collection of Provincial Taxes from Chinese* [2 September 1878], 42 Vic. Ch. 35, 129–132.

9   *Daily British Colonist*, 11 September 1878.
10  *Ibid.*, 18 September 1878.
11  *Ibid.*, 28 September 1878.
12  *Ibid.*, 22 September 1878.
13  *Ibid.*, 26 October 1878.
14  *Ibid.*, 28 September 1879.
15  David T.H. Lee, *Overseas Chinese History in Canada* (Vancouver: Canadian Freedom Publisher, 1967), 127.
16  *Daily British Colonist*, 3 July 1881.
17  Ten-ming Huang, *The Legal Status of the Chinese Abroad* (Taipei: China Cultural Service 1954), 82.
18  *Daily British Colonist*, 4 July 1884.
19  SBC, 2nd Session, 4th Parliament, 1884, Chap. 2, 3; Chap. 3, 5–6; and Chap. 4, 7–12.
20  *Daily British Colonist*, 4 November 1883.
21  *Ibid.*, 22 Jan. 1884.
22  *Mallandaine's Victoria Directory* (Victoria: Mallandaine, 1871), 94–95.
23  Canada, *Royal Commission on Chinese Immigration: Report and Evidence* (Ottawa: Printed by Order of the Commission, 1885), 363.
24  *Ibid.*, 42.
25  *Daily British Colonist*, 7 and 8 February 1882.
26  *Ibid.*, 24 November 1882.
27  *Ibid.*, 22 February and 8 March 1883.
28  *Ibid.*, 8 June 1883.
29  *Ibid.*, 1 June 1884.
30  *Ibid.*, 10 January 1884.
31  Chuen-Yan David Lai, "The Demographic Structure of a Canadian Chinatown in the Mid-Twentieth Century," *Canadian Ethnic Studies*, XI, 2 (1979), 56.
32  David T.H. Lee, *op. cit.*, 174.
33  Commemorative Issue of the Third National Convention of the Lee Clan, August 1985, 45.
34  Chuenyan David Lai, "Home County and Clan Origins of Overseas Chinese in Canada in the early 1880's," *BC Studies*, 27 (1975) 8–9 and 23.
35  Chuenyan David Lai "Shipment of Bones to China," *Likely Cemetery Society's Annual Newsletter*, July 1991 (unnumbered).
36  AC, Photo of the 60th Year Anniversary of the Victoria Yushan Chong How Zong Tang, dated 2 September 1945.
37  A Commemorative Issue of the Establishment of Yushan Zong Gongsuo, Vancouver Yue Shan Society, 1949, 3.
38  Chuenyan David Lai, *Chinatowns: Towns Within Cities in Canada* (Vancouver: University of British Columbia Press, 1988), 94–95.
39  *Special Issue of the Third Pan-Canadian National Convention of the Lee Clan, Calgary, 3–5 August 1985.* (Calgary: Special Issue Editorial Committee, 1986), 45.
40  Maurice Freedman, "Immigrants and Associations: Chinese in Nineteenth Century Singapore. "*Comparative Studies in Society and History*, 3 (1960), 35.
41  C.N. Reynolds, "The Chinese Tongs," *American Journal of Sociology*, 40 (1935), 617–19.
42  *Ibid.*, 621.
43  Cao Jianwu. "The History of the Hungmen's Participation in the 1911 Revolution" Unpublished Chinese manuscript, 1930. pages unnumbered (Archives of the Chinese Freemasons, Victoria). *The Daily Colonist* reported on 4 October 1898 that Lim Sam and Yip Wing, directors of the Chee Kung Tong, told a reporter in 1898 that the Society had been in existence for the last twenty years.
44  *Daily British Colonist*, 20 January 1877 and *Daily Colonist*, 4 October 1898.
45  *Daily British Colonist*, 4 January 1879.

46  *The Daily British Colonist* was renamed the *Daily Colonist* on 1 January 1887.

47  *Daily Colonist*, 22 November 1884.

48  *Ibid.*, 13 November 1886.

49  AC, draft letter, Victoria's merchants to Huang Tsim Hsim, Consul General in San Francisco, March 1884.

50  *Ibid.*, Huang Sic Chen's Letter to Victoria merchants, 28 April 1884.

51  *Ibid.*, circular for fund-raising campaign for the establishment of Zhonghua Huiguan, 10 April 1884.

52  *Ibid.*, *Rules and Bylaws of the Chinese Consolidated Benevolent Association*. Approved and filed on 18 August 1884 by Chas Leggatt, Acting Registrar General.

53  *Ibid.*, regulations of Victoria's Zhonghua Huiguan, 1884 (in Chinese script).

54  Henderson's British Columbia Directory and Street Index, 1890.

55  *Daily British Colonist and Victoria Daily Chronicle*, 27 January 1872.

56  The boards of director in 1892 had 22 members.

57  LRO. D.D. Roll 109B, 987, No. 6291a, registered 21 March 1885 in Absolute Fees Book, Vol. 8 February, No. 895; Col. 4 July 1885.

58  Chuenyan David Lai, *The Forbidden City Within Victoria: Myth, Symbol and Streetscape of Canada's Earliest Chinatown* (Victoria: Orca Book Publishers, 1991), 122.

59  *Daily British Colonist*, 28 May 1885.

60  AC, handwritten invoice submitted by John Teague, 29 September 1885. The total cost amounted to $9,475.66: drawing up 5 contracts and advertising for tenders: $272.17; five contracts: brick work by Humber ($5,140), carpentry by Gray ($3,162), painting by Lettice ($350), tin work by Stephens ($384), and gas and water by Bradue ($167.49); *Daily British Colonist*, 4 and 15 July 1885.

61  AC, hand-written note on "The auspicious date and time for the installation of Lie Sheng Gong of Zhonghua Huiguan".

62  David Tung Hai Lee, former secretary of CCBA, private interview, October 1979.

63  David T.H. Lee, *op. cit.*, 174.

64  AC, *Regulations of Bidding for the Custody of the Temple, 14 December 1885 and 13 September 1886.*

65  AC, "The Proposal for the Establishment of Taipingfang, 1884".

66  Chuenyan David Lai, "Home County and Clan Origins of Overseas Chinese in Canada in the early 1880's," *BC Studies*, 27 (1975) 4–5.

67  AC, circular to Welcome Zhang Yinhuan Yinchai Dachen, 1886.

# 3

# Oligarchic Rule, 1884–1890s

—3—

# Oligarchic Rule, 1884–1890s

*Chinatown is an offence to at least two senses — sight and smell. It reeks of opium, and is suggestive of low gambling-hells. There sit the fat "merchants" who are probably deep in usurious practices of the most blood-sucking description. It is impossible not to suspect that the hard toil of many a poor John goes to increase the paunch of some of these fat tyrants who sit lurking like spiders in their dark and silent dens, concocting in their minds webs for the unwary. Yet be it remembered that many of these men have invested large sums in the country, and are deeply interested in pushing trades but for them would not be existing today.*[1]

This was what Francis Macnab thought of Chinese opium merchants in Chinatown when he wrote about settlers in British Columbia in 1898. He failed to mention that the "fatter tyrants" might be British merchants: they grew opium in India, made it into balls of crude opium in Hong Kong, and sold them to Chinese merchants who then shipped the semi-processed product to Victoria's opium factories for manufacturing. Furthermore, customs duties on opium and re-exports had been one of Canada's important sources of revenues. For example, the duties on opium imports into Canada totalled nearly $47,500 in 1906 and amounted to nearly $54,900 in the first nine months of 1907.[2] Hence, the "fat" Chinatown merchants had enriched not only themselves but also the coffers of Canada as well as the United Kingdom.

Most CCBA founders were proprietors of opium importing or manufacturing companies. A study of their background and the characteristics of the Chinese population will help reveal the leadership pattern and monolithic power structure of Chinatown in the 1880s and 1890s.

## Home Origins

CCBA archives have about 5,060 stubs for the $2 donation receipts dated 1884 and 1885, of which 672 stubs came from Victoria.[3] The description on each stub provides valuable information about the home county and clan origins of the donor (see Figure 3). Of the 672 donors in Victoria, 52% came from *Siyi* (Four Counties) and 29% from *Sanyi* (Three Counties) on the Zhujiang delta (Table 4). The Siyi people have a common dialect and speak differently from the Sanyi people. The competition for business and jobs between these two groups of people was so keen and bitter that occasionally it resulted in a "tong war."

The 672 donors are classified into 81 clans according to their surnames (Table 5). Classification reveals that the three largest clans were surnamed Li, Ma, and Huang; together they accounted for nearly 30% of the Chinese population in the city. Within these three clans, the Lis outnumbered those from other clans, constituting over 16% of the Chinese population.

## Merchant Class

In the traditional society of China, the scholarly and official class had both power and wealth because the literati were placed above peasants, artisans, and merchants in traditional China's four-tier social structure. In the early days, most Chinese in Canada were poor, unskilled, and illiterate labourers, and gentry and scholar officials were absent. The Chinese community in Victoria was thus polarized into two extreme groups: an overwhelming majority of a socially depressed and illiterate group and a very tiny group of wealthy merchants who could easily become dominant. Merchants gained power and respectability through wealth which derived from their positions as wholesale importers and exporters, opium manufacturers, and labour contractors. Many extended credit and negotiated employment for poor rural labourers seeking passage to Canada. In addition to providing employment, merchants or contractors also provided room and board for

Table 4  Home County Origins of Donors in Victoria, 1884–1885

| County | No. of Persons | | % of Total | |
|---|---|---|---|---|
| Siyi (4 Counties) | 352 | | 52.2 | |
| Taishan | | 183 | | 27.2 |
| Enping | | 72 | | 10.7 |
| Xinhui | | 53 | | 7.9 |
| Kaiping | | 44 | | 6.5 |
| Sanyi (3 Counties) | 194 | | 28.9 | |
| Panyu | | 153 | | 22.8 |
| Shunde | | 28 | | 4.2 |
| Nanhai | | 13 | | 1.9 |
| Huaxian | 7 | | 1.2 | |
| Zhongshan | 35 | | 5.2 | |
| Zengcheng | 25 | | 3.7 | |
| Dongguan | 17 | | 2.5 | |
| Heshan | 15 | | 2.2 | |
| Baoan | 7 | | 1.0 | |
| Yangjiang | 3 | | 0.4 | |
| Other counties | 17 | | 2.5 | |
| Total | 672 | | 100.0 | |

Sources: Stubs of donation receipts, 1884 and 1885, CCBA

Table 5  Clan Origins of Donors in Victoria, 1884–1885

| Surname | No. of Persons | % of Total |
|---|---|---|
| Lee (Li) | 109 | 16.2 |
| Mar, Mah, or Marr (Ma) | 46 | 6.8 |
| Wong (Huang) | 43 | 6.4 |
| Chan or Chin (Chen) | 34 | 5.1 |
| Leung (Liang) | 27 | 4.0 |
| Tse, Der, Dare or Hsieh (Xie) | 24 | 3.6 |
| Chow, Joe, or Chou (Zhou) | 23 | 3.4 |
| Chui, Tsui, Chu or Hsu (Xu) | 20 | 3.0 |
| Fung (Feng) | 15 | 2.2 |
| Sum or Shum (Shen) | 15 | 2.2 |
| Lum or Lam (Lin) | 13 | 1.9 |
| Ng, Eng or Ing (Wu) | 13 | 1.9 |
| Kong or Chiang (Jiang) | 13 | 1.9 |
| 68 other surnames | 277 | 41.2 |
| Total | 672 | 100.00 |

Sources: Stubs of donation receipts, 1884 and 1885, CCBA. A Chinese surname may be transliterated into different English spellings. The Pinyin spelling is in brackets

newly arrived labourers, and offered certain benevolent services to the needy. For example, after completion of the Canadian Pacific Railway, many Chinese railway workers drifted backed from the mainland to Victoria in January 1886.[4] They were out of work and starving, begging at houses and street corners. The merchants pooled their resources to help them. By virtue of their wealth, provision of jobs, and the ability to read and write, they were recognized leaders in the Chinese community. With the support of the Manchu officials from San Francisco, they were entrusted to establish CCBA and govern all Chinatowns or Chinese settlements in British Columbia and acted as spokesmen for all Chinese in Canada.

To achieve social status back in China, wealthy merchants in Victoria identified with the elite culture of the literati in three ways: buying official titles, purchasing properties in home villages in China, and emulating the literati-gentry's lifestyle. They educated their sons in the hope that they could pass the civil examinations and become members of the literati in their own right.[5] After the Opium War ended in 1841, the Manchu government was in great financial difficulty, and tried desperately to raise money by granting official titles and rank to ordinary citizens inside or outside China who made large contributions of funds. The sale of titles and rank not only helped solve the Manchu government's financial problems, but also helped it to cultivate overseas Chinese loyalty.

This pro-Manchu movement developed among overseas Chinese until the late nineteenth century. Apart from having close contacts with the Manchu consuls and visiting officials, many overseas Chinese merchants rendered overt political, financial, and social support to the Manchu government when opportunities arose.

In the 1860s, the Manchu government signed treaties with Western powers in recognizing the right of Chinese people to leave China, and issuing visas to those who wished to return to China. Visas had three grades. The third grade, the lowest, was issued to labourers, the second grade to small merchants. The first grade was given to *Shen Shang* (meaning gentry-merchants), that is, very rich merchants in overseas Chinese communities. A first grade visa thus became a status symbol of overseas wealthy Chinese merchants because the Manchu government encouraged them to return home and invest in China.[6]

## Profile of Founders

CCBA was founded in 1884 by about 10 merchants in Victoria. Most engaged in import and export of Chinese merchandise, opium manufacturing, labour recruiting, land development, and/or other businesses. A few had started their own businesses but most were inherited from their fathers in San Francisco and/or Guangzhou in China, and had established branches in Victoria and other cities in British Columbia. Soon after CCBA was formed, the founders became respectively president, vice-president, and members of the board of directors, and were re-elected again the following year.

Lee Yau Kain (alias Lee Poon Chee), was a Taishan native. He was a merchant in Portland's Chinatown before he came to Victoria in the 1860s and established the Kwong On Lung & Co. on Cormorant Street.[7] The company sold Chinese commodities wholesale and manufactured opium behind the store. Balls of crude opium were cooked in boiling water for about 12 hours until they were converted into jelly and then canned for sale. Lee was a well-respected, public-spirited merchant. Soon after the Legislative Assembly of British Columbia passed the Chinese Tax Act on 2 September 1878, by which every Chinese in the province had to pay $40 head tax a year, Lee immediately asked other Chinese merchants to join him in writing a letter to Guo Songtao, the high commissioner in London, to protest. The three provincial acts of 1884 prompted Lee and other merchants to form CCBA and urge the Manchu government to set up a consulate or an embassy in Canada. Lee was elected CCBA co-president in 1884 and 1885 and president in 1887. In 1884, the Dominion government passed $50 head tax on Chinese immigrants. Together with Tong Him Tai (alias Dong Tai or Tong Kee) of Tai Soong & Co., he spearheaded launching a lawsuit to contest the validity of the $50 head tax by contributing $550 (Figure 7). In recognizing his generous donations and public service, the Manchu government later conferred an honorary official title on him of Imperial-Awarded First Class Sub-Prefect.

Wong Yim Ho (alias Wong Soy Chew), CCBA co-president in 1884 and 1885, was a Panyu native. He was the son of Wong Tien Lui, who operated Tai Chuen Co. in Hong Kong and Kwong Sang Tai Co. in San Francisco.[8] In 1858 Wong Tien Lui and his partner, Tong Him Tai (alias Tong Kee), established the Tai Soong & Co. as a wholesale company on Johnson Street in Victoria. Two or three times a year, the company

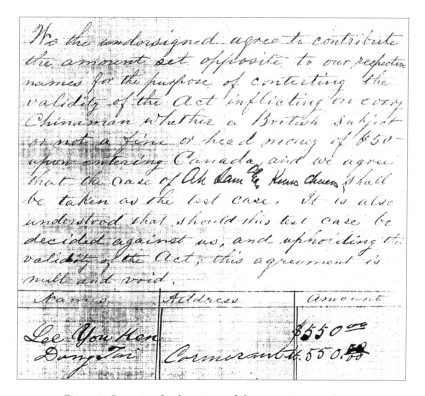

Figure 7  Campaign for donation to fight against $50 Head Tax

chartered a clipper to ship tons of dried goods and Chinese merchandise from Hong Kong to Victoria, and then distributed the goods to Chinese stores in New Westminster, Quesnellemouth, Barkerville and other gold-mining towns in the interior.[9] Tai Soong & Co. was not only the second largest Chinese import and export company, but also a leading opium manufacturer in British Columbia. Wong Yim Ho and Chow Quong, took over the management of the company after the retirement of Wong Tien Lui and the death of Tong Him Tai.[10]

Loo Chock Fan, a CCBA director, and his brother, Loo Chew Fan, owned Kwong Lee & Co., the largest Chinese import and export company in British Columbia. They also operated Kwong U Shing in Canton (Guangzhou), Kwong Man Fung in Hong Kong, and Hop Kee & Co. in San Francisco.[11] In 1858, the Loo brothers established Kwong Lee & Co. on Cormorant Street, and asked Lee Chong and Tong Fat to manage it. By 1868, branches of Kwong Lee & Co. had been set up in Yale, Lillooet, Quesnelle

Forks, Quesnellemouth, and Barkerville.[12] Loo Chock Fan was not only an import and export merchant but also a labour contractor. In April 1860, for example, he arranged for the first group of 265 Chinese labourers to come from China and provided room and board in Chinatown.[13] Many worked in his gold mines.[14] After the gold rush was over, Loo recruited labourers to work for other companies. For example, in August 1884, he got a contract to plough and level about 25 acres of land in Sooke District at $19 per acre, and to cut 2,000 piles of red fir at three cents per lineal foot for the piles, and $2 per cord for the red fir cordwood.[15] Loo was also a land developer and speculator. In July 1858, he and Chang Tsoo of Yang Wo Sang & Co. purchased 13 lots in Block N on the north side of Cormorant Street and divided the land between them.[16] At the beginning of the 1880s, the Loo family's wealth began to decline. Owing to heavy borrowing and family disputes, the Loo brothers went to court often, eventually going bankrupt.[17] By the late 1880s, all their properties in Chinatown had been sold by public auction.

Lee Yick Tack, another CCBA director, managed Tai Yune Co. His uncle, Li Tianshi, was a prominent, wealthy Chinese merchant who had established import and export companies in Macao, Hong Kong, Honolulu, and San Francisco, and operated a large opium factory in Macao.[18] In recognition of his generous donations and community service, the Manchu government awarded Li Tianshi Imperial-Awarded First Class Sub-Prefect (Plate 2). In 1875 he came to Victoria and established Tai Yune Co. and asked his nephew, Lee Yick Tack, to look after it. When Lee Yick Tack retired in 1887, he asked his brother, Lee Yick Wei (alias Lee Sui Ting), to take over management. Tai Yune Co. owned one of the largest opium factories in Victoria and produced the finest opium, known as the "Tai Yuen brand."

Plate 2  Li Tianshi, founder of Tai Yune Co.

Lee Tin Poy, known to the white public as Lee Chuck, was a Taishan native, and a CCBA vice-president. He operated Lee Chuck Company in Victoria and recruited Chinese railway workers for Andrew Onderdonk. During the construction, many Chinese railway workers died not only of accidents but also from winter cold, illness, and malnutrition. Neither the railway company nor Lee Chuck Co. provided medical assistance to sick workers. The exploitation of workers by Lee Chuck Co. was made public after railway workers refused to work. On 10 May 1881, for example, they went on strike in Yale, and rioted for four days later because the White contractor permitted Lee Chuck Co. to provide supplies and to retain 2% of their wages as commission.[19] The workers complained that they were forced to buy all supplies from Lee's company at prices higher than in other stores. The supplies were deficient in weight and quality, and the price of rice was raised by two cents a pound. If a Chinese worker patronized other suppliers, his wages would be cut. Lee Tian Poy refused to look after the railway workers after they were laid off and left impoverished along the railway track. After the news brought to the attention of Huang Tsim Hsim, consul general in San Francisco, he wrote to Lee and compelled him to ship the workers back to China. Lee Tin Poy was probably an unpopular CCBA director because he had no concern for his railway workers.

Mar Sau, another CCBA director, was also a prominent labour contractor in Victoria. He operated Tai Chong Yuen & Co. on Cormorant Street. In December 1884, Robert A. Graham and C.W. Busk, who got the contract to build the Nanaimo-Chemainus section of the Esquimalt and Nanaimo Railway (E. & N. Railway), arranged with the company to hire several hundred Chinese labourers.[20] Mar Sau immediately sent a hundred Chinese workers to Nanaimo in January 1885, and recruited about 900 Chinese labourers from San Francisco. Many of them landed in Victoria on 22 June 1885.[21] By the time they arrived at Nanaimo, they were no longer needed. Robert Graham and C.W. Busk had financial problems, and began to lay off their workers. Mar Sau then had the problem of finding jobs for his labourers since the E. & N. Railway would be finished within a year. Furthermore, Mar Sau was charged for non-payment of the provincial tax on his Chinese railway workers. As a result, he had to declare the bankruptcy on 29 July 1885.[22] Five creditors immediately made claims against his company of nearly $1,670.[23] In November, Kwong Tai Lung Co. purchased his business and continued to operate it from the same premise.[24]

## Chinatown Elite

Selling rank and office became more common after the Taiping Rebellion and was sanctioned by imperial decree on 13 December 1850.[25] For example, Annam (now Vietnam) was under the sovereignty of China until the French invaded Hanoi and set up a protectorate in 1882. Accordingly, in 1883 the Manchu government sent troops from Yunnan and Guangxi provinces into Tongking (now northern Vietnam), where they met the French in pitched battles.[26] Since Guangdong was the chief base area for forces in Tongking, its viceroy appealed to overseas Chinese for financial supports in the Sino-French War. On 25 June 1885, Huang Sic Chen, secretary of the consulate general in San Francisco, sent a letter to CCBA, acknowledging its donation of about $400 towards the military needs of Guangdong Province (Figure 8). On 15 August, he sent another letter to CCBA, stating that the Chinese in Victoria had contributed 337.795 taels, and asking for the names of donors and the type of titles and ranks they wanted, based on regulations for the sale of official ranks and titles (Figure 9). Since most rich overseas Chinese merchants were immigrants from poor economic backgrounds, imperial honours greatly satisfied their psychological need and enhanced their prestige and power in local Chinese communities.[27] They could achieve social mobility through the award or purchase of honorary official titles and ranks.

The honour system was also the Manchu government's way of acquiring loyalty and overseeing its overseas subjects in countries where there were no Chinese consulates. If the Manchu government wanted to control Chinatown associations and Chinese schools, they had to enlist the support of the merchants because they were usually association and/ or school board directors. So the government awarded merchants imperial honours after they had done special services such as raising capital for investment in China and donating money or raising funds for drought, flood, and other types of relief in China and overseas countries. For example, on 20 December 1897, two honourable titles of *Liupin Dingdai* (Milky White Crystal Button of the Sixth Rank worn on Head Dress) were put up for auction to provide relief funds for the Chinese community in Cuba (Figure 10). The two successful bidders in Victoria were Jiang Jingke, who paid $159.5 and Lee Kam Tao (alias Lee Dye or Lee Kum Chow), who paid $125. On 8 April 1898, the Manchu government tried to raise

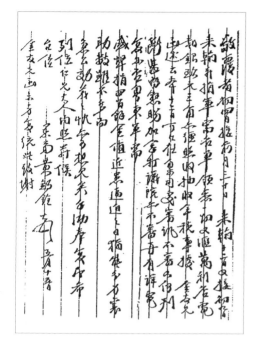

Figure 8  Letter from Chinese consulate in San Francisco, 25 June 1885

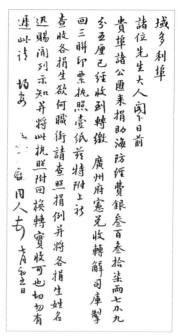

Figure 9  Letter from Chinese consulate in San Francisco, 15 August 1885

more relief funds for the Chinese community in Cuba by offering three honourable titles of *Wupin Dingdai* (Transparent White Crystal Button of the Fifth Rank worn on Head Dress). These titles were won by Lin Bangxi for $161, Huang Fukang for $120, and Lee Kam Tao for $115.

In the 1890s and 1900s a small Chinese elite formed by well-to-do merchants emerged in Victoria's Chinatown. In 1902, for example, merchants of 13 big Chinese companies or stores were nominated to sit on CCBA board of directors (Figure 11). They had lived in Chinatown for many years and were well known to the Chinese community. As they were wealthy and powerful, mention of their names was a sufficient guarantee of their respectability and high standing among Chinatown residents. A few merchants who had received honourary titles from the Manchu government thus formed the backbone of leadership in Chinatown. For example, seven merchants had honourary titles: Li Hongqia (alias Li Runhua) was Imperial-Awarded First Class Sub-Prefect of the Fifth Rank; Loo Yang

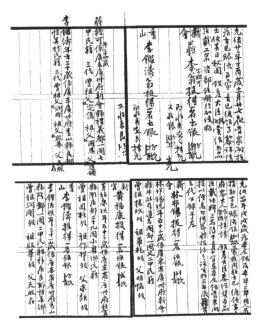

Figure 10  Successful bidders for honorary titles, 1897, 1898

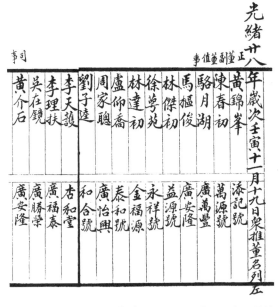

Figure 11  CCBA Board of Directors, 18 December 1902

Kiu was the Single-eyed Pea-
cock Feather Intendant; Huang
Fukang had a Military Merit
Award of the White Crystal
Button of the Fifth Rank worn
on Head Dress; Huang Zhenwei
had the title of Collegian of the
Imperial Academy of Learning;
Liu Tongchun had the title Sub-
District Magistrate of Guangxi;
and Huang Yulin had the title
of Lieutenant.[28] Some promi-
nent merchants had received an
Honorary Medal from Qinchai
Dachen (Imperial Commis-
sioner) (Plate 3).

Plate 3 Award Medal by Imperial Commissioner of Manchu government

The Lee clan was undoubtedly the most influential power block in
terms of wealth and constituted a large proportion of the elite class in Chinatown, as shown by its strong representation on the first few boards of
directors of CCBA.[29] Some prominent members were Lee Yau Kain, Lee
Tin Poy, and Lee Yick Tack who helped founding CCBA. Other prominent
Lees included Lee Hoon Yuen, Lee Mong Kou, Lee Yick Wei, Lee Dye, Lee
Folk Gay, and Lee Ying San.

Lee Hoon Yuen, a Zhongshan native, worked in Hawaii and Australia
before he came to Victoria in the 1870s.[30] There he opened Hoon Yuen & Co.
on Cormorant Street, and engaged in import and export business as well as
labour recruiting. He was probably one of the few Chinese merchants who
was naturalized as a British subject.[31] Later he and his son, Lee Kam Tao
(alias Lee Dye or Lee Kum Chow), established Wah Yuen Co.[32] In 1897, Lee
Dye donated money to help the Chinese in Cuba and was later awarded by
the title Imperial Student of the Expectant of Assistant District Magistrate
of Blue Feather of the Fifth Rank. In the late 1900s, Lee Dye formed Lee
Dye & Sons Co. on Cormorant Street, one of the largest wholesalers of
Chinese food in Chinatown. Lee Yick Wei (alias Lee Sui Ting), a Taishan
native, managed Tai Yune Co. in 1887. He amassed a fortune in land
speculation and became prominent in China. On 14 September 1898,
he and Lee Mong Kow, Loo Yang Kiu and Yip Sang (alias Yip Chun Tin)

went to Vancouver to meet Li Hung Chang, viceroy of the Guangdong and Guangxi provinces.[33] In 1900, he was CCBA president when the Boxer Rebellion in China started. He had a lot of difficulty protecting the Chinese when some Western people attacked Chinese in revenge. He died in 1909 and was honoured by an elaborate funeral.

Lee Mong Kow, a Panyu native, spoke English well. During his childhood in Hong Kong, he had lived with his mother in an English family where she worked as a maid.[34] He went to San Francisco in 1881 and moved north to Victoria in the following year.[35] He worked as a labourer in Esquimalt for three years. Because of his ability in speaking and writing English, he was employed in 1885 by Canada Customs and Immigration as an interpreter. At the same time, he entered into a partnership with Sewn Yuen, a Chinese Herbal store. Later he managed Tai Soong & Co. when Tong Him Tai (alias Tong Kee) retired, and became a prominent merchant in Chinatown. He was also one of the founders of the first Chinese free school in Victoria. As an interpreter he became an important liaison official between the Chinese community and the government. In recognition of his contributions, the Manchu government conferred him the Imperial-Awarded First Class Sub-Prefect of the First Rank of the Privilege of Wearing Peacock Feather in 1897. In 1915, the government of the Republic of China conferred him Gar Wo Medal of the Sixth Rank.[36] He retired to Hong Kong in 1921.

Lee Folk Gay (alias Lee Man Wai ), a Taishan native, operated Quong Man Fung & Co. located at 26 Cormorant Street, specializing in silk, embroidery, and hats.[37] He helped Kang Yuwei, a political reformer in exile, to establish the Chinese Empire Reform Association (CERA) in 1899 and became

Plate 4  Chinese Empire Reform Association building, 1900s

the president of the association. In 1905, on behalf of CERA, he purchased a building at 1715 Government Street to where he moved his company on the ground floor and housed the association office on the 3rd floor (Plate 4). The building was next to Tam Kung Temple which was built in 1875 by the Hakka people.

Lee Ying San, another Taishan native, was CCBA president in 1891. He was a merchant in Portland's Chinatown before coming to Victoria in the 1870s.[38] He opened Boon Yune & Co., a wholesale company for Chinese merchandise, and manufactured opium behind the store. His son, Lee Min Sun, was also a public-spirited person. Together with his father, he established Ying Chong Lung and ran a large greenhouse, and did pig farming. In 1898, Dr. Sun Yat Sen, the famous revolutionary leader against the Manchu government, came to Victoria and stayed at Ying Chong Lung for several day. In 1911, Lee Min Sun did fund-raising campaigns to support Dr. Sun's Huang Hua Gang uprising.

All these Lees were involved in CCBA activities. Other Chinatown elite members who wielded heavy influence, included the managers of the three large opium factories (Won Alexander Cumyow of King Tyre Co., Loo Yan Shan of Fook Yuen Co., and Cheung Ah Kin of BowYune Co.) and merchants such as Chue Lum Fook (alias Chue Lai) of Wing Chong & Co. and Fung Kum Shoong (alias Kum Shoong) of Chu Chung & Co. The background of some individuals is unknown, however, because of lack of information, such as Chen Fengchang, Xu Riheng, and Zhai Ganchen, who was CCBA president in 1886, 1890, and 1897.

## Endnotes

1   Francis Macnab, *British Columbia for Settlers* (London: Chapman and Hall 1898), 88.
2   Canada, House of Commons, Sessional Papers, 1907–8, Vol. Paper No. 10, 52–53.
3   Chuen-yan David Lai, "Home County and Clan Origins of Overseas Chinese in Canada in the Early 1880s," *BC Studies*, No. 27 Autumn (1975), 4–5.
4   *Daily British Colonist*, 31 January 1886.
5   Wang Gungwu, *China and the Chinese Overseas* (Singapore: Times Academic Press 1991), 183.
6   Ching-hwang Yen, *Coolies and Mandarins Chinese Protection during Late Ch'ing Period* (Singapore: Singapore University Press 1985), 268.
7   *A Commemorative Issue of the Third National Convention of the Lee Clan in Canada, Calgary, August 1985* (Vancouver: Lee's Benevolent Association of Canada 1986), 48.
8   *A Commemorative Issue of the Grand Opening of the Yue Shan Society Building in Vancouver.* (Vancouver: Yue Shan Society 1949), Section 2, 2.
9   In the late 1860s, Tai Soong & Company was moved from Johnson Street to Cormorant Street and managed by Chan Tan.

10　Tong Kee deceased without a will, and in June 1878 Chun Tan, administrator of his Estate, sold his property (Lot 597) to Loo Chock Fan and Loo Chew Fan of Kwong Lee & CO. (LRO DD 29063). Chow Quong, the manager of the Tai Soong, signed the deed to buy Lot 443 in July 1883 (LRO DD7142).

11　*First Victory Directory and British Columbia Guide* (Victoria: E. Mallandaines 1868), 77.

12　*Ibid.*

13　*British Colonist*, 25 April 1860.

14　For example, he owned 20 shares of Grouse Creek Flume Co. at $5 per share (document signed by Lee Chang on behalf of Kwong Lee, BCARS Add. MSS 1053: Dr. Wilson E. Knowlton, Call No. MG55/29 #149).

15　BCARS, An Agreement between William Charles Siffken and Kwong Lee, signed by Yick Tai on 27 August 1884 (Add. MSS 1053: Dr. Wilson E. Knowlton, Call No. MG55/29 #149).

16　David Chuenyan Lai, *The Forbidden City Within Victoria: Myth, Symbol and Streetscape of Canada's Earliest Chinatown* (Victoria: Orca Book Publishers, 1991), 18–19.

17　Loo Chock Fan was sued by his brother Loo Chew Fan on 29 July 1887 (LRO. AFB Vol. 9, Fol. 845, #7492. DD27813 and DD29063).

18　*A Commemorative Issue of the Third National Convention of the Lee Clan in Canada, Calgary, op. cit.*, 48.

19　*Daily British Colonist*, 15, 17, 22 May 1881.

20　*Nanaimo Free Press*, 10, 31 December 1884; *Daily British Colonist*, 8 December 1884.

21　*Ibid.*, 7, 14, 21, 24 January, 1 February 1885.

22　*Daily British Colonist*, 30 July 1885; *Nanaimo Free Press*, 1 August 1885.

23　*Daily British Colonist*, 2, 5 August 1885.

24　*Ibid.*, 27, 29 November 1885.

25　H.S. Brunnert and V.V. Hagelstrom, *Present Day Political Organization of China, 1911* (Taipei: Book World, 1911), 507.

26　John Fairbank, *et al.*, *East Asia: Tradition and Transformation* (Boston: Houghton Mifflin, 1978), 605.

27　Yen Ching-hwang, "Ch'ing's Sale of Honours and the Chinese Leadership in Singapore and Malta 1877–1912," *Journal of Southeast Asian Studies*, Vol. 1 no. 2 (September 1970), 21.

28　David T.H. Lee, *Overseas Chinese History in Canada* (Vancouver: Canadian Freedom Publisher 1967), 330.

29　*Special Issue to Commemorate the 75th Anniversary of Victoria's Chinese Consolidated Benevolent Association (1884–1959) and the 60th Anniversary of Victoria's Chinese Public School (1899–1959)* (Victoria: Chinese Consolidated Benevolent Association 1960), 28–32.

30　*A Commemorative Issue of the Third National Convention of the Lee Clan in Canada, Calgary, op. cit.*, 49.

31　*Daily British Colonist*, 11 July 1880. His name was spelled Lee Hung Yune.

32　*A Commemorative Issue of the Third National Convention of the Lee Clan in Canada, Calgary, op. cit.*, 49.

33　*Daily Colonist*, 15 September 1896.

34　*A Commemorative Issue of the Third National Convention of the Lee Clan in Canada, Calgary, op. cit.*, 49–50.

35　Jack Wai Yen Lee, *The Legacy of Lee Mong Kow Prefecture*. Manuscript, Victoria, 2008, 9.

36　*Ibid.*, 3.

37　*A Commemorative Issue of the Third National Convention of the Lee Clan in Canada, Calgary, op. cit.*, 49.

38　*Ibid.*, 50.

**4**

# Functions and Activities, 1884–1890s

# Functions and Activities, 1884–1890s

Perusal of the correspondences, circulars, notices, and minutes of meetings in CCBA archives reveals that CCBA was a multi-functional organization. Like a philanthropic organization, it served specific purposes such as welfare and philanthropy. Like a social unit, it united the Chinese in British Columbia and other parts of Canada. Like a consulate, it functioned as a diplomatic representative for Chinese in Canada until 1909, and communicated their opinions to Manchu officials and the Canadian government. Like a local government, it exercised semi-judicial power to deal with the internal affairs of Chinatown. It learned to overcome discriminatory regulations and laws and fight against ill treatment by the host society. Its efforts minimized the sense of insecurity, cultural deprivation, and economic exclusion of Chinese in Canada. The three levels of government in Canada probably were aware that CCBA's work involved arbitration of both criminal and civic disputes among the Chinese. They did not care what it was doing as long as it only ran Chinatown and ruled the Chinese people without affecting the Western community.

The functions and activities can be broadly classified into nine groups: (1) work for the consulate general in San Francisco; (2) protests against discriminatory laws and regulations; (3) protection of Chinese citizens in Canada against abuses; (4) enforcing self-discipline and maintaining peace and order in Chinatown; (5) arbitration of internal disputes; (6) running the Chinese hospital, cemetery, and school; (7) shipment of bones;

(8) fund-raising for relief work in Canada; and (9) fund-raising for relief work in China and other areas. In this chapter, I cited one or two examples in each group, and highlighted some Chinese documents of the CCBA that illustrate the diversity of its work.

## Consular Duty

Before 1909, CCBA acted as the representative of Huang Tsim Hsim, the consul general in San Francisco (1882–85), and worked for him in Canada. Examples of this function, are seen in two letters written by his secretary, Huang Sic Chen, who told CCBA directors what the consul general had asked them to do. The first letter requested for a donation for erecting a monument to honour Charles Gordon, who was killed in January 1885 in Khartoum in fighting against Mahdist forces. On 12 May 1885 Huang Sic Chen wrote to CCBA (Figure 12), stating that:

> *During the reigns of Emperor Xianfeng and Emperor Tongzhi, Charles Gordon, a British general, led the foreign soldiers in vanquishing the Taiping rebels for the Chinese government, and recaptured several cities in Jiangsu and Zhejiang provinces from them ...*

Figure 12  Letter from Chinese consulate in San Francisco, 12 May 1885

*Gordon died in the battle in Egypt last year. The British people proposed to erect a monument to commemorate him ... the British Consulate asked us to appeal to the Chinese people for contributions. The consulate general and various Chinese associations in San Francisco have donated $130, and the consul general asked your association to contribute $30. Since the due date for contributions was the 20th day of the 3rd lunar month (4 May 1885), we have to make the contribution on your behalf ...*

Another letter (Figure 13), dated 14 January 1886, stated:

*Many Chinese in San Francisco suffer from severe poverty. The Consulate is now appealing to shipping companies to reduce their fares so that poor Chinese can return to China. Twenty-five copies of the notice have been mailed to you, please distribute them immediately.*

*We were told that after completion of the railway, many Chinese workers recruited by Lianchang Co. were thrown out of jobs and suffered from severe poverty in Victoria. We heard complaints that the proprietors of Lianchang Co. had profited from the contract, whereas its recruited workers were penniless and unable to return home. If these complaints are true, any contractor will find it difficult to recruit labourers in China in the future. The shipping companies have now agreed to reduce the fare, and various associations in San Francisco are doing fund-raising campaigns to help sick, poor, or elderly workers to return home. This letter is to request the help of CCBA directors to urge proprietors of Lianchang Co. to give*

Figure 13  Letter from the Chinese consulate in San Francisco, 14 January 1886

*financial help to its recruited labourers so that they are not left stranded to die in a foreign country.*

*P.S. We have heard that the railway company used trucks to transport stranded Chinese labourers from the interior to the coastal cities. Since these trucks had no railings, many Chinese passengers were thrown into ditches when they turned too sharply around road corners. We do not know how many have been killed and how many hurt. Would you investigate this matter and report to us?*

In return for its service, CCBA requested the help of the consulate general in San Francisco to resolve the grievances of Chinese who left Victoria to work outside Canada. For example, Wing Wah Co. of San Francisco sent an agent to Victoria in March 1887 to recruit about 240 labourers to work in Mazatlan, Mexico. Later, CCBA received letters from those workers that they were ill-treated in Mazatlan and that many were not employed and unpaid. CCBA immediately reported this to the consulate general in San Francisco. On 10 January 1887, Huang Sic Chen sent a letter to CCBA (Figure 14) stating:

*Having investigated this matter in April, I immediately instructed San Francisco CCBA to send you a telegram, asking you to advise the Chinese public not to believe the lures of the company. I together with San Francisco CCBA directors chided the share-holders of Wing Wah Co. such as Kwong Ying Kee, Wei Zide, Wei Bai father and son, and Lei Wang etc. for causing the suffering of Chinese labourers in Mazatlan and told them to ship them back to Victoria. Since they keep postponing repatriation, I have reported this matter to the ambassador. The ambassador instructed us to summon Kwong Ying Kee and Wei Zide to the office and told them that if they did not bring back the Chinese labourers from Mazatlan, he would inform the authority of Guangdong Province to punish their families in the village. On 9 January, San Francisco CCBA sent Chen Cai of Taishan County and Liang Yizhou of Xinhui County to Mazatlan. We will bring back those labourers who wanted to return to Victoria or China.*

*Would you investigate for us how many of the 240 Chinese who left Victoria have paid and obtained the certificate of departure and how many have not? Could you ask the Immigration Department to exempt returnees from paying the head tax again if they have not got the certificate of departure?*

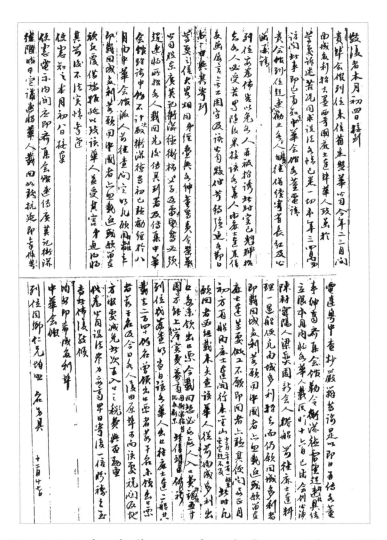

Figure 14  Letter from the Chinese consulate in San Francisco, 10 January 1887

## Protests Against Discrimination

One of the main CCBA tasks was to fight against discriminatory acts imposed by municipal, provincial, and dominant governments. Since its establishment, it had waged one campaign after another to fight discriminatory laws and regulations by means of legal counsel. It lodged protests and made appeals while anti-Chinese municipal or provincial legislations were pending approval from Ottawa or England.

In addition, CCBA carried out passive protests against discrimination. The fight against the "cubic air" bylaw of the City of Victoria in 1885 was a good example. According to this bylaw, each room should contain at least 384 cubic feet of space for each occupant, and should have a window, able to be opened at least two feet square.[1] In other words, a room measuring eight feet square and six feet high, for example, should not have more than one occupant. This restrictive bylaw caused much financial hardship for poor Chinese labourers. Their privacy was disturbed as police frequently came to raid their living quarters, arrested them, and fined them for overcrowding. Sometimes over ten Chinese were arrested and over $100 in fines was collected. City council encouraged the police to make more raids and arrests since the fines were an attractive source of income for the city. On 2 November 1893, CCBA decided on a passive means of ending the raids. It passed a resolution that if any Chinese resident was arrested during a police raid and fined for overcrowding, he should go to jail instead of paying a fine (Figure 15). After he was released, he would be given $10 by the association. If he paid a fine, he would be fined $10 by the association for disobedience. A Chinese old-timer recalled his father's saying that soon after CCBA enforced its resolution, all arrested Chinese pleaded guilty and accepted the jail sentence for overcrowding, which took the police completely by surprise. If all offenders were thrown into the one-room jail, the police themselves would violate the "cubic air" bylaw. Eventually, all offenders were released. From then on, the police stopped

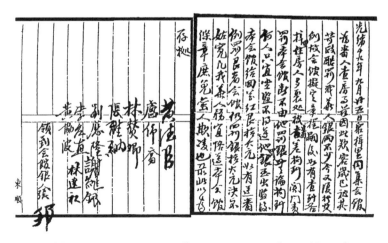

Figure 15  CCBA meeting minutes on Chinatown overcrowding, 3 November 1893

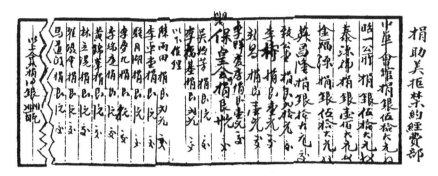

Figure 16   Donations to Chinese in the US, 1905

raiding Chinatown for overcrowding and let the offensive bylaw lapse.

CCBA fought not only against discriminatory laws in Canada but also against discrimination in the United States. In 1905, for example, Victoria CCBA raised nearly $625 to help San Francisco CCBA to fight the American Exclusion Act in court (Figure 16).

## Protests Against Abuses

There were many Chinese documents and some English newspaper reports on assaults, injuries, or murders of Chinese people by Westerners. For example, on 16 November 1899, the *Daily Colonist* reported that there were increasing assaults on Chinese servants. In the most recent incident, a small Chinese little boy was badly beaten and his property taken by several older White boys at the corner of Johnson and Blanshard streets at 4 p.m. Two men looked on and did not interfere. "While the presence of Chinese is not considered desirable," the paper said, " they should be afforded the same protection as White citizens while they are members of this community."

In remote mining settlements, White violence against Chinese was more common and often unknown to Victoria until the establishment of CCBA. For example, on 17 October 1885 Chinese store owners and miners in Williams Creek sent a letter to CCBA (Figure 17), stating:

> *Insolent policemen in towns and cities came to the mining creeks and checked whether we have Free Miner's Certificates ($15 each). They demanded us to show the certificates immediately without delay. Many of us did not understand what they said and looked for someone to interpret their*

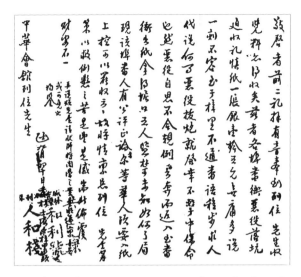

Figure 17  Letter from Chinese Store Owners in Williams Creek, 17 October 1885

*requests. An imperious policeman suddenly pulled out his gun and fired at us. Fortunately, he missed us and no one was hurt. Then he rushed back to the police station and got a warrant to arrest five Chinese miners. They are still in prison. Some of the righteous Westerners suggested we should go to court to appeal. We are reporting this incident to you and ask for your help.*

## Self-discipline and Keeping Order

CCBA helped maintain law and order in Chinatown, promote social harmony, and encouraged self-discipline in order to avoid conflicts with Westerners. For example, upon completion of the CPR and the Esquimalt and Nanaimo Railway a year later, hundreds of Chinese labourers were laid off and out of work for months. Many of these starving labourers drifted back to Victoria' Chinatown and began begging at street corners. While CCBA and clan and county associations already felt the increasing pressure of supporting them, Chinese labourers from China continued to arrive. Accordingly CCBA sent a letter to Tung Wah Hospital which, like CCBA, was the largest Chinese charitable organization in Hong Kong. The letter requested the hospital's help in telling Chinese not to come to Canada, but it received the following reply dated the 7th lunar day of the 7th lunar month in Guangxu 11th year (16 August 1885) (Figure 18):

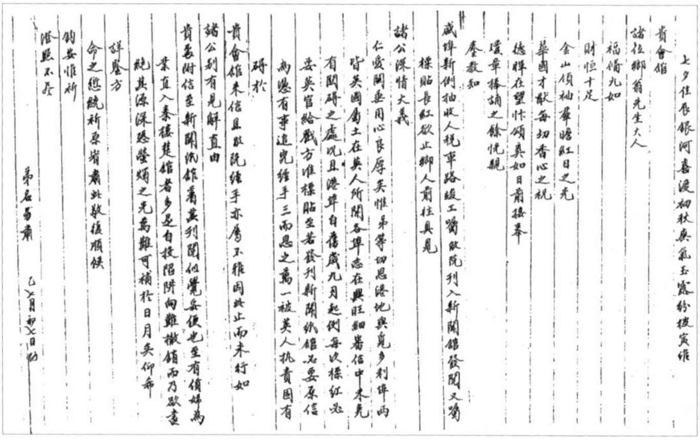

Figure 18  Letter from Tung Wah Hospital, Hong Kong, to CCBA, 16 April 1885

*We received your letter stating that a new head tax was imposed on each Chinese. You asked us to advertise in the newspaper and post notices advising our fellow countrymen not go to Canada because the railway had been completed. We appreciate your concern and kindness. However, both Hong Kong and Victoria are British colonies and the British want them be prosperous. Your request seems to contradict their objectives. Furthermore, the Hong Kong Government passed a law last September that before public notices were posted, prior approval of the government was required. We also need your written notice for the newspaper advertisement in case the British reprimand us for this advertisement. That is the reason why we have not carried out your request. We wish to suggest that it would be more appropriate if you would send the notice directly to the newspaper for publication. Furthermore, most girls who became prostitutes did so through their own fault. It is difficult to abolish the sale of women and eliminate the source of prostitution. We are sorry that we cannot be of much help to solve this problem.*

The hospital declined help because imperial decrees of the Manchu government demanded that Chinese emigrants must be licensed for going abroad and returned to China within a time limit. Unlicensed emigrants who left China without permission would not be allowed to return to China. However, the British government demanded the Manchu government to permit Chinese labourers to emigrate and work in British colonies. Hence, the hospital directors in Hong Kong did not dare discourage emigration as requested by CCBA.

The $50 head tax did not discourage Chinese emigration to Canada either. For example, during 1897 and 1898, a total of 8,345 Chinese landed in British Columbia.[2] White workers complained again about the influx of Chinese labourers and demanded the end of Chinese immigration. CCBA drafted a notice in mid-April 1899 and sent it to China to be posted in villages and cities in Guangdong Province (Figure 19). Its content is summarized briefly as follows:[3]

*In recent years, the commerce and industry of Victoria have not been prosperous. Chinese are prohibited from underground work in Nanaimo coal mines. Those gold mines that are still in operation are nearly exhausted.*

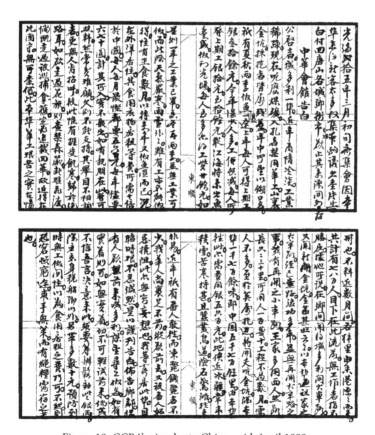

Figure 19  CCBA's circular to China, mid-April 1899

*The only means of earning a living here is to work in the fish-canning industry during the summer and autumn fishing seasons. Each worker earns only about $20 during the two fishing seasons. After the seasons are over, workers are laid off in winter and spring when it is bitterly cold, rainy and snowy. They can do nothing but sit idly and wait for the next fishing season. An annual income of $10–$20 per person does not cover the annual minimum expenditure of $60–$70. Therefore, those who have no relatives or friends in Victoria will receive no help and will suffer from starvation and cold.*

*In the last few months, about 700 to 800 of our fellow countrymen have come from Hong Kong. Many are unemployed and loiter aimlessly in Victoria. Some said that they had heard railways were being built in Victoria and that new gold mines had been discovered. In fact, the railway has long been completed. Although there may be plans to construct branch lines, the government will employ White labourers only. The new gold mines in northern British Columbia are about 1,700 miles away from Victoria. The travelling cost from here to these mines is $500 to $600. They are in a bitterly cold area and in a region which is rugged, precipitous, and nearly inaccessible. Only Westerners dare go there and many have died of cold or hunger. Even if we had the courage to make the trip, we would be hindered by envious Westerners.*

*We see our fellow countrymen coming here only to be plunged into a sea of trouble and sorrows. This is why we are sending this notice to inform you that if you are not sure of a job here, never think of coming to Canada. If you are determined to come, you should have enough money to pay for the fare to Victoria and the head tax and have an extra $30 to $90 to pay your board and lodging while you are still seeking work. Otherwise, you will have to sleep in the open with no job, no food, and no salvation.*

Most Chinese immigrants came from poor villagers and were ignorant of Western culture and customers. One old-timer told me that he was so poor that he was barefoot and had underwear only when he left his village and went to Hong Kong to board a ship to Canada. As a result, once the Chinese boarded the ship, they were looked down on by Western passengers for their shabby clothing and uncivilized behaviour. In April, 1901, CCBA sent over 10,000 copies of a notice to villagers in China and told them what they should and should not do aboard ship (Figure 20):

*Regulations to be observed by Chinese immigrants*

1. *Whether you will be met by relatives or friends at the pier in Canada, make sure you have $5 for travelling after you go ashore.*
2. *Buy dresses, trousers, hat, and socks in Hong Kong before you get on board the ship, and put them on before you disembark. This will not disgrace yourself in front of Westerners.*
3. *On board the ship, do not undress and catch fleas. Go to the toilet and never urinate overboard. Westerners will not excuse you if you commit this offence.*
4. *Line up for meals and do not jump the queue.*
5. *When Westerners are taking a meal inside their rooms, do not pop your head in and look, otherwise you will be chided.*

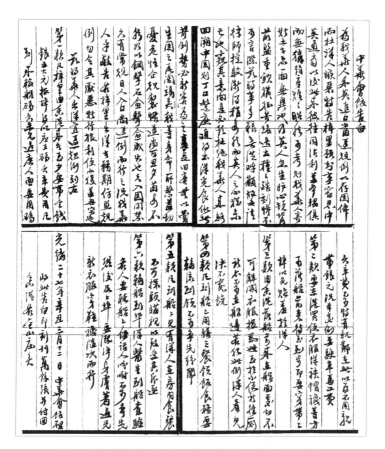

Figure 20  CCBA's circular of regulations, 30 April 1901

*6. After arrival of the ship, a Western doctor will come aboard to check the health of passengers. Listen to the interpreter and line up to disembark orderly. Clean yourself first and put on new clothing before disembark.*

CCBA directors also set up rules for themselves.[4] At the meeting on 8 April 1892, it was decided that there would be a fine of $1 for being late for a meeting; a fine of $2 for being absent or leaving a meeting before it finished. If a director was not free to attend a meeting, he was to send a representative. If any complaint or dispute could be settled by CCBA, the settlement should be written and signed by the directors as well as by both the complainer and defendant. If the dispute could not be revolved and both parties refused to sign the settlement document, the director still had to sign it and keep it as a record.

CCBA cleaned up Chinatown streets as they were not maintained clean by the city. On 22 March 1886, it tendered a contract for picking up litter and debris in Chinatown. "The successful bidder was expected to go to every street and alley in Chinatown twice a day to pick up litter, to empty the fifteen waste baskets each night, and to burn the collected debris in the incinerator behind the association building."[5] Li Jiang got the job for $6 a month.

CCBA also dealt with minor offences by arbitration before or even after they were reported to the police. For example, Ho Ng was robbed by Lee Hung in a gambling den and reported the robbery to the police. Upon the advice of the association's directors, Ho Ng accepted $50 from Lee Hung, and withdrew his complaint.[6] After a Chinese shop was burgled, CCBA announced that a reward would be given to anyone who gave information leading to arrest of the burglar or burglars.[7] The informer would be paid $300 if the burglar(s) was sentenced to three years or less in prison, and $600 if the burglar(s) was imprisoned for four years or more. If he gave evidence against the burglar and was threatened, the association would see him safely aboard ship to Hong Kong. The big reward was definitely one way to stop burglary in Chinatown.

Ah Sue, who was the concubine of an employee of Kwong Lee & Co., was abducted by members of the Hip Sing Tong on 10 November 1886; the following day, a reward of $50 for her apprehension was advertised in the *Daily British Colonist*.[8]

## Internal Disputes

CCBA had handled many controversies and personal grievances, and settled disputes before they became too serious, thus preventing contending factions from using the Western legal system or resorting to violence. Furthermore, most Chinese labourers did not understand English and were helpless in Canadian courts. Instead of exercising their legal rights through the legal channels in Canada, they appealed to CCBA to protect their interests and settle their disputes. The parties involved usually accepted the association's quasi-judicial decisions, and took cases to Canadian courts only after CCBA failed. For example, Zhou Mei won a lottery of $4,200 in Wo Lee Gaming Club but the club refused payment, stating that the lottery ticket was a fake. CCBA directors verified that the ticket was real and was asked by the Oi Lien Tong, a Zhou clan association, to resolve this small dispute before it became serious.[9]

CCBA also served as a witness in business transactions, including selling and redeeming young girls. For example, its directors signed as witnesses on a note stating that Yip Cheung Lun had sold a girl, named Ah So, to Chan Chun as a maid for $600, and on another note witnessed that Sum Wai had paid $330 to Yip Cheung Lun for redemption of a girl named Sum Ah Kwai.[10] In March 1885, On Hing & Co. in Victoria paid customs duties of $99.25 on behalf of Wah Chong Co. in Seattle, but Chan Yee Hay, manager of the latter company, was unaware of this payment and refused to reimburse On Hing & Co. Through CCBA mediation, an agreement was signed on 23 January 1897 by Chan Tung Yu of On Hing & Co. and Chan Yee Hay of Wah Chong Co. (Figure 21), to the effect that

> Chan Yee Hay will pay $100 to CCBA in trust, waiting for the reply of Cheng Yuk to clarify the payment of the customs duties. If he does not reply or refuses the payment after three months, the $100 in trust will be paid to On Hing & Co. If On Hing Co. takes Wah Chong Co. to court and wins the case, Wah Chong Co will pay all legal fees in the United States and Canada, and interest of the debt. On the other hand, if Wah Chong wins the case, On Hing will pay all the expenses and interest. CCBA was the witness to this agreement.

Chinese labour disputes were often settled by the medication of CCBA. For example, in May 1888, Kwong Chong & Co. and Kun Wo Jan Co. in Kamloops recruited 26 Chinese labourers for a mining company in Dog

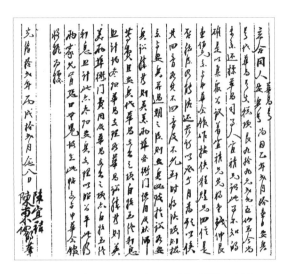

Figure 21  Dispute Agreement witnessed by CCBA, 23 January 1897

Creek, and agreed to pay their wages and travelling expenses. On 6 June, the labourers, led by their foreman Woo Tim, arrived at Dog Creek and found that the mining company needed 15 labourers only. A week later, the Chinese labourers stopped working as provisions of food were exhausted. They resumed working a week later after they were assured of the payment of wages. However, the foreman disappeared in September and the Chinese labourers had still received no wages, and were stranded in Dog Creek without food. A month later they were told to quit. The workers wrote to CCBA on 15 December 1888, saying that on 16 October, they had started walking from Dog Creek to Kamloops, begging for food on their long trip. Trekking for days in cold and hunger, 7 out of the 26 persons were sick and lagged behind. They subsequently got lost and did not arrive in Kamloops. It was unknown whether they had survived or not. They could not get the contracting company to pay them and appealed to CCBA for help.[11]

CCBA mediated not only disputes among the Chinese but also family dissension and quarrels. Sometimes, it was even asked by the consulate in San Francisco to resolve disputes. For example, Huang Sic Chen, its secretary, sent a letter on 15 February 1886 to CCBA directors (Figure 22):

> Loo Ying Chun of Hop Kee & Co. of San Francisco takes his brother, Loo
> Chock Fan of Kwong Lee & Co. to court in Victoria. We are not sure about

Figure 22 Letter from the Chinese consulate in San Francisco, 1886

*the dispute between the brothers; one looks after the family business in San Francisco, and the other in Victoria. The Consul General hopes that they would resolve their problem internally and should not hurt the feelings of their parents by settling it in court. His Honour, the consul general, instructed me to ask for your help in mediating the family dispute, and report to him later.*

## Chinese Hospital

In the old days, Chinese in British Columbia did not see Western doctors or go to Western hospitals when they were sick, mainly because they could not communicate with doctors and nurses in English and preferred using Chinese herbs to taking Western medicine. In 1881, there were 1,767 Chinese residents in Victoria in 1884 of whom only 106 were females (41 married women, 31 singles, and 34 prostitutes). Most of the rest were single males.[12] Sick married women and children were looked after at home and prostitutes in the brothels where they worked. *Taipingfang* thus housed only the poor, homeless, and very sick single men. In fact, it functioned like a "hospice" today although it was known to Westerners as a Chinese "hospital." CCBA employed a caretaker to do chores such as tidying the hut, preparing meals and herbal medicines for patients, feeding them in bed if necessary, and removing corpses to the mortuary. As only one caretaker was on duty day and night every day, he was unable to do so many tasks. As a result, *Taipingfang* was poorly managed. In February 1893, a local reporter visited it and described the horrifying scene he saw:

> *Lying on the floor of the filthy apartment was the body of the unknown Celestial, with mouth wide open, tongue protruding, and eyes aglare. In the corner of the room lay another dead body, covered up with a lot of repulsive looking rags. This was a man who had been removed to the hospital the previous day ... Two other dead bodies lay on benches similarly covered while the poor paralytic [patient] crouched upon a piece of matting, groaned in his torment of mind and body, and shivered for the want of sufficient bed clothing. The room was miserably cold, and no doubt the knowledge of being in a dead house added to the miseries of the already miserable man.*[13]

The reporter portrayed *Taipingfang* as a house of horrors, but to the impoverished lonely Chinese patients, it was still a home. Nevertheless, disclosure of the dreadful condition of the *Taipingfang* property prompted CCBA directors to start fund-raising for construction of a hospital. On behalf of CCBA, Wong Soon Lum and Lee Mong Kow purchased the dilapidated hut on Lot 461 in Block F from W.H. Oliver for $2,500 on 27 June 1899.[14] The dilapidated hut was demolished

Plate 5  Chinese Hospital, 1899

and a two-storey brick building built and completed in the winter of 1899; it was called *Zhonghua Yiyuan* (Chinese Hospital) (Plate 5).

In order to maintain the hospital, CCBA directors decided that every Chinese in Canada who was about to leave for China had to donate $2 to the hospital (Figure 23). They arranged with Chinese shipping agents not to sell a ticket to any Chinese who did not have a hospital donation receipt. Several large stores or prominent merchants in Victoria, Vancouver, and Nanaimo were commissioned to collect hospital donations and issue

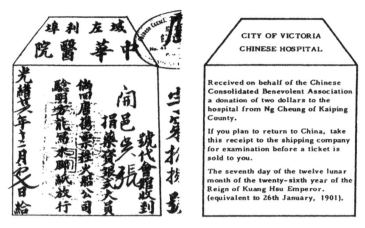

Figure 23  Stub of donation receipt issued by the Chinese Hospital, 26 January 1901

receipts; each store or merchant received a commission of $5 for $100 collected.[15] In those days, all the ships bounded for China departed from Victoria. On the day a boat was leaving for China, the hospital caretaker or an inspector appointed by the CCBA would go to the pier and collect donation receipts at the gangplank as the Chinese passengers boarded the ship. If an individual showed up without a receipt to surrender, he had to make the donation on the spot. Virtually no one argued and refused to pay since every returnee was eager to return to China as soon as possible to see his family and relatives.

This mandatory contribution, like CCBA foundation fee, virtually amounted to another departure fee for Chinese leaving for China. CCBA could wield this power without opposition from the city government because this was an entirely Chinese business. Nor did Chinese who paid this compulsory donation complain because only the returnees who were employed were asked to make the contribution. Poor and old returnees did not have to donate provided that they had asked a reputable firm to write a letter requesting an exemption. They could use this letter as a substitute for the donation receipt.

## Chinese Cemetery

The Ross Bay Cemetery in Victoria were laid out in October 1872 and opened for burials the following year.[16] The first Chinese interred there, on 18 March 1873, was listed as "Chinaman No. 1" and the Chinese buried

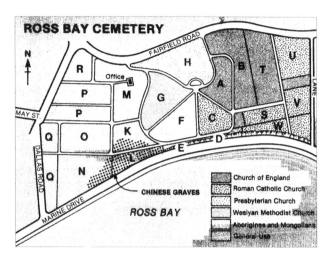

Figure 24   Chinese burial site in Ross Bay Cemetery, 1873

were recorded in similarly derisive terms as "Chinaman No. 2," "Chinaman No. 3," and so on.[17] Probably the caretaker found it difficult to spell Chinese names and did not bother to try. It was not until 4 October 1880 that Chinese names were recorded.

The cemetery was divided into 21 blocks of which Block L, at the low-lying southwestern corner, was specifically set apart for burials of "Aborigines and Mongolians" who were not attached to churches[18] (Figure 24). CCBA set up a Chinese altar at the corner of Block L and that part became known as the "Chinese Cemetery." The site was almost at sea level and always flooded after heavy rainstorms. Chinese graves were lashed by high waves also whenever the sea was rough.

CCBA decided to acquire land for a Chinese cemetery because some Chinese graves were always covered by water after a heavy downpour of rain or by seawater after a windy storm. In 1891, it purchased a lot of 8.75 acres on the southern slope of Lake Hill (now called Christmas Hill), about half a mile north of Swan Lake (Plate 6).[19] The area was still a wilderness where no more than ten farming families lived. The Hick and McKenzie families lived near the plot purchased by CCBA, and did not want the land used as a Chinese cemetery. As soon as they saw a Chinese funeral procession, they took out shotguns and fired at the mourners, so CCBA dared not use the site and left it empty for over ten years. In the winter of 1901, strong wind and waves eroded a few waterfront graves in the Chinese section of Ross

## The First Auspicious Feng Shui Site in Canada

Plate 6  Swan Lake Chinese Cemetery Site

Bay Cemetery. Some coffins were exposed and broken and remains washed away. This prompted CCBA to decide to sell the Swan Lake site and use the money to buy another more suitable piece of land to be used as a Chinese cemetery.

## Shipment of Bones

Many Chinese railway workers were seriously injured or died of accidents during railway construction. It is unknown how many died because provincial coroners normally did not investigate the deaths of Chinese labourers as they were never reported. Numerous deaths were also caused by cold weather, malnutrition, and lack of medical treatment. Many Chinese railway workers were buried in the southeastern corner of the present Kamloops Chinese Cemetery, but an unknown number were wrapped up in mattresses or pieces of cloth and covered with piles of rocks and earth near the railway track. Burial sites were marked by a piece of wood or brick on which the name of the dead and his home county and date of death were written or carved. In many former gold-mining creeks, some Chinese graves might also be identified by bricks or blocks of wood used as headstones.

After it purchased the Swan Lake Chinese cemetery site in 1891, CCBA invited various county associations to set up a Committee of Bones

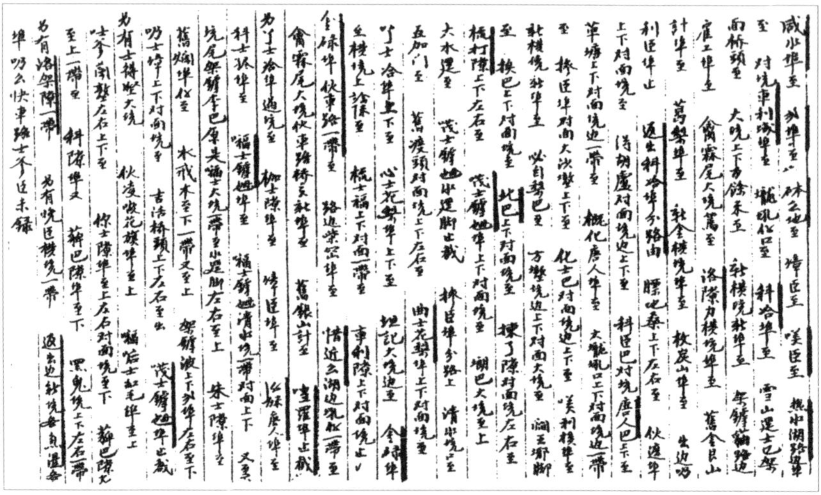

Figure 25   Locations suggested by CCBA to look for Chinese graves, 1891

Collection and Shipment. It engaged Chinese workers to walk along the railway tracks from Vancouver to Shushwap Lake to look for Chinese graves and retrieve the bones.[20] A retriever was paid $4 for digging up a grave, cleaning the bones, and then packing them properly in a box. If the body had not completely decomposed, the retriever covered up the grave again and was paid $2. The committee paid the travelling and other expenses such as sacks and wooden boxes, but the retriever had his own spade, shovel, and other equipment to open graves.

CCBA also engaged retrievers in 1891 to go to various former gold-mining towns and creeks to look for Chinese graves and retrieve bones. One piece of Chinese document listed the towns and creeks for retrievers to look for Chinese graves (Figure 25). These places, transliterated from English and written in Chinese characters, are difficult to identify. I marked the identified locations with a thick line in the document and deduced the routes as follows:

>   1. *One route from Vancouver — New Westminster — Port Moody —*
>      *Mission — Harrison Hot Springs — Chilliwack — Hope — (possibly*
>      *following the Dewdney Trail from Hope to the Similkameen and China*
>      *Creek near Princeton) — China Creek near Osoyoos — Rock Creek —*
>      *returning to Hope and to fish-canning towns on the Fraser River delta*
>      *(Figure 26).*

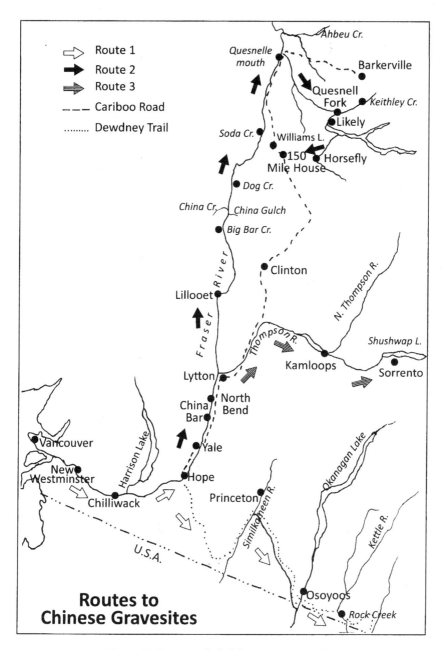

Figure 26 Routes to find Chinese gravesites, 1891

2. *Another route from Hope (following Cariboo Road up the Fraser River) — China Bar — Lytton — China Creek near Lillooet — Big Bar Creek (continuing up the Fraser River to China Gulch and China Creek) — Dog Creek and Williams Lake) — Soda Creek — China Creek near Quesnellemouth — Quesnelle Fork — Keithley Creek — (to Likely and Horsefly ) — 150 Mile House.*

3. *The third route from Lytton (following Cariboo Road and up the Thompson River to) — Kamloops — along the railway track — Shuswap Lake and ending at Sorrento.*

Several hundred boxes of bones were collected throughout the province and taken to Victoria. CCBA immediately contacted different *shantang* to collect the boxes of their own county, and each *shantang* then organized its own shipment of bones back to China.

## Chinese School

On 18 March 1874, the Methodist Church opened a Sabbath School near Chinatown for Chinese children and adults.[21] Although they were more eager to learn English than to become Christians, the missionaries thought that they would eventually be converted. The school was closed probably in the late 1870s for lack of funding.

John Endicott Vrooman, born of missionary parents in China, spoke Chinese and was an interpreter at the Customs House in 1885. He thought a mission school was needed in Chinatown to preach the gospel. His idea was supported not only by the Methodist Church but also by some Chinese merchants. For example, Loo Chock Fan of Kwong Lee & Co. immediately contributed $50 and promised further financial assistance if required.[22] Vrooman rented an upstairs room in a building on Cormorant Street and furnished it with desks and benches. On 3 February 1885, the Chinese Mission School was inaugurated to serve 25 Chinese ranging in age from 8 to 40 years.

Soon after the CCBA building at 554–60 Fisgard Street was completed in the summer of 1885, CCBA permitted Vrooman to run the Mission School in the room adjoining the Palace of Sages on the third floor of the association building.[23] In 1887, Vrooman resigned his government post as interpreter, became a Methodist clergyman, and devoted all his time to missionary work in Chinatown. He also ceased to use his stepfather's surname and instead used his own father's name, John E. Gardner (alias John E. Gardiner), when he was ordained.[24] With a grant of $10,000 from the Methodist Mission Board, Reverend Gardiner purchased a lot at 526 Fisgard Street and built the Chinese Methodist Church.[25] It was officially opened on 13 March 1891, and the Chinese Mission School then moved to the upper floor of the church.[26]

In the early 1880s, children of few merchant families were taught at home by private tutors. By the 1890s, there were about 100 Chinese children in Chinatown, and CCBA saw a need for a Chinese school in Chinatown. In January 1899, 12 prominent merchants such as Lee Mong Kow, Lee Yick Wei (alias Lee Sui Ting), Loo Yang Kiu, Tong Him Tai, Huang Fukang, and Lee Folk Gay (Plate 7) raised more than $3,000 to establish *Lequn Yishu* (Sociability Free School), the first free Chinese school in Canada.[27] It was opened on 1 July 1899 and attended by 39 pupils[28] (Plate 8).

In the early 1900s, other associations also organized their own schools or classes. For example, the Chinese Empire Reform Association ran *Aiguo Xuetang* (Patriotic School), the Chinese Freemasons organized *Qinge Xiaoxue* (Young Primary School), the Yue Shan Society operated *Yushan Xiaoxue* (Yue Shan Primary School). The Chinese Methodist Church and the Chinese Presbyterian Church ran English classes and Sunday schools for Chinese children and adults.

Plate 7  Founders of Lequn Free School, 1899

Plate 8  Chinese students attending school, early 1900s

## Charity and Relief

CCBA did much charitable work not only in Victoria but also in other cities in Canada, and in China. For example, after the fire in New Westminster on 10 September 1898, about 2,000 Chinese residents were homeless or without food, so CCBA raised funds for fire victims.[29] CCBA always showed great concerns about disasters in China. When floods, droughts, or other natural disasters struck China, CCBA would immediately launch fundraising campaigns and supervise all activities designed to aid the mother country. In 1889, for example, CCBA fund-raised to help ease the famine effects of Henan, Jiangsu and Anhui provinces (Figure 27). In Victoria, 102 companies, stores, and individuals donated $1,012, whereas in Vancouver 46 stores and individuals donated $95.45. This reflected the strength of the economy in Victoria's Chinatown compared to that in Vancouver in the late 1880s.[30] Also in 1889, CCBA raised $1,216.60 to help the droughts and famines in Guangxi Province, and raised $870 to help the famines in the provinces of Henan, Hebei and Liaoning.[31] One of the major donors was Zhaoyi Gongsuo in Victoria which was Canada's first Chinese Chamber of Commerce. It was established in 1893 by several prominent Chinese merchants such as Lee Folk Gay, Lee Yick Wei, and Lee Ying San.[32] This organization was probably encouraged by the Manchu government which promoted the establishment of Zhaoyi Gongsuo in China and among overseas Chinese in order to enlist the loyalty of wealthy merchants at home and abroad.

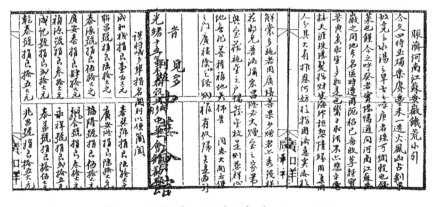

Figure 27  Circular appealing for donations, 1889

In addition, CCBA also raised funds for Chinese communities in other parts of the world. For example, after the Cubans' unsuccessful revolution against the Spanish in 1895, the Spanish military commander, Valeriana Seyler Y. Nicolau, instituted the *reconcentrado* system in 1896, by which Cuba's rural population, including many Chinese, was confined to centrally located garrison towns, where thousands died from disease, starvation, and exposure. In 1897 and 1898 Lai Wing Yiu, Chinese consul-general in Cuba, appealed to CCBA for relief aid, offering honourable official titles for sale by auction in Victoria.[33] A total of $680.50 was raised by selling five honourable official titles to merchants in Victoria.

## Endnotes

1  *British Colonist*, 8 May 1885.
2  B.C. Legislative Assembly, Sessional Papers, 1899, 1383–4.
3  For a complete translation of the letter, refer to Chuen-Yan Lai, "Chinese Attempts to Discourage Emigration to Canada: Some Findings from the Chinese Archives in Victoria," *BC Studies*, 18, (1973) 35–36.
4  CCBA, 8 April 1892.
5  AC, Notice, 22 March 1886.
6  CCBA, 1 June 1893.
7  *Ibid.*, 27 November 1894.
8  *Daily British Colonists and Victoria Daily Chronology*, 12 and 13 November 1886.
9  AC, A Letter from Oy Lien Tong to the CCBA, 21 May 1885.
10  Chuen-yan Lai "The Chinese Consolidated Benevolent Association in Victoria: Its Origins and Functions," *op. cit.*, 59.
11  AC, Letter by labourers in Kamloops to CCBA, 13th lunar day of 11th lunar month in 14th year of Guangxu (15 December 1888).
12  The Royal Commission on Chinese Immigration: Report and Evidence (Ottawa: Printed by the Order of the Commission, 1885), 363.
13  *Daily Colonist*, 19 February 1893.
14  LRO Documents Deposited Roll, 109B-987.
15  AC, A brief on the operation of the Chinese Hospital, 1895
16  John Adams, *Historic Guide to Ross Bay Cemetery* (Victoria: Heritage Architectural Guides, 1983), 4–5.
17  Burial Records, Ross Bay Cemetery, Victoria.
18  "The Ross Bay Cemetery: Rules and Regulations," *B.C. Gazette*, 9 August 1873, 7.
19  Chuen-yan David Lai, "A Feng Shui Model as A Location Index," *Annuals of the Association of American Geographer*, 64 (1974), 506–13.
20  AC, Notice of Committee of Bones Collection and Shipment.
21  *Daily British Colonist*, 20 March 1874.
22  *Ibid.*, 4 February 1885.
23  *Ibid.*, 6 January 1886.
24  Letter, from Noni Vrooman McCamley, Chairperson of Genealogical Committee, the Vrooman Family in America, to Adam Vrooman of the City of Victoria, 13 August 1984.
25  British Columbia, Land Registry Office, *Absolute Fees Book*, Vol. 10, Fol. 504. The property at Lot 454 was bought for $3,500.
26  *Daily Colonist*, 15 March 1891.

27   CCBA, 8 January 1899.
28   *Daily Colonist*, 30 June 1899.
29   AC, Canadian Pacific Railway Company's Telegraph, 11 September 1898.
30   *Ibid.*, A Record of Fund-Raising for famines in Hebei, Jiangsu and Anhui provinces, 1889.
31   *Ibid.*, A Letter and Receipt sent by Tung Wah Hospital, Hong Kong to the CCBA, 23rd lunar day of 4th lunar month in 26th Year of Guangxu (21 May 1900).
32   David T.H. Lee, *Overseas Chinese History in Canada* (Vancouver: Canadian Freedom Publisher 1967), 208.
33   AC, Letter from Lai Wing Yiu to CCBA, 25th lunar day of 6th lunar month in 24th Year of Guangxu (12 August 1898).

# 5

# Organizational Growth,
# 1890s–1930s

# Organizational Growth, 1890s–1930s

After the 1890s, Victoria Chinatown expanded from Cormorant Street to Fisgard Street and its population increased from 3,458 in 1911 to 3,702 in 1931. With increased membership, many *fangkou* and *shantang* were reorganized as clan and county associations. After the 1920s, a new generation of local-born Chinese youths emerged. They established business associations and new types of organizations. As the power of the Manchu government waned towards the end of the nineteenth century, revolutionary parties emerged not only in China but also in Chinatowns.

## Chinese Empire Reform Association, 1899

A new political force developed in China after the Manchu government was defeated in the first Sino-Japanese War in 1894–95. Kang Yuwei, a brilliant Chinese statesman, advised Emperor Guangxu to adopt Western technology and education and establish a constitutional monarchy like Britain's. He convinced the emperor to carry out extensive political, educational, military, and financial modernization programs. Accordingly, in the summer of 1898, Emperor Guangxu issued a series of reform edicts for China modernization without consulting his dominating mother, the Empress Dowager.[1] His radical reform angered her so much that she confined him to an island, revoked his reform edicts, and ordered the execution of Kang Yuwei and other reformers. Kang escaped from China to Canada as a political refugee, arriving in Victoria on 7 April 1899 en route to London.[2] As a bounty of $60,000 was placed on him, the British government told the Canadian government to provide Kang protection. W. Fiffe, a member of the Northwest Mounted Police, was assigned as his bodyguard.[3] In Victoria, he was warmly greeted by Lee Mong Kow, who arranged for his accommodation at Tai Yune Co. and introduced him to other prominent merchants such as Lee Folk Gay, Lee Yick Wei, Huang Xuanlin, and Lin Lihuang.[4]

In July, Kang returned from London to Victoria and sent out a letter to all the Chinese communities in Canada, proclaiming establishment of Baohuanghui (meaning literally "Protecting Emperor Association") (Figure 28). The proclamation read as follows:

> *China is approaching extinction. Overseas people are insulted or expelled. At home, territories are ceded and lost... I sacrifice myself to request government reform in order to save China ... In spite of having no actual power, the Emperor carried out reforms ... and now he is imprisoned in Yingtai. I received his secret edict to save him ... I left China and sought help from overseas. If five million overseas Chinese are united, we can save our country ... Many patriotic comrades have responded to my appeal for establishing Baohuanghui to save our Emperor and China.*
>
> *Righteous fellow countrymen in your city: after you receive my letter, please tell me the following:... how many people in your city, how much*

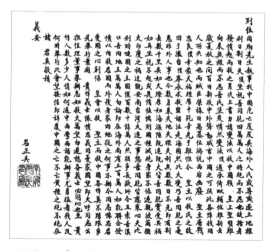

Figure 28  Letter from Kang Yuwei to overseas Chinese, July 1899

*fund can be raised, how many people know both Chinese and Western languages, how many are capable organizers, how many are brave fighters, when you can establish Baohuanghui.*

On 20 July 1899, Baohuanghui was established in Victoria by Lee Folk Gay of Quong Man Fung & Co., and Chue Lai of Wing Chong Co. The English name of the association was the Chinese Empire Reform Association (CERA). It was officially opened by Kang Yuwei and Emperor Guangxu was named the honorary president.[5] Kang together with Liang Qichao, another prominent Reform leader, had close relationships with two prominent merchants in Victoria. Kang's daughter was married to Luo Chang, and Liang's daughter to Zhou Guoxian[6] (Luo Chang and Zhou Guoxian were consul generals in Canada after the Republic of China was established). The Luo and Zhou clansmen were thus strong supporters of CERA. On Empress Dowager's birthday on 6 November 1899, CERA, in the name of "Chinese People and Merchants" sent a left-handed compliment to her. The telegram read: "Birthday congratulations. We request your abdication. Restore power of Quang Sui [sic] Emperor to whom our compliments."[7] Meanwhile, CERA launched a campaign to recruit members and by 1904, it had about 7,000 members in 12 cities across Canada.[8] In 1905, CERA in Victoria established its headquarters at 1715 Government Street.[9]

On 24 July 1899, Charley Yip Yen (alias Yip On), Won Alexander Cumyow, Chen Cai, Huang Yushan and other prominent Chinese merchants established CERA in Vancouver. The complete Chinese name was Baojiu Daqing Guangxu Huangdi Hui (Protecting and Saving Great Manchu Guangxu Emperor Association)(Plate 9). A considerable amount of money was subscribed in sums ranging from $50 to $500.[10] In 1903, Vancouver CERA set up the Sun Bo Co. and published the *Chinese Reform Gazette* (known as *Rixin Bao* in Chinese), the first Chinese newspaper in Canada, which propagated Kang Yuwei's ideology of a constitutional monarchy.[11]

Soon after the Manchu government announced in 1906 that the government was planning to establish a constitutional monarchy, Kang Yuwei and Liang Qichao renamed CERA as Constitutional Party (Digu Xianzhengdang or Xianzhengdang). It had much support from prominent leaders in Victoria such as Lee Mong Kow, Lee Fook Kay, Quon Yen, and Lee Dye. After Owyang King, the first Chinese consul appointed for

Plate 9  Chinese Empire Reform Association Directors, Vancouver, 1899

British Columbia arrived, Lee Mong Kow, a staunch and influential CERA member, arranged a banquet at the Empress Hotel on 27 November 1909 to welcome his visit to Victoria.[12] All the wealthy Chinese merchants in Chinatown, Mayor Hall, Dr. D.H. Helmcken, and many other Western dignitaries attended the banquet.

## Dr. Sun's Revolutionary Party

In August 1897, Dr. Sun Yat Sen, leader of the revolution against the Manchu, arrived at Victoria from Europe and was received by Reverend Chan Sang Kai of the Chinese Methodist Church, and Lee Ying Chang and Lee Min Sun of Ying Chong Lung Co.[13] He propagandized his revolutionary ideas among educated young people. In 1907, Wu Zihuan, Seto Ying Shek, Wu Shangying, and a few other youths established Jijishe (Striking Oar Society) in Victoria to support Dr. Sun's revolution.[14] They also published a newsletter irregularly to promote the revolutionary ideas.[15] Jijishe was dissolved two years later after its organizers were unemployed and left Victoria to look for jobs.

Plate 10  Kuomintang Building and its New Republic office on Cormorant Street, 1950s

In 1910, Dr. Sun visited Victoria again en route to China and set up Tongmenghui (MTH) or Revolutionary Alliance in Victoria and other cities in Canada. In the following year, Dr. Sun visited Victoria for the third time. He instructed Gao Yu Shan and other TMH members to convert the irregular newsletter of Jijishe into *Xinminguo Bao* (the *New Republic*), a daily newspaper. It was published daily in 1912 after the Manchu government was overthrown and the Republic of China established (Plate 10). In the same year, TMH was reorganized as Kuomintang (KMT). The TMH in Victoria was renamed KMT (Victoria District) and some members formed Han Yuen Club, a recreation club, in 1913, for promoting friendship among themselves.

Yuan Shih Kai, President of the newly formed Republic of China, had no intention to establish a republic government in China. On 4 November 1913, he banned KMT and sent troops to attack several provinces with KMT governors. Accordingly, Dr. Sun formed a new party known as the Chinese Revolutionary Party (Zhonghua Gemingtang) in June 1914 to replace KMT and started the Second Revolution against Yuan. China was then divided into Northern Government controlled by the Northern warlords, and Southern Government led by Dr. Sun. In October 1919, he renamed the Chinese Revolutionary Party as Zhongguo KMT (Chinese Nationalist Party). In Canada, it was registered as the Chinese Nationalist League of Canada and a total of twelve branches were set up in Victoria, Vancouver, Edmonton, Calgary, Lethbridge, Winnipeg, Ottawa, Toronto, Thunder Bay, Hamilton, Montreal, and Quebec City.

## Chee Kung Tong

The Hongmen Society (or Triad Society) was established in the 1760s in China as a secret political organization with the objective of overthrowing the Manchu regime and restoring the Ming Dynasty.[16] When Hongmen members migrated to the US and Canada, they set up lodges under different names such as Chee Kung Tong, Hip Sing Tong, Bing Kung Tong, and Suey Sing Tong. These secret societies accepted every Chinese irrespective of clan, county, religion, or occupation. Initially they relied on gambling, prostitution, and opium for finance; nearly all members were poor labourers who needed mutual help and protection.

Chee Kung Tong (CKT) in Victoria was established in 1876 with about 30 members. By the 1890s, its membership included not only labourers but also small merchants. Its leader was Quong Yuen (alias Quong Cum Yuen), who was a labour contractor and owner of Hip Lung Co. When he died in February 1898, CKT had about 200 Hongmen members and no rival in gambling and other lucrative business in Chinatown.[17] On 3 July 1899, Lee Yow Young represented CKT to buy a lot at 615-21 Fisgard Street

Plate 11  Chinese Freemasons Building on Fisgard Street, 1964

for $2,600 and built a two-storey brick building on the site (Plate 11).[18] The society moved its shrines and headquarters to the new building on 23 November 1900.[19]

The Hongmen Society still had the quasi-political objective of overthrowing the Manchu government and Dr. Sun recognized its power in overseas Chinese communities. Soon after he joined it in 1903, he proposed a new constitution which would transform it from a secret society into an open revolutionary party.[20] Under his proposed constitution, each Hongmen member would pay a membership fee of US$3. With an estimated 70,000 members in North America, Dr. Sun hoped to raise $210,000, an amount that would be enough to support an uprising. Accordingly, he went to different cities in the US and Canada to promote his proposed constitution.

On 4 July 1908, Victoria CKT was officially registered as "Chee Kung Tong Society" with the BC government, with Mar Yin Yuen as president.[21] On 6 February 1911, Dr. Sun went to Vancouver and asked CKT members to raise funds for the uprising.[22] On 14 February, the Hongmen Fund-Raising Bureau (Hongmen Chouxiang Ju) was established and members were encouraged to buy its Golden Bonds (Jinbiquan), which could be cashed after the revolution succeeded. To the public, the bureau was known as National Relief Bureau (Guomin Jiuji Ju). In mid-February, Dr. Sun went with Fang Ziyou, a newspaper editor, to Victoria to fund-raise, and hoped that overseas Hongmen could raise $300,000. Fang pointed out that most Hongmen members were workers and could not afford large donations. The quickest way to raise a large amount was to mortgage the association building. On 24 February, over 80 CKT members in Victoria signed an agreement to mortgage its building on Fisgard Street for $12,000 to support the uprising. The same year, GaoYu Shan, Fang Ganqian, Wang Bodu, and other revolutionaries in Victoria established TMH and recruited many CKT members as its members.[23] TMH members in Victoria also established the Minsheng Reading Club in Herald Street to propagate revolutionary ideas. After establishment of the Republic of China in 1912, CKT ceased to be a secret society and was recognized in December 1913 by President Yuan Shih Kai as a legitimate organization.[24]

## Expansion of Clan Associations

A few Chinese merchants who had started with humble businesses earned more money by speculating in real estate, and so expanded their businesses. They paid for the passage of relatives and friends from their villages to Victoria, where they worked in their businesses either without pay or with only some pocket money for a certain period. The employer-employee bond was strengthened by the same clanship. The employer acted like the head of a family to control his clansmen or relatives, with all respect and power attributed to him. At the same time, many workers of the Canadian Pacific Railway had been laid off and could not find jobs in the interior, so drifted back to Victoria. Without jobs and being hunger, they appealed to their clansmen for help. They were accommodated in *fangkou* which became very overcrowded. Some *fangkou* were reorganized as clan associations and purchased property and established headquarters in Chinatown. They usually used the top floor of the building for assembly halls and office, and rented out lower floors to generate income to support their clansmen and clan activities. As a result, clan associations played an increasing role in the welfare of the Chinese community.

Table 6   Surnames and County Origins of Chinese Buried in the Chinese Cemetery, December 1902–July 1920

| County | Surnames | | | | | | | | | | | |
|---|---|---|---|---|---|---|---|---|---|---|---|---|
| | Li | Huang | Zhou | Chen | Lin | Liu | Ma | Yu | Zhang | Guan | Other | Total |
| Siyi (4 counties) | 83 | 66 | 32 | 47 | 38 | 18 | 28 | 19 | 17 | 19 | 187 | 554 |
| Taishan | 50 | 40 | – | 27 | 13 | 15 | 27 | 12 | – | 1 | 73 | 258 |
| Xinhui | 31 | 19 | – | 18 | 25 | 3 | 1 | 3 | 7 | 1 | 48 | 156 |
| Kaiping | 1 | 7 | 32 | 2 | – | – | – | 4 | 9 | 17 | 43 | 115 |
| Enping | 1 | – | – | – | – | - | – | – | 1 | – | 23 | 25 |
| Sanyi (3 counties) | 1 | 1 | 41 | 9 | 2 | 3 | – | – | 2 | 1 | 50 | 110 |
| Panyu | 1 | 1 | 41 | 1 | 2 | 2 | – | – | 1 | – | 42 | 91 |
| Shunde | – | – | – | 7 | – | 1 | – | – | – | 1 | 7 | 16 |
| Nanhai | – | – | – | 1 | – | – | – | – | 1 | – | 1 | 3 |
| Zhongshan | 8 | 8 | 1 | - | 6 | 6 | 3 | 4 | 3 | – | 43 | 82 |
| Zengcheng | 3 | 4 | 6 | 2 | 1 | 8 | – | – | 8 | – | 8 | 32 |
| Dongguan | – | 1 | – | – | – | – | – | – | – | – | 11 | 12 |
| Baoon | – | 2 | – | 1 | – | – | – | – | – | – | 8 | 11 |
| Heshan | – | 1 | – | – | 3 | – | – | – | – | – | 5 | 9 |
| Other | 7 | 4 | 0 | 2 | 2 | 1 | – | – | – | – | 23 | 39 |
| Total | 102 | 87 | 80 | 61 | 52 | 36 | 31 | 23 | 22 | 20 | 335 | 849 |

Source: Burial Records of Chinese Cemetery at Harling Point, December 1902–July 1920

There are no official records of the Chinese population in Victoria by clan and county origins. CCBA's archives have a record of Chinese in Victoria who were buried in the Chinese Cemetery from 1902 to 1920. The record lists the name and county origin of the deceased and reveals that the largest clans were Li, Huang, Zhou, Chen, Lin, and Ma, and that most people had come from Taishan, Xinhui, Kaiping, Panyu, and Zhongshan counties (Table 6). Table 6 also reveals the operation of the "chain migration" whereby a new arrival in Victoria would later send for his sons, brothers, nephews, or other close relatives or friends in the same village to join him. Hence, most Lis and Huangs came from Taishan and Xinhui counties, and most Zhous from Panyu and Kaiping counties.

The Li clan was the strongest in finance and membership in Victoria. In December 1909, for example, Lee Mong Kow, Lee Dye, Lee Dan, and Lee Wing Yew represented Lee Long Sai Tong to purchase a lot at 612-14 Fisgard Street.[25] In 1910, the clan association built two brick buildings which "added greatly to the prominence of the thoroughfare" as described

Plate 12  Lee's Association Building on Fisgard Street, 1990

by a local reporter (Plate 12).[26] In October 1920, the association sold one of the buildings (#612) and kept #614.[27] In 1931, Lee Long Sai Tong united with Li Dunzong Gongsuo, another Lee clan society in Victoria, into one association known as Lee's Benevolent Association (Lishi Gongsuo).[28]

Clansmen with the surnames Liu, Guan, Zhang, and Zhao untied in the 1880s to form a rudimentary clan society known as Ming Yee Tong. Their clan relationship was based on the legendary sworn-brotherhood for four heroes of the Three Kingdoms Period (220–80 AD): Liu Bei, Guan Yu, Zhang Fei, and Zhao Zilong. In 1902, Ming Yee Tong was reorganized as Lung Kong Tin Yee Association under the leadership of Charles Bo (Loo Gee Guia), Quan Chongde, Zhang Xiliang, Zhao Liu, and other clansmen.[29] In 1905, the association bought the building at 1717 Government Street and established its headquarters on the third floor (Plate 13). The defunct Lum Sai Hor Tong was rejuvenated in 1908 by Lim Fat, Lin Lihuang, and other Lin merchants.[30] As Victoria Chinatown declined in the early 1920s, many Lin clansmen moved to Vancouver's Chinatown. In 1923 the clansmen there established Lum Sai Hor Tong on Canton Alley. George Yuen Lim, a clergyman at the Chinese Anglican Church, was elected president, and Lim Po

Plate 13  Lung Kong Kung Shaw, and Yen Wo Society Building on Government Street, 1990

Han, consul-general of China in Vancouver, became honorary president. In 1924, the society moved to 531 Carrall Street and changed its name as Lum Sai Hor Zongtang (Zongtang means "society headquarters"). This led to disputes between Lin clansmen in Victoria and those in Vancouver over which association was headquarters. As the number of Lin clansmen in Victoria continued to decline in the 1930s, the Victoria association eventually accepted its position as a branch chapter.

With few members, some clans were grouped together as one clan because they believed to be descendants of a group of putative ancestors. For example, in 1903, Gee Tuck Tong was formed by Chinese surnamed Ng, Chow, Choy, Yung, or Cho (Wu, Zhou, Cai, Weng or Cao). The same year, Yee clansmen formed Yee Fung Toy Tong. In June 1903, the two societies pooled their money

Plate 14  Gee Tuck Tong on Fisgard Street, 1990

to buy a property at 622–26 Fisgard Street and constructed a two-storey building.[31] Gee Tuck Tong owned the western portion and Yee Fung Toy Tong the eastern portion of the building (Plate 14).

By 1909, there were at least 12 clan associations, namely, Lee Long Sai Tong, Ming Yee Tong, Lum Sai Hor Tong, Chan Wing Chun Tong, Mar Gim DooTong, Wong Kong Har Tong, Seto Kou Lun Tong, Ho Lo Kong Tong, Chow Oylin Kung Shaw, Suoy Yuen Tong, Gee Tuck Tong and Yee Fung Toy Tong. These informal societies did not have regular meetings and did not keep records of meetings. Most small clan societies were virtually defunct by the early 1920s.

## Expansion of County Associations

*Shantang* was set up initially to ship bones back to China but gradually it extended its work to charity and other activities for its fellow countrymen. Membership usually increased faster than the membership of *fangkou* because *shantang* included people of different surnames in a county. In May 1902 when CCBA was planning to buy the property at Foul Point to be used as a Chinese cemetery, total donations from the 11 *shantang* amounted to

$2,400.[32] These *shantang* were Yee Hing Tong (Xinning County), Chong How Tong (Panyu County), Fook Yum Tong (Nanhai County), Hang On Tong (Shunde County), Hook Sin Tong Society (Xiangshan County), Po On Tong (Dongguan County), Ying On Tong (Zengcheng), Fook Hing Tong (Xinhui County), Hong Fook Tong (Enping County), Kwong Fook Tong (Kaiping County), and Yen Wo Company (Hakka people) (Figure 29). Hence, on 3 April 1903, the CCBA bought the cemetery site of about 3.5 acres at the corner of Penzance and Crescent Road at Foul Point (now known as Harling Point).[33]

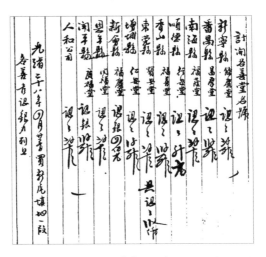

Figure 29   Donations of Eleven Shantang, May 1902

After the turn of the nineteenth century, several prominent merchants reorganized their traditional *shantang* into more formal county associations. For example, Xinning Yee Hing Tong, a rudimentary *shantang* of Xinning (Taishan) people, was established in 1887 and had no office. In 1893, Lee Ying San, Lee Yick Wei, Lin Zanqing, Li Hongqia, and other Taishan merchants raised enough money to establish headquarters on Cormorant Street and renamed the association Ning Yung Benevolent Association in 1902.[34] Two years later, they purchased a building at 536–40 Cormorant Street (Plate 15).[35] In 1914, Xinning County in China was renamed Hoy Sun County (Taishan County). So, the association was renamed Hoy Sun Ning Yung Zhonghuiguan (Hoy Sun Ning Yang Benevolent Association).

In the 1910s, a group of Panyu merchants reorganized Chong How Tong as a county association and established its office at 1715 Government

Plate 15  Hoy Sun Ning Yung Benevolent Association on Pandora Street, 1990

Plate 16  Zhongshan Fook Sin Tong on Herald Street, 1980

Street. Similarly, 11 Zhongshan merchants expanded their *shantang*, Hook Sin Tong, into a more formal organization in 1902.[36] Chinese stores owned by Zhongshan people in Vancouver, New Westminster, and Nanaimo readily sent donations to Victoria. Within two years, Zhongshan people raised enough funds for construction of an association building. In August 1904, Lee Dye of Wah Yuen Co., on behalf of the association, purchased a lot at 658–64 Herald Street and built a wooden hut on the site.[37] In 1912, the hut was demolished and replaced by a large brick building which was officially opened on 2 March 1913 (Plate 16). Tiecheng Chongyihui (Shon Yee Benevolent Association), another Zhongshan County association, was established on 9 May 1915 by a group of Zhongshan natives in Vancouver.[38] They set up a branch in Victoria in 1921.

Other small county associations such as Fook Hing Tong, Hong Fook Tong, and Kwong Fook Tong did not hold meetings regularly and left no records of their activities. Some *shantang* changed its name after it became a county association. For example, Xinhui people changed the name of their *shantang* from Fook Hing Tong to Kong Chow Benevolent Association in 1925.

## Dialect Associations

The Hakka people migrated from North China to South China during the Eastern Jin Dynasty (317–420 AD) and settled in Wuhua, Huizhou, Chixi, and a few other counties in Guangdong Province. Although they lived in different places in China, they maintained their own dialect and practised their own customs. Hakka people in Victoria built their temple, Tam Kung Temple, at 1713 Government Street, and dedicated it on 21 January 1876.[39] (see Plate 4) The property was purchased on 22 January 1877 by Tsay Ching and Dong Sang on behalf of the Hakka people and transferred to Yen Wo Co. after it was established in 1905.[40] Yen Wo Co. demolished the temple in 1911 and replaced it with a four-storey building, using the top floor as Tam Kung Temple (see Plate 13).[41]

Initially natives from Nanhai, Shunde, and Huaxian counties who speak the same Sanyi dialect, had their individual *shantang*. In 1922, they united together and formed a county association known as Nanhuashun United Association.

## Business Associations

The period from the 1890s to the 1930s witnessed not only the reorganization of many rudimentary clan or county associations but also the establishment of new types of associations. In the 1890s, the Manchu government encouraged Chinese merchants in China and overseas Chinese merchants to establish Zhaoyi Gongsuo, which functioned like a Chamber of Commerce so that the government could have a focal point to enlist the loyalty of wealthy merchants at home and abroad. Zhaoyi Gongsuo in Victoria was established in 1893 by Lim Fat, Lee Ying San, Lee Folk Gay, and other prominent Chinese merchants.[42] In 1896, Gongyi Gongsuo, another society formed by Chinese merchants in Victoria, appeared in Chinatown. In 1908, the two societies were united as the Victoria Chinese Merchants Association.

In the summer of 1922, the Chamber of Commerce in Victoria requested that City Council prohibited Chinese peddlers to sell vegetables door to door except on Wednesdays and Saturdays. This proposal prompted a group of Chinese peddlers to form an organization to fight against this request.[43] Hence, on 7 August 1922, Shangmen Xiaofan Lianhehui was formed (literally meaning, From Door to Door Peddlers United Association). In English, it was called the Chinese Vegetable Peddlers Association. As some members did not sell vegetables from door to door, the society was later renamed Guacai Lianhehui (Melon and Vegetable United Association). Later, a member thought that the name might imply that business was wholesale, so on 26 March 1939 the association was renamed Maicai Tongye Gonghui (Selling Vegetables Business Association).[44] However, the English name remained the same until the association became defunct after the Second World War. In 1925, Chinese greenhouse owners established the United Green House Association.

## Christian Organizations

Christian organizations played an important part in assisting Chinese people to assimilate into Canadian society. The Chinese Anglican Church (Good Hope Mission), established by Bishop Hill in 1891 at 719 Caledonia Street, was the first church for Chinese.[45] In 1925, it moved to 523 John Street; its minister was the Reverend Clarence Lee. The second Chinese church was started by the Reverend John Endicott Gardiner. With a grant of $10,000 from the Methodist Mission Board, he purchased a lot at 526 Fisgard Street and built the Chinese Methodist Church.[46] It was officially opened on 13 March 1891 by the Reverend C. Bryant, president of the BC Conference.[47] The Reverend Chan Sing Kai served the church throughout the 1890s and 1900s, and was replaced by the Reverend Chan Yiu Tan in 1912 after he retired to Hong Kong.

The Victoria Presbyterian Gospel Hall for Chinese was the third Christian organization and started by the Reverend A.R. Winchester in April 1892 at the corner of Government and Cormorant streets.[48] On 22 January 1899, the mission was upgraded to a church known as the First Chinese Presbyterian Church.[49] In 1908, it was moved to a building at the corner of Government and Pandora streets, and led by the Reverend Leung Moi Fong throughout the 1910s. In 1921, he formed the Christ Church United Society (Yesujiao Lianhui) with Wong Wah as president and Mar Yick as secretary. He also represented the Society on the CCBA Board of Directors in 1922.

In 1925, the Presbyterian Church, Methodist Church, and two other churches were united as the United Church of Canada. Hence two Chinese churches in Chinatown became Chinese United Church at 526 Fisgard Street.

## Youth Organizations

A visible new local-born generation of Chinese youths emerged in the early 1910s. The 1901 Royal Commission report listed 145 Canadian-born Chinese children (63 male and 82 female).[50] In addition there were also Chinese youths who had come from China at an early age and been educated in Canada. In 1915, for example, the Victoria Chinese Public School graduated its first full high school class, a group of 12, including both boys and girls.[51] By 1924 the school had an enrolment of 41 students.[52] In addition, many young people graduated from missionary schools in Victoria and a few youths from mission schools in China came to Canada. They were members of the Chinese Christian Youth Association. Educated in Canada, they were very concerned about their future and anxious to be equal with White youth. For example, a group of local Chinese students formed the Chinese Young Men's Progressive Party around May 1911. They appealed to police to stop gambling in Chinatown and sent a letter to the British monarch that "the law as regards all immigrants from Hong Kong to this country be ameliorated so that their reception on landing may be easier for them."[53] On 31 July, Lau Nu, Lau Fung Tsun, and Lau Tsung Sui of the Progressive Party sent a letter to CCBA and asked its directors to take the lead in getting subscriptions in aid of their proposed establishment of a Chinese library in Victoria.[54]

In 1914, a few Chinese youths organized a social club and named it Victoria Chinese Canadian Club (Tongyuanhui, meaning Common Origin Association) whose members included Canadian-born Chinese youths, China-born Chinese youths who studied in Chinese Public School, and mission schools in Victoria as well as in mission schools in China. Gradually its members became involved in local political, social issues, and charity work. For example, they organized benefit performances to raise relief funds for sufferers of natural disasters in China. In the 1920s and 1930s, these youths became the new generation's leaders and worked alongside the senior community leaders in Chinatown.

A short-lived Victoria Chinese Aviation School was organized in 1922 by Chan Dun and Lee Quong Yee, who were members of Chinese Nationalist League in Victoria. The main objective of the school was to train Chinese pilots for the National Chinese Air Force or for commercial airlines for China. Lieutenant Harry Brown, a First World War pilot, was the moving force behind the Victoria Branch of the Aerial League of Canada, composed of war-trained pilots who had no jobs to go to.[55] He and his partner Norman Goddard formed a flying school and purchased a Jenny "Canuck" JN-4. He was approached by Chan Dun and Lee Quong Yee to be instructor for the Chinese flying school. The school opened with eight Chinese students and later had ten. On 24 February 1923, Hip Quong, a Chinese student, crashed the Jenny at the entrance to Esquimalt Harbour. He escaped with minor injuries but the aircraft was demolished. That was the end of Victoria's first flying school.

In 1929, the Philippines Chinese Basketball Team played their first game in Victoria during its North American tour. This inspired local Chinese youths to form the Chinese Students' Basketball Club in 1931 with Albert Mar as the founder and first chairman.[56] The club was soon well known as it regularly won championships. In the 1940s, the club was renamed the Chinese Students Athletic Club (Huasheng Tiyuhui) and branched out into table tennis, softball, and tennis. Other youth organizations were also formed. For example, the First Chinese Scout Group was formed in 1932 by the Good Hope Mission of the Chinese Anglican Church.[57] The group initially had 13 members and was led by Reverend Clarence L.T. Lee. After he left, there were no trained scout leaders to guide the group, so it was dissolved in 1934.

## Organizational Leadership

After the 1900s, all Chinese voluntary organizations began basic units of Chinatown's institutional structure. Membership in each organization was the first step for entrance to leadership in Chinatown because these organizations provided a network of contacts. For example, once a person joined a clan or other community association for several years and was active in its activities, he might gain respect of his fellow members and be elected president or other official posts of the association. With the support of his own association and personal ties with other Chinese organizations, he might be nominated for CCBA directorship. Hence, after the 1900s, Chinatown leadership which was previously held by wealthy merchants, was gradually replaced by leaders of clan, county, and other associations who were small merchants emerging in Chinatown.

## Endnotes

1  Cameron, M.E. *The Reform Movement in China, 1898–1912* (New York: Octagon Books, 1963), 21.
2  *Daily Colonist*, 8 April 1899.
3  *Ibid.*, 20 July 1899.

4 David T.H. Lee, *Overseas Chinese History in Canada* (Vancouver: Canadian Freedom Publisher 1967), 276.

5 *Daily Colonist*, 20 July and 10 October 1899.

6 David T.H. Lee, *op. cit.*, 274.

7 *Daily Colonist*, 7 November 1899.

8 David T.H. Lee, *op. cit.*, 282.

9 LRO, *The Indenture between Lee Folk Gay and Trustees of the Chinese Empire Reform Association*, 2 February 1905, Absolute Fees Book, Vol. 22 Fol. 229, No. 1084.

10 *Daily Colonist*, 10 October 1899 and 25 July 1900.

11 David T. H. Lee, *op. cit.*, 348.

12 *Daily Colonist*, 28 November 1909.

13 Kuomintang, *A Brief Introduction to Party History* (Victoria: Kuomintang, Victoria Branch), August 1996, 26.

14. David T.H. Lee, *op. cit.*, 298.

15 Kuomintang, *A Brief Introduction to Party History, op. cit.*, 27.

16 Chuen-yan David Lai, "Contribution of the Zhigongtang in Canada to the Huanghuagang Uprising in Canton," *Canadian Ethnic Studies*, XIV, 3 (1982), 98.

17 *Daily Colonist*, 1 March 1898.

18 LRO, Conveyance of Lot 599 Block N from Joshua Davies to Lee Yow Young, dated 3 July 1899 (DD 17399). On 5 February 1910, Lee Yow Young sold the property to Chee Kung Tong Society for one dollar (LRO, DD17399).

19 *Daily Colonist*, 25 November 1900.

20 *Reminiscence and Expectation of Hongmen History* (Toronto: Commemoration of 100th Anniversary of the Establishment of Hongmen Minzhidang, 1894–1994, 1994), 15.

21 LRO, DD 13838.

22 Cao Jianwu, " History of Chee Kung Tong's Revolution to Re-establish the Nation," unpublished Chinese manuscript, 1930, kept in the Chee Kung Tong office in Vancouver.

23 Kuomintang, *A Brief Introduction to Party History, op. cit.*, 27.

24 *The Chinese Freemasons Contribution for 140 years, 1863–2003* (Vancouver: Zhongguo Hongmen Minzhidang Headquarters in Canada, 2003), 156.

25 LRO, AFB Vol. 28 Fol. 310 #23502c DD 17303

26 *Ibid.*

27 *Daily Colonist*, 22 September 1910.

28 LRO, 47976-I.

29 The 65th anniversary and 1st convention of Lung Kong Association in Canada, 1967, 45.

30 *A Commemorative Issue of the Golden Anniversary of the Union of Lum Sai Hor Zongtang and Lin Jiumu Gongsuo*, 1980.

31 LRO, AFB Vol. 21 Fol. 235 #8828c and 83407-I.

32 Xinning County was later known as Taishan County, and Xiangshan County as Zhongshan County.

33 *Ibid.* DD987 Deed for Lot 8 of part of Sec. 46: District of Victoria, B.C. on Map 222a in Land Registry office, Victoria.

34 Special Issue on the Second National Convention of Taishan people in Canada, Victoria, May, 1975, 130.

35 LRO, AFB Vol. 9 Fol. 727 #7487and AFB Vol. 22. Fol. 143 #10459a and #10640a.

36 Pamphlet on "Xiangyi Hook Sin Tong Chengli" held in the office of Hook Sin Tong.

37 LRO, AFB Vol. 22 Fol. 10 4 #10305 DD 28349 and F99718 AFB Vol. 22 Fol. 120 #10372).

38 Commemorative Issue of the 70th anniversary of Shon Yee Benevolent Association of Canada, 1914–1984, 16.

39 *Daily British Colonist*, 23 January 1876.

40 LRO, AFB Vol. 5 Fol. 324, No. 182A-20581. Subdivision Lot 7 of Lots 602 and 603, City Block M.

41 *Ibid.*

42 David T.H. Lee, *op. cit.*, 208.

43 Record of minutes of Shangmen Xiaofan Lianhehui, 7 August 1922.

44 Record of minutes of Maicai Tongyet Gonghui, 1939.

45 Anglican Diocesan Archives, 912 Vancouver Street. Good Hope Mission Text 57 Box 6. File 3, 1860–1892, p. 144–173.

46 LRO, AFB, Vol. 10 Fol. 504 The property at Lot 454 was bought for $3.500.

47 *Daily Colonist*, 15 March 1891.

48 *The Chinese Presbyterian Church, Victoria, B.C. 1892–1983* (Victoria: Chinese Presbyterian Church 90th Anniversary Celebration Committee, 1983), 15.

49 *Ibid.*, 18.

50 Report of the Royal Commission on Chinese and Japanese Immigration (Ottawa, 1902), 12–13.

51 *Commemorative Issue of the Establishment of the Chinese Consolidated Benevolent Association (1884–1959) and Chinese Public School (1899–1959),* (Victoria: Chinese Consolidated Benevolent Association, 1959), Section 3, 63.

52 *Ibid.*, 68.

53 *Daily Colonist*, 4 August 1911.

54 *Ibid.*, 2 August 1911.

55 Jim Brown, "When Victoria had a Chinese flying school," *Times-Colonist,* 13 January 2002.

56 *Souvenir Program on Chinese Students Athletic Club 20th Anniversary Celebration and Re-Union, 1931–1950,* (Victoria, 1950) pages unnumbered.

57 H.K. Chen, "History of Chinese Scouting in Victoria, BC" (Vancouver: *Chinatown News,* 18 January 1990) 15.

# 6

# Democratic Rule, 1900s–1930s

# Democratic Rule, 1900s–1930s

After the turn of the nineteenth century, CCBA found it hard to unite the Chinese community because of political dissension in Chinatown, inter-association disputes and contention, financial difficulties, and other factors. Replacement of Victoria by Vancouver as an important port of entry on the Pacific coast in the 1910s weakened the economy of Victoria's Chinatown and reduced the business of Victoria's Chinese gentry-merchants. Chinese leaders in political parties, county, and clan associations who might be merchants or labourers became involved in community services. In 1916, they were elected to the CCBA Board of Directors. This marked the beginning of bifurcation of power and gradual change from monolithic control to more democratic rule in Chinatown.

## Political Dissension, 1900–1910s

CCBA board directors were formerly very united and dedicated to the Manchu government. However, they were divided politically after Emperor Guangxu was imprisoned. In the early 1900s, some CERA members such as Lee Folk Gay, Lum Lop Fong and Luo Yuehu were CCBA directors. They were shunned by some other directors who feared that an association with them might be reported to Empress Dowager by her secret emissaries and their relatives in China would be executed. Unconfirmed reports stated that some CERA members had resorted to violence when they faced opposition in Chinatown. For example, the Reverend Chan Sing Kai, pastor of the Methodist Chinese Mission, advised his followers not to be involved in CERA activities, probably because he worried that Chinese Christians inside China might suffer if overseas Chinese Christians participated in the anti-Empress Dowager movement. On Christmas Eve in 1899, a bomb was placed in the Chinese Methodist Church and exploded, causing slight damage to the building.[1] Many people believed that the explosion had been caused by CERA members, although they denied that.

CERA was renamed Constitutional Party (CP) after 1906 and always fought with Sworn Oath Society (Jijishe) which supported Dr. Sun Yat Sen's revolution.[2] Seto Ying Shek and Wu Zihuan, founders of the Society (SOS), were English secretary and Chinese secretary respectively of CCBA. At meetings, they always argued with some board directors who were CP members. For example, soon after the death of Empress Dowager and Emperor Guangxu in 1908, Mei Boxian, the consul in Portland, sent a telegram to CCBA and told it to fly its flag at half-mast. After SOS members failed to stop this move, they rushed into CCBA assembly hall and interrupted the memorial service being held by CP and other conservative directors.[3] The altercation might have ended in a brawl had the police not stepped in.[4] Conflicts between CP and SOS members weakened the solidarity of CCBA board of directors.

SOS lasted only for two years because its members had to leave Victoria for a living. The few remaining members later joined Tong Men Hui (TMH), Dr. Sun's revolutionary party.

On 22 May 1911, TMH and Chee Kung Tong (CKT) in San Francisco made a joint announcement that they would accept members of each other's organization.[5] Soon after the Republic of China was established in 1912, TMH was renamed Kuomintang (KMT). In Victoria and other Chinatowns in Canada, KMT membership consisted of well-established merchants, traders, school teachers, and newspaper editors, cutting cross clan and county lines. The nationalist movement in overseas Chinese communities was widespread and KMT branches were established even in small cities. For example, a KMT branch was set up in 1913 in Brandon, Manitoba, where the Chinese population was so small that a Chinese Benevolent Association had not even been formed.

As KMT increased in power in Canada, it challenged CKT leadership. In spite of their considerable contribution to Dr. Sun's revolution, CKT members were not rewarded in the form of offices by the republic. Instead, KMT considered former TMH members as originators and supporters of the 1911 Revolution and paid little tribute to CKT's contribution. Furthermore, some KMT members who had joined CKT did not see the benefit of being CKT members and suggested that CKT be dissolved and transformed to a new society known as the National Public Society (Guomin Gonghui). This led to confrontation between CKT members and KMT members and they parted acrimoniously.

In Victoria, the conflict between the two groups ended in an assault. For reasons unknown, a KMT member assaulted a CKT member after CCBA meeting on 28 February 1915.[6] CCBA directors condemned this barbaric behaviour and called for a meeting on 4 March 1915 at which the directors tried to mediate the conflict between KMT and CKT for the sake of community unity. Meanwhile, CKT leaders felt a growing threat from KMT. On 12 November 1915, 71 die-hard CKT members such as Li Jiguo and Mar Yin Yuen established Dart Coon Club (Achieving Power Club) which aimed at "preserving the public power of CKT."[7] The club accepted only very dedicated CKT members unaffiliated with other political parties, especially KMT. Anyone who wanted to join Dart Coon Club had to join CKT first for a few years before applying for membership in the club. In other words, Dart Coon Club was a high "inner circle" or "cabinet" of CKT, whose Hongmen members were strictly screened. From 1915, Dart Coon Club and CKT were mortal enemies of KMT. They also allied with Constitutional Party to oppose Dr. Sun and KMT.

KMT also faced other opposition in Canada. Yuan Shih Kai, President of Republic of China, planned to declare himself as emperor and banned KMT in 1913. Dr. Sun consequently re-organized KMT as a Chinese Revolutionary Party, set up the Southern Government of China in Canton, and launched a second revolution against Yuan. KMT members in Canada supported the Southern Government of China and did not obey instructions from the Chinese consuls in Canada who represented the Northern Government headed by Yuan and other northern warlords. After World War I broke out, the Northern Government of China allied with Britain and France against Germany and its consuls hinted to the Canadian government that KMT in Canada might be intriguing with Germany. On 1 September 1918, Tang Hualong, ex-Minister of Education in the Northern Government, visiting Victoria's Chinatown on his way to China from the

US, was shot to death by Wang Chang, a KMT member, who then killed himself.[8] This murder persuaded the Canadian government that KMT was a clandestine uprising organization so it banned both KMT and the Chinese Labour Association (Zhonghua Gongdang) in November.[9] The proscription lasted only six months. KMT was in operation again soon after Dr. Sun's Southern Government declared war on Germany.

Sometimes CCBA tended to neglect the welfare of Chinese citizens because of political feuds. For example, Mayor C.T. Dupont wrote a letter to the *Daily Colonist* on 10 February 1903, disapproving Canon Arthur Beanlands' defence of his cathedral choir boys, who had assaulted a Chinese boy on Fort Street.[10] He was pushed and felt down on a street rail. He was run over by a street car and one of his legs had to be amputated. The case came before the police court after the "most extraordinary delay," but the judge "unhesitatingly acquitted the accused because no evidence was produced."[11] On 6 April 1904, Mayor Dupont wrote to the *Daily Colonist* to say that "the assault was committed. The poor boy is maimed for life. Simply because he was a China boy, no one else is punished, not even lay a police court fine for simple assault. Surely there is a failure of justice."[12] For nearly a year after the assault, CCBA had not taken any action to help the boy. It was not until late April 1904 that the association sent out a circular asking for donations (Figure 30).

*Last winter, Jiang Huixi was assaulted by Western boys in Fort Street, pushed down onto the rail and shorn of his leg by a street car. Without*

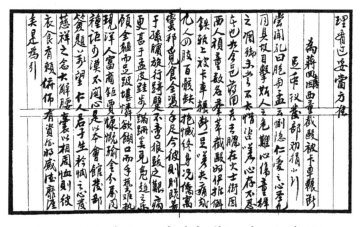

Figure 30  Circular to raise funds for Chinese boy, April 1904

*a leg, he would find it difficult to eke out a living. Now some Western wealthy merchants have generously donated money to help him. As he is our fellow countryman, how can we disregard this matter? Accordingly, the association is now distributing donation booklets and sincerely hopes that you will donate generously for the sake of charity.*

Some Chinese outside Victoria had also complained about CCBA and other organizations not caring about them. For example, on 27 June 1905, over 15 *fangkou* sent a resentful letter to CCBA, complaining that the association and other organizations did not care about Chinese in lower status (Figure 31):

*Last Tuesday, a Chinese sailor was hammered and badly hurt by a Western sailor on board a ship in the harbour of Ladysmith. As a Chinese fellow countryman, he should be helped. CCBA was established for the protection of fellow countrymen, CKT was set up to protect its blood brothers, and CERA was formed to protect its comrades. Every Chinese person tried to join these associations for protection. It turns out that CERA protects only its president and vice-president, and not its comrades. CKT protects only its officers and not ordinary members. CCBA cares for the merchants but not the roamers and drifters. It charged any Chinese who returned to China. May we ask for what purpose the money would be used? You have enriched yourself without doing anything for your fellow countrymen.*

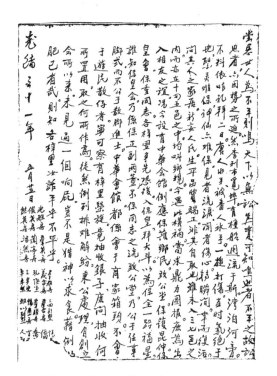

Figure 31　Letter of complaint, June 1905

Although the complaint was not entirely justified, it did reflect that CCBA no longer had the high respect from the Chinese community that it did in the 1880s and early 1890s. Its supreme authority had also gone with the creation of new political organizations and the growth of a small merchant class.

## Small Merchant Class

After the manufacture of opium was banned in 1908 in Canada, all opium factories in Victoria closed. Many wealthy opium merchants who once controlled CCBA were getting old and retired to China. Furthermore, CCBA began to lose its "consulate-like" power after the Manchu Government in 1909 established a consulate-general in Ottawa and a consulate in Vancouver. Meanwhile, some hard-working labourers who had saved enough money or received financial support from relatives or friends started small businesses such as restaurants, tailor shops and barber shops in Chinatown. Some Chinese gardeners purchased farmlands in the suburbs to grow vegetables; their businesses served not only the Chinese community but also the Western community. A growing number of Chinese workers who had some savings, joined a business network, like an artificial brotherhood, operating as members under family discipline. Some other workers worked for relatives who had businesses. If they were close and direct kin, they could improve their position rapidly. If the relationship was less close, they might work hard as shop assistants and save enough money to start their own business. A small class of such merchants began to emerge in Chinatown (Plate 17 and Plate 18).

Plate 17  Fong Ching and his family, 1890s

Plate 18  Lee Mow Kow with his friends, 1904

A few Chinese merchants who had started humbly, earned more money by speculating in real estate. By 1909, Chinese merchants owned about half the land in Chinatown which covered five city blocks.[13] The major land investors were Chan Tong Ork, Lim Dat, Lee Garm Chau (alias Lee Dye), Lee Mong Kow, and Lee Folk Gay; each owned three or more lots. After some merchants expanded their business, they paid the passage of relatives and friends from their villages to Victoria where they worked without pay or only with pocket money for a certain period. The clan-tie strengthened the employer-employee bond. The employer acted like the head of a family in order to control his clansmen or relatives, with all the respect and power attributed to him. Gradually, these small merchants became leaders in clan and/or county organizations, and their business cards often listed leadership posts with several clan, county and other community organizations. All these associations shared the objectives of having fraternal and socioeconomic interaction and arbitrating disputes of individuals within associations. They provided a degree of social security based on mutual benefit and aid. Assistance was provided to members when they were unemployed or had trouble with other people or authorities. They also helped migrants adjust to the new environment in Chinatown and Western society. Members of clan or county associations were related through the tie of the same surname or county and more closely integrated than CCBA membership, so they did not rely so much on CCBA for help and support.

The coordination of bones shipment to China was taken over by a county association indicated the decline of CCBA leadership. After 1909, CCBA did not arrange each county association to organize its own shipment and entrusted Hoy Sun Ning Yung Benevolent Association with the responsibility to centralize shipments. Crates of bones were collected across Canada and shipped once every seven years to the mortuary of Tung Wah Hospital in Hong Kong.[14] The hospital would notify the shantang in Hong Kong to pick up the bones for delivery to villages. Centralized shipments of bones occurred in 1909, 1916, 1923 and 1930. A fifth shipment was scheduled for 1937 but was stopped by the outbreak of the Sino-Japanese War. All the crates of bones which had been sent to Victoria from other cities across Canada were then stored in the brick building in the Chinese Cemetery at Harling Point, awaiting delivery after the war (Plate 19).

Plate 19  Bone House in Chinese Cemetery, 1950s

The Chinese Immigration Act of 1923, which prohibited Chinese from entering Canada, had a great impact on Chinese society in Canada. As the number of families grew, the centre of gravity of Chinatown life gradually shifted from bachelor society to the families of small businessmen and their social relations and concerns. Bachelor labourers and small business families continued to live side by side in Chinatown, but increasingly family life dominated community attention and defined the external image of Chinatown in Canadian society. Men from these prosperous merchant families entered the institutional life of the community and reinvigorated CCBA's merchant leadership. Meanwhile local-born Chinese youths were in English language and began to fight for their civil rights in Canada.

## National Subscription, 1912

All overseas Chinese celebrated the downfall of the Manchu government and enthusiastically supported the new republic government. The new government knew, for example, that if it wanted to solicit the opinions and support of the Chinese community in Victoria, it had to contact CCBA first because its board directors were important community leaders. Other Chinese associations, small merchants, store employees, and labourers were still bound to CCBA through a web of business, familial, and political ties. To appeal to overseas Chinese in Canada for donations to help pay foreign debts, the republic government asked CCBA in Victoria and CKT in Vancouver to establish a National Subscription Bureau (Guomin Juanju) to collect donations.[15] The republic government also followed the Manchu government's example by giving awards for donations. For example, a

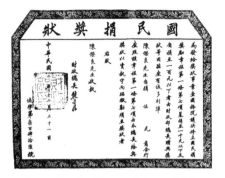

Figure 32  Certificate of National Subscription Award, 1913

Certificate of National Subscription
Award was given to an individual
who either donated $100 or less
himself or herself, or solicited
$1,000 or less from other donors
(Figure 32). Wealthy merchants
contributed generously and set the
pace for others. Within three years,
total donations in Victoria alone
amounted to $35,840.[16]

CCBA still has 1,575 stubs
for donation receipts from the
National Subscription Bureau, which reveals that most Chinese in Victoria
had come from the Siyi counties (Taishan, Xinhui, Kaiping, and Enping),
and from Zhongshan County (Table 7). In other documentary sources, the
Sanyi counties (Panyu, Nanhai, and Shunde) also included a lot of peo-

Table 7  Home County Origins of Major Clans, 1912–1914

| County | Clan | | | | | | | | | Total |
| | Wong | Lee | Mar | Lum | Chan | Chow | Lau | Yee | Others | |
|---|---|---|---|---|---|---|---|---|---|---|
| Taishan | 152 | 71 | 155 | 31 | 52 | 2 | 23 | 20 | 162 | 668 |
| Xinhui | 66 | 41 | 1 | 41 | 18 | 1 | 7 | 19 | 120 | 314 |
| Kaiping | 6 | 5 | 3 | 3 | - | 48 | 1 | 11 | 130 | 207 |
| Enping | - | 1 | - | - | 2 | - | 1 | - | 30 | 34 |
| Zhongshan | 17 | 52 | 5 | 18 | 15 | - | 16 | 3 | 96 | 222 |
| Panyu | - | - | - | - | - | 3 | - | - | 6 | 9 |
| Nanhai | - | 1 | - | - | - | - | - | - | 2 | 3 |
| Shunde | - | - | - | - | - | - | - | - | 3 | 3 |
| Huaxian | 1 | - | - | - | - | - | - | - | 12 | 13 |
| Heshan | 2 | 6 | - | - | - | - | - | - | 15 | 23 |
| Zengcheng | - | 1 | - | - | - | 1 | 10 | - | 4 | 16 |
| Dongguan | - | - | - | - | 1 | - | - | - | 7 | 8 |
| Baoan | - | - | - | - | - | - | - | - | 2 | 2 |
| Yangjiang | 1 | - | - | - | - | - | - | - | - | 1 |
| Unknown | 1 | 4 | - | 1 | 2 | 2 | - | 1 | 41 | 52 |
| Total | 246 | 182 | 164 | 94 | 90 | 57 | 58 | 54 | 630 | 1,575 |

Sources: Stubs of donation receipts of National Subscription Bureau of Victoria, 1912–1914

ple (see Table 4 and Table 6). The largest clans were Wong, Lee, Mar, Lum, and Chan. The 54 honourary canvassing members of the National Subscription Bureau represented 27 Chinese associations in Chinatown: 11 county associations, 9 clan associations, 3 political parties, 2 Christian churches and 2 other types of organizations (Figure 33). All these documents indicate the prosperity of Victoria Chinatown and the growing power of small merchants.

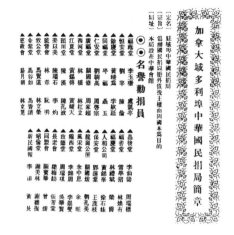

Figure 33  Chinese Associations, 1912–1914

## Feuds Between County Associations

County associations increased their membership much faster than clan associations because they included persons of different surnames from the same county. Many people's affiliation to the county association took precedence over their clan association. County associations looked after the welfare of their members and protected their interests against people from other counties. For example, Siyi people and Sanyi people were united by their dialects and solidarity often caused so-called "Tong Wars" in Chinatown. For example, when a Siyi person quarreled with a Sanyi person over a woman or money, both called for help from their own county people. An initial argument between only two individuals might become an open confrontation between two groups of people. CCBA weakness became apparent after it failed to resolve disputes between county associations. In September 1898, for example, the old hatred between the Siyi and Sanyi people in Victoria was stirred up, and "iron bars are being brought out, and preparations advanced for possible hostilities on either side."[17] According to one report, the unrest was caused by CKT members, who were mostly Siyi people. The society demanded $15 a month for each gambling house in Chinatown, but gambling houses owned by Sanyi refused to pay.[18]Accordingly, CKT immediately instructed its members not to gamble in the houses owned by Sanyi.[19] However, Lim Sam and Yip Wing, CKT directors of the society, explained to a Western reporter in

October 1898 that since many members were short of money because of the failure of the salmon run on the Fraser and the New Westminster fire, the society advised its members not to gamble. If they lost money for they would not be able to survive in the winter.[20] CCBA failed to resolve the feud between the Siyi and Sanyi in Victoria.

In the evening of 31 October 1903, another county association conflict happened. A Sanyi actor struck a Zhongshan actor during a performance in the Chinese Theatre. This incident triggered a fracas between the Sanyi and Zhongshan people in the theatre. The fight moved to the street and continued until the police arrived. Throughout the following week, several other fights occurred in Chinatown. According to one report, the actual cause of the fight was the murder of Charley Sing, a Sanyi leader in Victoria who "had his throat cut from ear to ear by unknown parties" during his visit to Steveston.[21] Charley Sing, who dressed in European clothes and had cut off his queue, was known to Chinese gamblers as "No Queue Charley." He was accused of giving information to the police that led to raids in Chinatown. He had nearly been killed some years before and had been recently beaten, possibly by Zhongshan people. His murder triggered fights between the Sanyi and Zhongshan natives. The atmosphere in Chinatown was uneasy as revolvers and knives were purchased by both sides. A Chinese interpreter told the reporter that he expected that the "tong war" in Victoria would extend to Vancouver, where younger Chinese of the contending factions were armed with lead pipes and preparing to fight.[22]

CCBA was not only incapable of stopping inter-association conflicts but also failing to mediate conflicts within an association. For example, some Zhongshan people surnamed XXX had a large number of members in Hook Sin Tong and bullied other Zhongshan people of small clans.[23] Accordingly, on 9 May 1915, over 20 Zhongshan persons in Vancouver formed a separate Zhongshan county association known as Shon Yee Benevolent Association (Tiecheng Chongyihui) and set up a branch in Victoria in 1921. Throughout the month of April in 1925, CCBA tried in vain to resolve disputes between Zhongshan people of Shon Yee Benevolent Association and Hook Sin Tong. On 9 May, two ShonYee members in Vancouver, namely Lin Taigu and Wu Minghe, were murdered by members of the XXX political party.[24] The Shon Yee Benevolent Association then decided that it would not accept membership from Zhongshan persons bearing the surname XXX or belonging to the XXX political party.

## Labourers vs Merchants

The issue on the Palace of Sages also revealed CCBA's weakening prestige and power. After the Chinese Public School at 636 Fisgard Street was built in 1909, its lower floor was used for classes, and the upper floor for CCBA office which was moved from its old association building at 554–560 Fisgard Street. After the school building was completed, CCBA still had a debt of $9,000. Lee Mow Kow, school principal, suggested that the Palace of Sages in the old association building be closed and temple idols, relics of superstition, be destroyed. The floor would be made available for renting and the rents would help pay the debt on the new school.[25] Some CCBA directors and several enlightened merchants supported his idea. However, many Chinese labourers in Chinatown still respected their idol gods and strongly opposed Lee's idea. Rumours spread that the merchants were going to close the Palace of Sages and sell the building to the Canadian Pacific Railway Co. for $9,000 to pay off the school debt. This story infuriated many Chinese labourers, who charged CCBA directors for exploiting the debt situation to aggrandize themselves and looting the joint funds of the Chinese community.

To resolve the dispute, CCBA called for a public meeting on Sunday afternoon, 10 October 1909, at the Chinese Public School.[26] A vote was to be taken and if a majority favoured abolition of the Palace of Sages, the idols would be cast out. The meeting never came to order. Three hundred labourers burst in and smashed the ballot-boxes. In the melee, one merchant was severely hurt and police was called. A Chinese was arrested but released afterwards. After that, CCBA held many meetings but could not resolve the dispute between enlightened merchants and labourers. On 28 November, CCBA met with merchants and made a second attempt to remove the Palace of Sages.[27] The meeting was again swarmed by opposing labourers and several people were hurt. By the time the police arrived, the disturbance had finished and the meeting stopped. Eventually CCBA directors dropped the controversial issue. These incidents reflected the growing power of Chinese labourers in Chinatown and the weakening control of the merchants and CCBA in Chinatown.

## Shortage of Funds, 1900s

When the wealthy merchants controlled CCBA in the 1880s and 1890s, they were extremely generous in contributions to support the association.

However, after the 1900s, CCBA faced disunity and concomitant financial problems. As an increasing number of small merchants became board directors, continuous demand for their donations had drained their purses. With few donations from directors, CCBA had to rely on rental income, the $2 foundation fee, and the $2 departure fee of the Chinese Hospital.

In late July 1900, CCBA sent out circulars to all Chinese communities in British Columbia and encouraged people to make a contribution of $2 to the association (Figure 34):

> *The objectives of establishing the association were to promote relationship among fellow countrymen, help dissolve disputes and community difficulties, organize public welfare, and fight against discrimination. Without funding, the association found it difficult to carry out its tasks. It has now decided to adhere to the 1884 constitution and collect the $2 foundation fee. The association would not help anyone who had not paid the fee. Any new immigrant had to pay the fee within a year of arrival. We encouraged our fellow countrymen to contribute this small donation so that we could get enough fund for emergency.*

CCBA did not always send representatives to the pier check departing Chinese for departure permit receipts and collect fees systematically. Some unscrupulous fee collectors even kept the fees as a loan from CCBA and failed to return them to the association. Hence, CCBA's income from this source was virtually nil by the 1920s.

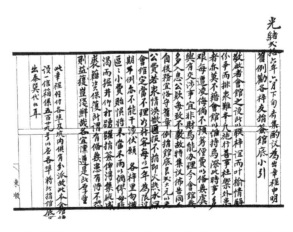

Figure 34  CCBA circular asking Chinese for $2 donation, July 1900

The Chinese Hospital also faced financial difficulties towards the end of the nineteenth century. Before the 1890s, Victoria was a major seaport on the Pacific coast. Since most Chinese returning to China had to leave from Victoria, CCBA could enforce other Chinatowns to collect the $2 donation on its behalf and make sure that Chinese passengers had donation receipts before boarding. Between 1891 and 1910, a total of 35,882 Chinese left for China.[28] Assuming that about 5% of them were exempt from paying the $2 donation because of poverty and advanced age, the total amount of donations in these 20 years would still be over $68,000, averaging a yearly income of $3,400, which would be the major source of revenue for the Chinese Hospital in Victoria. However, after completion of the CPR, more Chinese immigrants settled in Vancouver. Towards the end of the nineteenth century, Vancouver replaced Victoria as the major port of departure for China and CCBA in Victoria lost its influence over other CBAs across Canada. Vancouver's Chinese merchants thought that as the Chinese population in Vancouver's Chinatown had greatly increased and would need a hospital, it was unfair to continue to collect departure fees on behalf of the Chinese Hospital in Victoria and sent them to CCBA instead. On 19 February 1904, Vancouver CBA wrote a letter to CCBA, stating that it would keep donations for the purchase of a hospital property in Vancouver's Chinatown (Figure 35). It stated that

*We have already informed you that the hospital donation collected by Ye Huibo will be kept here for purchasing a property for our hospital. If you insist on having the donation, please do not list Ye Huibo as the debtor but list that the donation is borrowed by Vancouver CBA and will be paid back after we have paid our loan and still have a surplus. If CCBA insists on its claim to the donation, then the money should be considered a loan to us and be returned to CCBA after we have paid off our debt.*

However, after the Chinese Hospital in Vancouver was built, Vancouver CBA

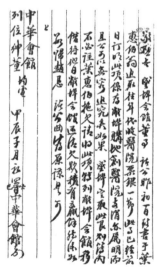

Figure 35 Letter from Vancouver CBA to CCBA, 19 February 1904

collected the departure fees for its own hospital instead for the Chinese Hospital in Victoria. Meanwhile, CBAs in other cities began to collect their departure fees to support their own benevolent activities instead of remitting the money to CCBA. For example, Montreal CBA , established in 1912, issued its own departure permits to Chinese in Montreal and asked CCBA not to demand departure fees from them. Accordingly, on 10 June 1914, CCBA replied to Montreal CBA that it would not issue permits to any person holding departure permit issued by Montreal CBA.[29]

In addition to a reduction of departure fees, CCBA directors faced the problem of overcrowding in the hospital. To solve this problem, they decided to use the hospital fund to send poor elderly patients back to China. They also appealed to all Chinese agents of steamship companies in Victoria not to sell tickets to Chinese on Vancouver Island if they did not have the hospital's departure permit.[30] However, the Yesujiao Lianhui (Christ Church United Society) in Vancouver sent a letter to the Customs Office in Victoria and informed Customs Officers that CCBA forced Chinese to pay the departure fees and prevented them from boarding if they had not paid. Accordingly, CCBA sent out a letter on 23 April 1915 asking the Society to withdraw the letter because departure fees were donations used for the Chinese Hospital.[31]

## Work of CCBA, 1900s–1910s

Although Victoria CCBA languished in power, it still tried to lead the Chinese community to fight against racism and discrimination. In 1902, for example, the federal government set up a Royal Commission on Chinese and Japanese Immigration to gather information on Chinese and Japanese in the country.[32] Its 34 questions included the quality of the Chinese and Japanese immigrants, the class to which they belonged, to what extent he had participated in trades and industries, to what extent they were essential to development of the province's natural resources, fisheries, mines and lumber industries, and so on. CCBA directors thought that these questions aimed at controlling employment of Chinese in these industries and prohibition of Chinese immigration. They wanted to raise several thousand dollars to engage a lawyer to fight against the survey. A circular was sent out to appeal to merchants to donate generously for the lawsuit, and ask individual Chinese to contribute 50 cents each and pay a $2 departure fee.[33] Failing to obtain enough donations, CCBA directors dropped the idea of fighting. The commission later published its report and recommended that further immigration of Chinese labourers into Canada be prohibited and that the head tax should be raised to $500. In 1903, the head tax was raised to $500, so some of the commission's findings and recommendations came to fruition.

In the early 1900s, CCBA directors fought against educational segregation. On 29 August 1907, the School Board of Victoria ruled that no Chinese children were to be admitted to public schools "until they could so understand the English language as to be amendable to the ordinary regulations and school discipline."[34] It claimed that non-English speaking Chinese children retarded the progress of other children. However, French and German children, for example, who could not speak English were admitted to public schools. CCBA engaged Fred Peters, a well-known barrister, to bring a suit against the school board, but it lost.[35] Under the ruling of the Victoria School Board, many Chinese children were not qualified to attend public school. CCBA had to place all China-born children in the Lequn Free School, which became over-crowded. In 1908, CCBA directors campaigned among Chinese communities across Canada to raise funds for construction of a school. By August, CCBA had raised more than $7,000 to purchase Lots 606 and 607W1/2 in Block M on Fisgard Street and build the school.[36] The new school, known as the Daqing Qiaomin Gongli Xuetang (Great Manchu Overseas Chinese Public School), was officially opened on 7 August 1909 by Xu Bingzhen, Chinese Consul-General at San Francisco (Plates 20, 21, 22).[37] Unlike Lequn Free School, the Public School had both English and Chinese classes and concentrated on improving the English standard of Chinese children so that they could be admitted to public schools later.[38] After the downfall of the Manchu government, the school was renamed Huaqiao Gongli Xuexiao (Chinese Public School).

The Manchu government had not established a Chinese consulate

Plate 20  Opening ceremony of Imperial Chinese School

Plate 21  CCBA Board Directors,
August 1909

Plate 22  Chinese Students of the Imperial
Chinese School, August 1909

in Canada before 1909. Hence CCBA in Victoria still functioned like a consulate for Chinese communities across Canada and was looked upon by CBAs in New Westminster, Vancouver, and other cities as their leaders. When there was a demand in Canada for increasing the head tax from $50 to $500, Tong Him Tai and Lee Mong Kow of CCBA, Chen Yuxiu of New Westminster CBA, and Yip Yang of Vancouver CBA sent a joint letter in March 1900 to Zhitai, the provincial governor-general in China (Figure 36): [39]

*Since Chinese people live in the British colony, trade between the two countries has been buoyant and we have been sharing the mutual benefit. There has never been such a law like the head tax. In 1885 the Canadian*

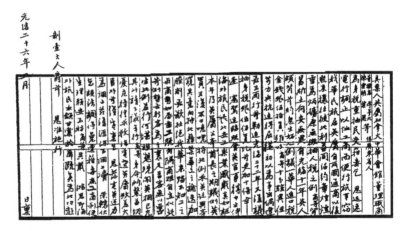

Figure 36  Joint letter of CCBA, and Vancouver and New Westminster CBAs, March 1900

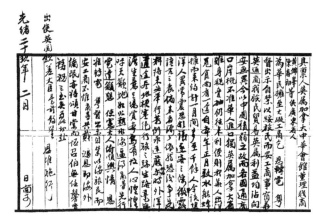

Figure 37  CCBA Letter to Chinese ambassador in England, March 1903

*government imposed a head tax of $50 on Chinese immigrants. We fought against this imposition in vain. In 1896, there was a demand for a head tax of $500. Fortunately, you argued with the British Government and stopped the increase. An election will be held this year and the British politicians here have been lobbying to obtain the permission of the British Government to increase the head tax again. This heavy tax will discourage the entry of Chinese labourers. The strong relationship between labourers and merchants is similar to that between the lips and teeth. Merchants will find it difficult to survive without labourers. We, merchants, beg your Honour to contact the British Government and deal with this matter.*

CCBA also worried that if China did not undertake a self-imposed restriction on emigration, sooner or later the Canadian government would completely terminate Chinese immigration. Accordingly, in March 1903, the association sent a letter to Luo Fenglu, Chinese ambassador in England, begging him to advise the viceroy of Guangdong Province to post a notice urging people to refrain from going to Canada (Figure 37):

*Many countries today are not open to Chinese immigration because China is weak. Canada is one of the few places where Chinese are still permitted to enter, although we have to pay a heavy head tax. Since January 1903, several ships loaded with Chinese arrived at Victoria, and within one month over a thousand had come. Because of this influx of our fellow countrymen, the White people here trembled with fear and talked of introducing laws to drive us away. If our fellow countrymen continue to pour into Canada, we fear that eventually laws will be passed to exclude us from immigration. This apprehension has been haunting us and forced us to resort to the help of Your Excellency. We beg Your Excellency to advise His Excellency the Viceroy of Guangdong Province to put up a notice restricting emigration to Canada. The efforts of Your Excellency will console the overseas Chinese and pacify the unrest of the workers and merchants here.*

CCBA also represented Chinese in Canada to communicate with overseas Chinese communities in other countries. For example, in 1882 the American Congress passed the Exclusion Act to prohibit Chinese labourers from entering the US for ten years only, but the act was extended for another ten years in 1892 and again in 1902. On 27 April 1904, the General Deficiency Appropriation Act was passed to extend the Exclusion Act without a time limit. American Chinese were greatly infuriated by this new act and sent out letters and circulars to Chinese traders and merchants in China, the US, and other countries to boycott American goods. CCBA immediately sent money to support the boycott and received a reply dated 28 June 1905 from the Association of San Francisco Chinese to fight against the act (Figure 38):

*We have received $622.75 from you and will publish the names of donors in the newspaper. We have suffered greatly from the American discriminatory laws. We had enthusiastic responses from merchants in the inland and they were going to stop selling American merchandize to support our protest against the new Exclusion Act. We are carrying fund-raising campaigns to help the merchants who would suffer from the loss in business. We appreciate greatly your help. It is hoped that the loss in trade and business might induce the American government to abolish the new Exclusion Act.*

Although its power declined in Victoria, CCBA was still looked upon by Chinese in other Canadian cities as a leader and asked for its arbitration and help against abuses. On 21 December 1908, for example, a group of Chinese merchants in Winnipeg, sent a letter asking CCBA to help raise funds for the victims in robbery (Figure 39):

*Last year, some Westerners came to rob a laundry and Li Zhuo and Lu Borong were killed. On 20 December, another laundry was robbed, and Zhang Liang and Gong Bao were killed. We have reported the robbery to*

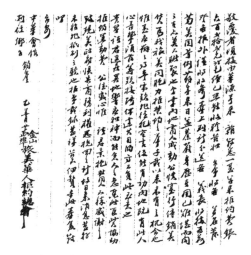

Figure 38  Letter from Chinese in San Francisco to CCBA, 28 June 1905

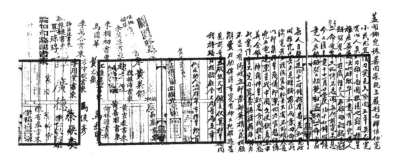

Figure 39  Letter from Winnipeg Chinese merchants to CCBA, 21 December 1908

*the local government and Chinese government. We are now asking CCBA to send out donation books to the Chinese communities and help raise funds for dealing with these robberies and murders.*

On 23 July 1900, some Westerners wanted to drive Chinese away from Kettle Valley (near Rock Creek) and Grand Forks in BC. Merchants there wrote to CCBA to ask for help.[40] On 11 March 1902, five Chinese farmers bought a piece of land in Grand Forks and got into a dispute. They sent a letter to CCBA and asked the association to mediate.[41] On 30 November 1904, Li Yuan, a Chinese store in Union Bay, was seriously damaged by a dynamitic explosion. After CCBA received the merchants' letter from Union Bay, it contributed a reward of $200 for arrest of the culprit.[42]

On 13 May 1900, Ma Lian, a Chinese cook in Rossland, was shot dead by a Westerner. According to Article 13 in Section 2 of the 1884 Constitution, CCBA offered a reward of $200 for information leading to the arrest and conviction of the murderer, and gave the victim's family a subsidy of $25. The association would ignore this matter if the $2 "foundation fee" had not been paid. Although Ma Lian had not paid the foundation fee, several board directors decided to give the Ma family with $100 instead of $200 for legal expenses, and to pay Chen Fu $30 per month to go to Rossland to help in the case against the murderer. [43] However, other directors thought that the association should adhere strictly to the constitution. Accordingly, CCBA decided in 1901 that after the Ma Lian murder case there should be no help for those who had not paid the foundation fee. Therefore, when Zeng Rongchuan informed CCBA on 13 May 1902 that his brother Zeng Baizi had been murdered by a ship captain, CCBA told him that no help would be given because the victim had not paid the foundation fee. [44] Similarly, on 31 March 1907, when the Chinese in Port William and Port Arthur, Ontario, reported to CCBA that Wu Xunjin had been shot dead by a Westerner, they were told that the association would not deal with the case because the victim had not paid the foundation fee. [45]

Although CCBA was short of funds, it usually set up a committee to response to requests for relief funds for natural disasters in China. The committee or Ad Hoc Charity Society would be dissolved after it had achieved its objective. For example, in May 1907, a famine threatened Guangdong Province and it was expected that the price of rice would be raised very high. [46] A telegram was sent by a charity society in Guangzhou to CCBA, asking for donations to purchase rice in advance which could be stored and sold at a low price when needed. CCBA launched fund-raising campaigns in Victoria and other cities in BC. In Victoria alone, $2,807.25 was contributed by various Chinese associations and individuals. [47] In the summer of 1908, Taishan, Kaiping, Xinhui and nearby counties on the Zhujiang delta were devastated by the floods of the Xijiang (West River). Within a few weeks, CCBA raised over $7,000 from individual donors in Victoria and remitted the money to China. [48] In response to the call for relief funds for another disastrous flood on the Zhujiang delta in 1914, CCBA raised nearly $4,000 within two months. [49] In 1907, it organized fund-raising campaigns for natural disasters in other parts of China and overseas Chinese communities outside Canada. For example, it raised

$1,216.60 for floods in Guangxi Province in 1900 and remitted $4,000 to help Chinese victims in San Francisco after the 18 April 1906 earthquake.[50]

Even after a Chinese consulate was established in Vancouver in 1909, the consul-general recognized CCBA as the *de facto* if not *de jure* "government" of Chinatown. He always consulted its directors on matters which affected Chinese people in Canada. Chinese communities outside BC still respected CCBA authority. For example, the Saskatchewan government passed an act to prohibit employment of White women or girls in any restaurant, laundry, or other business owned and managed by Chinese, Japanese or other Oriental people. The act came into force on 1 May 1912, but the words "Japanese or other Oriental persons" were deleted after the Japanese complained.[51] A similar act was enacted in Manitoba the following year. The Chinese in Saskatchewan asked CCBA, not the Chinese consulate in Vancouver, for help. CCBA raised a total of $1,175 in November 1914 and remitted it to the Chinese in Regina for legal expenses for abolition of the law.[52] However, a similar act was enacted in BC in 1914 and in Ontario in 1917. White girls across Canada also protested against the law which reduced their job opportunity. Finally, the law was amended in 1918, requiring a special licence from the municipality to hire a White female, without singling out Chinese by name.

## Changes in Election, 1916

Before September 1916, the board of directors were recommended and appointed by merchants in view of their weighty standing since they were the major financial supporters of CCBA. But the financial situation of the association deteriorated, few merchants wanted to serve on its board. Although board membership varied from 30 to 45 from 1903 to 1913, few attended meetings.[53] For example, the board of directors for September 1914–August 1915 consisted of only 30 merchants (Figure 40). On 17 August 1915, they held a meeting to discuss the new board of directors for the following year, but the meeting was cancelled because most directors were absent.[54] Twenty-two board directors agreed to hold their offices for another year; 8 new board directors were recruited later.

On 16 August 1916, board directors met to discuss the election of the board for September, 1916–August, 1917. They thought that the county associations, clan associations, political parties, and church organizations in Victoria had expanded and were much stronger financially than CCBA

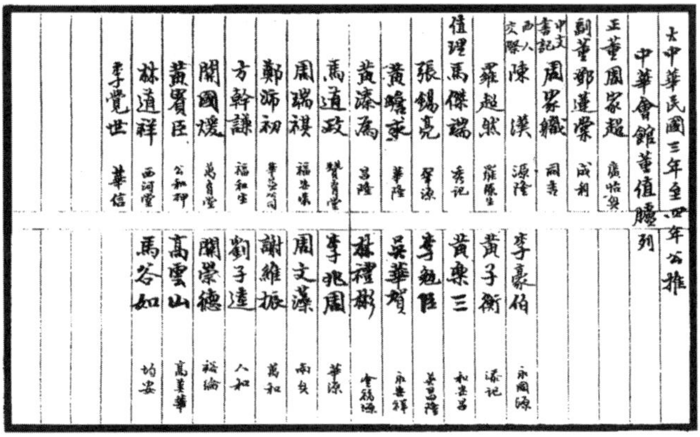
大中華民國三年至四年公推
中華會館董值職列
正董 周家超
副董 鄧蓮棠
中文書記 周家熾
西人交際 陳漢
羅超然
值理 馬傑端
張錫亮
黃曦家
黃滌為
馬道政
周瑞祺
鄭沛初
方幹謙
關國璣
黃賢臣
林道祥
李覺世
李豪伯
黃子衡
黃樂三
李勉臣
吳華贊
林禮彬
李兆周
周文藻
謝維振
劉子達
關崇德
高雲山
馬谷如

Figure 40 CCBA Board of Directors, 1914–1915

itself. It was decided that each organization would be asked to send two representatives to serve on CCBA board. An invitation was sent out, and thirty representatives came to the meeting on 21 August, 1916.[55] On 1 September, they elected Loo Gee Guia (alias Charlie Bo), a tailor who represented the Yen Wo Society, as president, and Lum Lap Wing as vice-president; both were CKT members. KMT members opposed the new system of election, which did not follow the constitution. They looked for an excuse to overthrow the presidency. The pretext came when the Chinese government in Beijing considered abolishing Confucianism as a state religion and promoting religious freedom in China. Some CCBA directors worried that the abolition would be followed by an influx of missionaries into China. On 20 September, Charlie Bo called a meeting at which a motion was made that a telegram be sent to China to protest against the proposed abolition of the state religion. The motion was passed by a vote of 15 to 6 and a telegram was sent to the Chinese consul in Vancouver.[56] Bo chose not to send the telegram although some Chinese believed that it had been sent to China.

On 24 September, an editorial in *New Republic* (*Xinminguo Bao*), a KMT publication accused Charlie Bo of sending the telegram to China without consulting the board directors. The following day, KMT initiated a meeting attended by some Chinese Christians as well. They demanded that Bo should cancel the telegram or alter it by stating that it represented his own view and not the views of CCBA.[57] On 26 September, another article appeared in *New Republic* attacking Bo and demanding his resignation.

Because of repeated accusations by KMT members led by Hoo Hee (Ho Tet Yen) and Ho Wen Sun (He Tiehun and Gao Yunshan), Bo called a meeting for 8 October in CCBA assembly hall. At the meeting, he read the telegram and acknowledged that it had not been sent to Beijing. However, Hoo Hee, Ko Pang and other KMT members attacked CKT members. Police were called in to stop the fight. On 28 October, Lee Hung Mow (Li Gongwu), editor, and Lee Gee Gin (Li Zijing), president of *New Republic* were arrested for taking part in the fight and later bailed out at $1,000.[58] On 1 November, Hoo Hee (He Tiehun) and Ho Wen Sun (Gao Yunshan), principal directors of *New Republic*, were charged for incitement to commit an aggravated assault but they were bailed out at $1,000.[59] Hoo Hee and Ho Wen Sun alleged that the brawl was started by Charles Bo and CKT members and counter-sued them. Bo, Lum Lap Wing, and six other board directors were charged with participation in an unlawful assembly and rioting.[60] However, evidence showed that most people arrested by the police were KMT members, while all the wounded were CKT members and friends; Bo was seriously cut on the face and arms and hospitalized for two weeks and Lum Lap Wing also suffered injuries necessitating hospital treatment.[61] The court case lasted four months. Eventually on 31 January 1917, He Tiehun and Gao Yunshan were found not guilty and four KMT members were fined $75 or three months in jail for assault.[62] This brawl inside CCBA had a significant effect because it sparked off the tong wars between KTM and CKT in the late 1910s and early 1920s not only in Victoria but also in other cities across Canada.

After September 1917, only a handful of Chinese in Chinatown were interested in the work of CCBA as its directors did not exhibit social integration nor have a positive group sentiment. The board of directors dropped to 17 persons with the same group of people from September 1918 to August 1920. CKT organized its own primary school, called Qinge School and did not send their children to CCBA's Chinese Public School. Undoubtedly the conflicts between KMT and CKT crippled CCBA in Victoria. To counteract this tendency, board directors attempted to expand control over small cities in BC, where fewer Chinese resided.

## Maintenance Committee, 1920

CCBA was left in the lurch by prominent community leaders when they refused to be directors. Furthermore, it owed the city for several years'

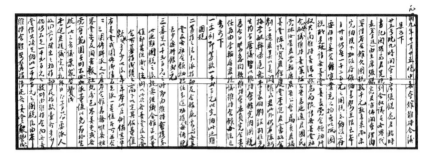

Figure 41   Minutes, CCBA Maintenance Committee meeting, 25 November 1920

tax. In September 1920, the board directors decided to set up a CCBA Maintenance Committee.[63] Zhang Xiliang, chair of the committee, invited county associations, political parties, churches, and other organizations to send representatives to a meeting on 25 November 1920. The minutes of the meeting (Figure 41) stated that.

> *CCBA was told that if it did not pay $1,200 tax in arrears by 30 November, the City government would auction the association's properties to pay for the tax. This is why we have invited the leaders of shantang (county associations) and political parties to come to discuss this matter. Three actions should be taken to maintain the association:*
>
> 1. *We must raise immediately $1,200 for the tax in arrears.*
> 2. *Leaders of shantang and other community leaders would canvass the Chinese people to make a donation of at least $2 to the association.*
> 3. *The Maintenance Committee would immediately pay the tax once it received the donation of $1,200, and also established a new CCBA Board of Directors. The amount of money raised by a shantang or a political party will determinate the number of directors on the board. Small shantang could be united as one group and pool their resources together to meet the required amount of donation for a seat on the Board. However, clan associations and reading clubs were encouraged to make contributions but were not qualified to send representatives to sit on the board because their members also belonged to either a shantang or a political party.*

It was decided that any county association, political party or church group could have a seat on CCBA board on the basis of a donation of

$100 per seat. The Maintenance Committee soon had $900 from nine organizations: CKT, United Chinese Christian Society, and seven county associations (Taishan *Yee Hing Tong*, Kaiping *Kwong Fook Tong*, Enping *Hong Fook Tong*, Zhongshan *Hook Sin Tong*, Xinhui *Fook Hing Tong*, Panyu *Chong How Tong*, and Zengcheng *Yan On Tong*). KMT contributed $200 and was entitled to have two directors.[64] Three small county associations, namely, Nanhai *Fook Yum Tong*, Shunde *Hang On Tong*, and Hua County's Overseas People Association, later united as a larger county association known as the Nanhuashun United Association and raised $100 to obtain a seat on CCBA board. These eleven associations were entitled to send 12 representatives to be directors on the board in the following year. Dongguan *Po On Tong*, Xinan *Tung Sin Tong*, and Yen Wo Society did not make the $100 donation and had no representative on the board. With two members on CCBA board of directors, KMT began to absorb other directors into KMT and finally controlled CCBA.

## First Revision of The Constitution, 1921

On 3 January 1921, CCBA Maintenance Committee drafted a new constitution to replace the 1884 constitution. The 1921 constitution consisted of 31 articles in 10 sections. Essential articles are as follows:

### Section I - Objectives

*Article 1. The objectives of the Association are to promote beneficial practices and eliminate malpractices within the Chinese community, and support the Nationalist Government.*

### Section II - Responsibility

*Article 2. The Chinese Public School, established by the Association, shall be administered according to a separate set of regulations but the Association still has the responsibility to operate it.*

*Article 3. The Chinese Hospital, established by the Association, shall be administered according to a separate set of regulations but the Association still has the responsibility to help and improve it.*

*Article 4. The Association is responsible for the management and improvement of the Chinese Cemetery.*

*Article 5. The Association is responsible for protesting against any local new regulations or laws which infringe on the rights of Overseas Chinese.*

*Article 6. If any Chinese complains to the Association about an injustice or a dispute, the Association shall call a meeting to deal with the issue.*

*Article 7. In the question of supporting the Nationalist Government, the Association will act impartially and remain independent politically.*

**Section III Membership**

*Article 8. Overseas Chinese who live on Vancouver Island are eligible for membership.*

**Section IV Duties**

*Article 9 (c) All Chinese residents on Vancouver Island should pay the Association's foundation fee.*

**Section VI Staff**

*Article 11. The Board of Directors consists of 12 members of whom the Executive Committee consists of the President, Vice-president, a Secretary, two Deputy Secretaries, a Treasurer, two Deputy Treasurers, a Social Convener, and two Deputy Social Conveners.*

**Section V Power**

*Article 12 The President, assisted by the Vice-president, represents the Association to deal with the public.*

**Section VII Duration of Term**

*Article 13 Executive Members are elected for one year term and permitted to be re-elected.*

**Section VIII Meetings**

*Article 17 Two-thirds of attending directors constitute a quorum.*

**Section IX Election**

*Article 18 . Election of the Executive Members shall be held once a year.*

*Article 19. The Board of Directors shall consist of representatives of the organizations which have previously made a donation to CCBA Maintenance Committee.*

*Article 21 The President will employ the Secretary, and Board Directors will employ the Public Relation Officer. Board Directors will be elected to take up other Executive posts.*

*Section X Incomes and Expenses*

*Article 23. Rents and foundation fees are the major sources of the Association's income.*

*Article 25. Only the Secretary and the Public Relation Officer will receive a salary. All other executive posts are voluntary.*

*Article 28. Any Chinese who lives in Victoria and leaves for China, shall make a donation of two dollars to the Chinese Hospital and be given a receipt. The money shall be used solely for the hospital.*

*Section XI Punishment*

*Article 31 Any Board Director who is absent three times continuously without first notifying the board will be fired and replaced by another representative of the association concerned.*

On 20 January 1921, CCBA held a meeting to make two amendments in the constitution. The first amendment was "Article 1. The objectives of the Association are to promote good relations in the community, to carry out charity work, to resolve disputes, to help the poor and the sick, eliminate malpractices within the Chinese community, and to fight against foreign oppression." The significant change was to delete "to support the Nationalist Government." This reflected that most board directors did not want CCBA to be a political agent of the Chinese government led by KMT. The second amendment was "Article 4. The Chinese Cemetery is the burial site of overseas Chinese and the property of the Association." Hence, the Association had the responsibility to maintain and keep the cemetery.

# New Board of Directors, 1922

The 1921 constitution was a great turning point and watershed in CCBA history. It marked the end of the oligarchic rule of wealthy merchants and the beginning of the power bifurcation. Representatives of the organizations which had donated money to save the association from bankruptcy would automatically be board directors. They were business owners, store employees, labourers, or whoever associations sent as their representatives. Some representatives might not be very well-to-do but they were usually active members in county, clan associations and/or other organizations.

Based on the new constitution, a board of 12 directors was elected on 1 December 1921; Ma Guru was elected president, and Joseph Hope vice-

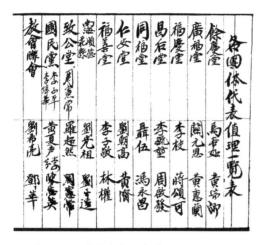

Figure 42  CCBA Board of Directors, 1922

president. At that meeting, the new board announced that the association had paid the City of Victoria tax of $1,083.50. However, CCBA did not have funds for recovering the Chinese Cemetery, which had been put up for auction by Oak Bay Municipality for tax in arrears. Hence, it was decided to take out $296.42 from the Chinese Hospital fund to redeem the cemetery.

After recovery of the cemetery, the new directors thought that the Chinese community would be readier to make donations to the school and hospital than to the association itself. At meetings on 13 and 26 December 1921, it was decided to create a Chinese School Committee and a Chinese Hospital and Cemetery Committee. Each CCBA member association was asked to send an additional representative as a board director to sit on either the school committee or the hospital-cemetery committee. Hence the total membership of Board of Directors in 1922 was increased from 12 to 24: 16 directors representing 8 county associations (Yee Hing Tong, Fook Hing Tong, Tong Fook Tong, Kwong Fook Tong, Hook Sin Tong, Chong How Tong, Yan On Tong, and Nanhuashun United Association), 6 directors representing 2 political parties (KMT and CKT), and two directors representing one religion organization (Christian Church United Society) (Figure 42). On 16 January 1922, the board sent a notice to Chinese communities on Vancouver Island (Figure 43), stating:

*In the past decade, there had been many changes in the political affairs in China. Our fellow countrymen had different political opinions and different political support. Their arguments and conflicts interrupted the operation of CCBA and nearly caused its dissolution. The association had tax arrears of $7,000 to $8,000. If the tax were not paid, its properties would be taken by the city. The Chinese Public School faced financial difficulties and would be closed if it received no further funding. If the financial problems of the*

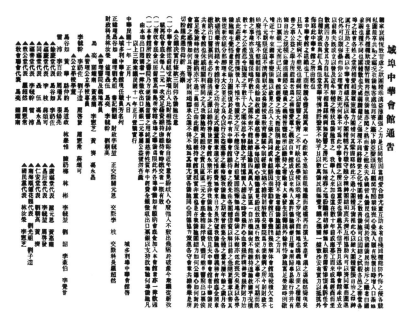

Figure 43  CCBA notice to Chinese communities on Vancouver Island, 16 January 1902

*Chinese Hospital were not solved, it would not be maintained. Other charity work and relief help to China were interrupted because of the discordance in our community. Alas! If just several thousand people in our community could not be united, how could we talk about unity of 400 million people in China? If just a small self-governed organization could not be maintained, how could we talk about saving our country? Could we bear the suffering of losing our properties after owing the city for decades? Would we feel sorry to see dissolution of an organization for several thousands of people in our community? ... Accordingly, CCBA Maintenance Committee was formed last year ... It resolved on the following three fund-raising methods on 1 January 1922:*

1, *Each Chinese should pay a foundation fee of $2 to CCBA to support the association.*

2. *All Chinese people on Vancouver Island have to pay the fee. Those who live outside the island and wish to join CCBA by paying the foundation fees will be most welcome.*

3. *Every Chinese who leaves Victoria for China must make a donation of $2 to support the Chinese Hospital.*

## Education Segregation, 1922–1923

The new Chinese School Committee's immediate task was to deal with the financial problem, which was mainly caused by 60 parents owing a total school fee of $2,962. Another urgent matter to deal with was education segregation.[65] In November 1921, J.D. Cameron, a member of the "Special Committee on the Problem of Oriental Aggression" of the Chamber of Commerce in Victoria said that "White children sitting side by side with Orientals tended to develop the idea of social equality," and John L. Beckwith, another member remarked that "the mixture of Whites and Chinese in public schools are abominable."[66] George Deane, Victoria school inspector, echoed the Chamber of Commerce. He reported to the school board that Chinese children came from unsanitary homes and that all 216 Chinese children studying in four schools in Victoria should be centralized in one school so that they would not affect the health of White children.[67] On 24 January 1922, Joseph Hope, Chairman of the Chinese School Committee, presented to the Victoria School Board a statement from the city's health officer that Chinese homes were not unsanitary.[68] After the "health menace" was not substantiated by the health officer's report, Deane came up with another reason to segregate Chinese children, saying that they "tend to retard the progress of the whole class" and recommending that all Chinese children in the city be assigned to Rock Bay Elementary School, three segregated classes in King's Road Elementary School, and Railway Street Elementary School.[69] White residents near King's Road and Railway Street strongly opposed the plan and claimed that their properties would be devalued by the presence of a segregated Chinese school in their neighbourhood.[70] Meanwhile, CCBA school committee called a meeting on 4 September 1922 at which it was decided that a lawyer would be engaged to fight the segregation and the legal expenses be raised from voluntary donations and compulsory contributions of two dollars per child from parents. Chinese children were told to return home if they were forced to go to the segregated schools. Upon the instruction of CCBA, they dispersed and returned home in the morning of 5 September when they were lined up and taken to the segregated schools.[71] This walk-out marked the beginning of a year-long strike of Chinese children. CCBA organized an Anti-Segregation Association (ASA) to fight the school board.

On 25 September 1922, the ASA sent letters to commercial, literary, and academic circles in Beijing, Shanghai, Guangzhou, and Hong Kong, and to other Chinese communities across Canada, informing them about segregation and asking for financial and moral support. In response, the CBAs in Vancouver and New Westminster and many other Chinese organizations donated generously. The ASA organized a Chinese Free School on 1 November for striking pupils. At the same time, it sent Yang Qizhuang to Shanghai to spread the news about segregation in Victoria and to urge the Chinese government to protest to the British and Canadian governments. Eventually, under pressure from Ottawa, the churches, and the public, the school board informed CCBA in August 1923 that all Chinese pupils could return to their original schools and that only 17 pupils whose English was poor would be assigned to the special class at King's Road School. They would be permitted to study with White children after they became proficient in English. CCBA accepted this arrangement and instructed Chinese children to return to school in September.[72]

## Loss of Hospital Property

The Chinese Hospital had been built for more than 20 years and was badly in need of repair. In April 1922 the Chinese Hospital and Cemetery Committee organized the first large-scale fund-raising campaign for renovations. Four teams of volunteers collected donations from Chinese stores in Chinatowns.[73] The fifth team collected donations from Chinese laundries and grocery stores outside Chinatown, and the sixth team, composed of women, approached Chinese housewives. The seventh team of 13 members travelled up Vancouver Island to solicit donations from Chinese communities in Cumberland, Nanaimo, and other places. Within about two weeks, over $5,000 was raised from Victoria and over $2,500 from other places on Vancouver Island.[74] Renovation of the hospital began in August and was completed two months later. A big celebration was held on 11 November 1922 to commemorate the renovation.

The successful fund-raising campaign could not, however, obscure the fact that the Chinese Hospital still had the basic problem of losing departure fees. After the 1920s, CCBA could not enforce the compulsory hospital donation on Chinese residents in Victoria as nearly all Chinese returning to China left from Vancouver instead of Victoria. Frequent appeals to Chinese returnees to donate to the hospital were ineffective. In desperate need of money, CCBA turned to Chinese gambling-den owners for help, although it had always tried to dissociate itself from them.[75]

The hospital financial situation went from bad to worse when the city changed its tax exemption policy for reasons still unknown: it taxed hospital property after the mid-1920s.[76] Since CCBA did not have the funds for the tax, it appealed to the Chinese community for donations. In March, 1926, the Min Sheng Club performed a play for the hospital and raised $1,551.30. In April, CCBA organized a lottery and raised $5,500. In May, the Tong-yuanhui put on a drama to raise several hundred dollars.[77] All these efforts raised a total of about $7,000 but CCBA was still short of $2,196.99 to pay a deficit of $900 and tax in arrears of $8,296.99.[78] CCBA appealed to the city several times to exempt the hospital from taxation, but its requests were repeatedly rejected.[79] Eventually the hospital property on Lot 461 in Block F was sold at a tax sale on 8 October 1929 for $799 in tax arrears. In the summer of 1930, CCBA organized a fund-raising campaign, but it could not raise enough funds to redeem the hospital. Since no one bid at the auction, the hospital property was taken by the city for non-payment of taxes after 8 October 1930.[80]

CCBA did not regret failing to redeem the Chinese Hospital because of two reasons. First, the directors had accepted that CCBA could no longer support a free hospital. Second, they did not think that there was a great need for a Chinese hospital as many Chinese were more willing to accept Western medical treatment when sick. Difficulties were caused more by language than by distrust of Western doctors. Furthermore, the number of poor, sick, and elderly patients had decreased because many elderly single men had saved enough money to retire to China.

Ironically, Victoria City Council wanted CCBA to maintain the hospital because it would be less expensive to the city for the Chinese to look after their own patients in an already existing facility. Hence, the Council decided to charge CCBA only $30 per month and asked CCBA to continue to operate the hospital. During the 1930s economic depression, many single Chinese men returned to China because of old age or being unable to find jobs. Chinese population in Victoria dropped from 3,702 in 1931 to 3,037 in 1941, a decrease of nearly 18%.[81] On 13 March 1938, CCBA decided to close the hospital at the end of the month because the hospital expenses threatened to bankrupt the association. To induce CCBA to change its decision, City Council reduced the monthly rent to $25,[82] and subsidized the Chinese hospital with a grant of $50 per month for the first four patients, and $10 per month for each additional patient.[83] This marked the beginning of the city's financial support for the Chinese Hospital, which was then registered as a convalescent home and placed under the jurisdiction of the city medical health officer.

## Exclusion Act, 1923

Canada experienced a general economic slump after the First World War. Factory workers were laid off and returned soldiers were unemployed. White workers again blamed Chinese labourers for taking away their jobs. Their resentment heightened as the number of Chinese immigrants soared — up from 650 in 1918 to 4,066 in 1919.[84] Clearly the head tax of $500 had failed to curb Chinese immigration.

On 8 May 1922, W.G. McQuarrie, MP for New Westminster, introduced a resolution that the federal government took immediate action to exclude future immigration of Oriental aliens.[85] The resolution was unanimously supported by all thirteen MPs from British Columbia, and in April 1923 the House of Commons completed the final draft of a bill on a new Chinese Immigration Act.

On 12 and 18 April 1923, CCBA called meetings to protest the bill. Meanwhile, the Chinese Association of Canada was established in Toronto with the objective of uniting Chinese communities across Canada to lobby against the bill. CCBA sent President Joseph Hope to represent Victoria to attend the meeting in Toronto on 29 April. Meanwhile, the attention of CCBA to protest against the bill was diverted by its argument with Dart Coon Club and CKT over rental payments and debts; their disputes lasted for several years. Many Chinese thought that they failed to amend or stop the bill because of China's weakness and disunity, and divisions among the Chinese in Canada.[86] Eventually, a Chinese Immigration Act was passed and went into effect on 1 July 1923.[87] Under this act, people of Chinese origin or descent were prohibited from coming to Canada, except for those in exempted classes, such as consular officials, children born in Canada, merchants, and students. The act consisted of 43 discriminatory articles against Chinese and was called by Chinese "the 43 Harsh Regulations on Chinese Immigration," or "the Exclusion Act."

In February 1924, six Chinese associations in Victoria, namely, Chinese Canadian Club, KMT, CKT, Constitutional Party, Fighting Against Discriminatory Immigration Act Association and Shi Shi Xuan wrote a joint letter to CCBA and requested it to start the "July First Humiliation

Commemoration Day." After several meetings, CCBA decided on 4 May 1924 that 1 July would be commemorated every year by Chinese communities across Canada as "Humiliation Day." On that day,

1. Chinese stores and organizations would not fly flags although it was the Dominion Day of Canada.
2. Chinese should not go out to watch the Dominion Day parade.
3. Mass meetings would be held in Chinese theatres at which community leaders would lecture on the Immigration Act of 1923 and its humiliation of Chinese Canadians.
4. English articles on the commemoration of Humiliation Day would be written and published in local English newspapers.
5. Chinese should wear badges designed specifically for commemoration of Humiliation Day.
6. Several cars covered with signs drew attention to the humiliating aspects of the 1923 Act by honking and driving past the Parliament buildings and through several White neighbourhoods.[88]

CCBA sent out circulars to Chinese associations and stores and instructed them to observe "Humiliation Day" every year on 1 July. This elaborate observance was made in Victoria for about five years but it began to be held less and less rigorously. Accordingly, CCBA decided on 26 June 1930 that commemoration of Humiliation Day would be held inside the association assembly hall only.

## Japanese Earthquake and Shanghai Strikes

While CCBA was busy fighting the Exclusion Act, it was still greatly concerned about Chinese in other countries. For example, the CBAs and Chinese Merchants Associations in Kobe and Osaka sent letters to inform CCBA of the death and injury of many Chinese in the Japanese earthquake and ask its financial help. At a meeting on 11 September 1923, CCBA decided that every director would canvass the Chinese community for relief funds.[89] It raised $1,000 and remitted the money to the CBA in Kobe on 19 September.[90]

CCBA also learned that on 30 May 1925 British-led police in Shanghai fired on Chinese workers demonstrating against Japanese spinning and weaving factories. Police killed many Chinese students and striking workers. CCBA sent a telegram supporting boycott of the British for justice and redress, and raised funds for Chinese workers in Shanghai. [91] As protests and strikes against the British spread to Guangzhou, British police suppressed a demonstration on 23 June, and killed over 50 students. When the news reached Canada, CCBA mobilized community-wide fund-raising campaigns which raised enough money to send $2,000 to the Shanghai Commerce Association for workers and students, $2,000 to the Shanghai Merchant Association, and $3,000 to Guangzhou strikers. [92] Consul Ho went to Victoria on 8 August 1925 and gave briefing on the strikes. [93] After his briefing, CCBA decided to set up a "Monthly Donation Committee for the China's Relief of Workers and Students." A monthly contribution of 50 cents was to start on 1 September and a badge bearing the inscription "Maintain the Fight" was presented to each donor. [94] When the strike organization in Shanghai was dissolved in December, it was decided that all donations would revert to striking organizations in Canada. [95]

## KMT vs CKT, 1920s–1930s

The CKT and KMT mutual resentment intensified conflicts between them throughout the 1920s and 1930s. The KMT power in China was strengthened after it accepted Communist party members in 1921. Throughout the 1920s CCBA directors were dominated by KMT members or their supporters. The community was still torn by the strife between KMT and CKT. Troubles arose again when Dr. Sun died in 1925. Chew On Kwok, a KMT member and CCBA president, and Chan Yu San, editor of *New Republic* and head of CCBA educational affairs, organized a mourning procession in Chinatown and a memorial service. On 12 April 1925 over 1,000 mourners marched through Chinatown to CCBA assembly hall, where the memorial service was held. Across the street was the CKT headquarters, from where there suddenly came a harsh burst of brazen noise, of beaten tom-toms, cymbals, shouting and laughter, disturbing the quiet, subdued service below. [96] Fights would have started if police had not stepped in. In face of the KMT's growing power, CKT allied with the declining Constitutional Party and they worked together more or less as a united force against KMT. [97] This explains why Ye Huibo (alias Yip On) who was one of the founders of CKT in Victoria, was also a very active Constitutional Party leader when he lived in Vancouver in the early 1910s.

In 1928, the conflict between KMT and CKT flared again and a series of assaults followed partly because of a dispute over disposal of funds to maintain the Chinese Hospital and CCBA, and partly because of robbery and closure of gambling dens.[98] On 18 January 1928, Fook Luk Sou, a gambling den owned by CKT members, was robbed of $400 by Lee Lim and Lee Sing.[99] After their arrest, they were bailed out by Lee Chee, KMT secretary. He then was attacked by Yip Tai, owner of the gambling den, while he was walking in Chinatown.[100] Police then learned that over eighty Chinese, armed with pistols and knives, had come to Victoria from Vancouver, Nanaimo, and other places, and an outbreak of violence was feared.[101] On 5 February, Lee Lum, Lee Sang, and Chow Liang Sing, KMT members, ambushed Wong Lim, a CKT member, near Herald Street and shot him in retaliation for the assault on their party secretary.[102] As gambling dens were a major source of income for CKT, a group of "Chinese merchants and citizens," who, according to CKT, were undoubtedly KMT members, petitioned the City Police Commission to close all gambling dens in Chinatown, claiming that they were the source of all fights in Chinatown.[103] Accordingly, on 9 February, the commission instructed John Fry, Chief of Police, to close all Chinese gambling houses in order to maintain law and order in Chinatown.[104] In fact, this action failed to restore peace in Chinatown; it was considered by KMT as their victory over CKT. CCBA ceased to be a mediator because it had internal conflicts between the directors of the two factions. Eventually, leaders of a few disinterested associations such Chinese Canadian Club set up a Peace Preservation Society and tried to mediate the disputes.[105] A group of prominent community leaders in Vancouver led by Bo Qwun Ko, Chinese consul general in Vancouver, also came to Victoria and tried to end the conflicts between KMT and CKT.[106] Noted community leaders in Victoria thought that their mediation had been in vain.[107]

## Two KMT Factions, 1926

KMT and Chinese Community Party (CCP) in China united under Dr. Sun, but the unity was only nominal. Soon after his death, KMT split into a right-wing faction led by Chiang Kai-shek, and a left-wing faction which included CCP members. The Northern Expedition to unite China was launched in July 1926 from Guangzhou. The right-wing KMT reached Nanjing in March 1927 and set up the Nationalist Government there, whereas left wing KMT officials, led by Wang Ching-wei, together with Communist allies, set up a rival government in Wuhan. The two KMT governments in China also led to the split of KMT members in Canada into right-wing and left-wing factions. In Edmonton, for example, the two factions fought for the Nationalist League's fund of $970.63; both claimed that they were pure Nationalists and charged that their opponents with being Communists.[108] In August 1927, Louie Ming Ha, editor of *Jianada Chenbao* (Canada Morning Post) in Vancouver, was shot and killed in his newspaper office.[109] He had been a left-wing KMT member and his assassination was thought to have been carried out by the right-wing faction.

In November 1928, after a massacre of CCP members in Shanghai, KMT started to register overseas Chinese Nationalists in Canada and other countries.[110] The dual objectives of the registration were to weed out CCP members or KMT members who were also CKT members, and to ascertain for the Nationalist Government in Nanjing the occupation and education of Chinese residents in Canada so that trained professional men could be picked for government positions in China.

In spite of political differences, China was at least united under the Nationalist Government and gained the support of overseas Chinese. The new government appealed to overseas Chinese to buy National Bonds to help rebuild China. On 16 September 1928, CCBA organized fund-raising campaign teams to encourage Chinese to buy National Bonds and for the first time included a team of merchants' housewives in the campaign.[111] Within less than three months, the campaign sold about $10,000 worth of National Bonds; the money was sent to Shanghai on 7 December.[112]

## Financial Problems, 1920s–1930s

Although the Chinese community in Victoria donated enthusiastically to help China and overseas Chinese inside or outside Canada, it was not keen about solving CCBA's financial problem partly because of its political divisions and partly because of the social status of directors. Before the 1900s, wealthy merchants ran the association and supported its operation with their own donations whenever necessary. However, after the 1900s, directors were small merchants, store employees, and labourers. Most did not have much money to donate or lend.

CCBA's financial problems were also partly caused by lack of a proper accounting system. It did not maintain an up-to-date account of receipts and expenditures. Some directors set aside sums for personal use and

Table 8 CCBA Income and Expenses, 1925

| Item | Incomes | Item | Expenses |
|---|---|---|---|
| Rental | about $2,500 | Tax in Arrears | about $ 2,000 |
| Annual donation | about 1,300 | Wages | about 1,900 |
| Departure fees | about 1,000 | Miscellaneous | about 900 |
| Total | about 4,800 | | about 4,800 |

Source: monthly meeting minutes, CCBA, 10 January 1926

considered them as loans. Records were not kept and were audited by a disinterested elected official. For example, in January 1925, the minutes recorded only the approximate amount of incomes and expenses for the year 1925 and listed only about $110 as the balance (Table 8). This amount was insufficient to pay the city tax. By February 1925, CCBA owned the City of Victoria several years' taxes, amounting to $6,385.26.[113] There were only 10 directors then and they had to recruit merchants in Chinatown to form a "Fund-Raising Committee for Maintaining CCBA."[114] The committee met on 14 March at which it was decided that every Chinese store on Vancouver Island would be asked to donate $2 a year and every Chinese resident on the island $1 a year to the association.[115] Clan associations, county associations, and political parties were asked to collect donations. By the end of March, only a donation of $500 had been received. CCBA directors were aware that they had to reply on the member organizations for the association's finances. On 4 April, they borrowed money from its eleven member organizations, amounts varying from $50 to $300 (Figure 44).[116] In addition to $1,500 loan from member organizations, CCBA had collected only about $1,000 in departure fees by the end of 1925. Such a small amount was collected partly because general strikes and riots against the British in China discouraged many people from returning home.[117] With its loan, donations, departure fees, and property rents, the association managed to pay a small portion of its tax in arrears in 1927.[118] In September 1928, the directors decided to ask gambling dens to make donations.[119] This decision departed again from CCBA's traditional policy of disassociation with gambling organizations. On 15 September, the directors asked Chinatown stores to lend CCBA from $50 to $100 per store and permitted them to collect and keep departure fees until loan was paid off.[120] Despite their efforts, the directors still could not raise enough money to pay the tax.

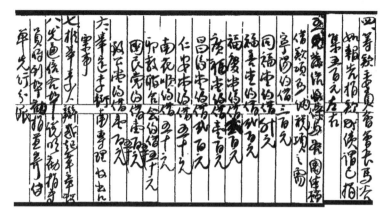

Figure 44  Loans to CCBA from Chinese Associations, 4 April 1925

In August 1929, CCBA received a warning notice from the city that if CCBA wanted to retain the two properties on Lot 458 and Lot 607W1/2, it had to pay the arrears together with interest amounting to $2,317.33.[121] On 5 February 1930, CCBA asked big Chinese business concerns to lend money and promised to pay them later from the departure fees.[122] By October, CCBA still could not raise enough money to pay for the tax in arrear.

Throughout the late 1920s and early 1930s, CCBA directors worked very hard to organize lottery and other fund-raising campaigns.[123] As a director said at a meeting in 1930, "most of us are labourers. We are not so familiar with the business situation as the merchants. We should invite them to come to our meeting and express their opinion whether we should go ahead with the lottery."[124] Another director who was a store keeper in Chinatown added that "the business of Chinatown was bad and the lottery should be carried only after the economic depression was over."

## Ecomonic Depression, 1929–1935

As the economic depression worsened, many merchants and property owners defaulted in payments of loans and taxes and had to foreclose businesses and lost properties. As a result, many workers were laid off. In the early 1930s, for example, many Chinese merchants lost land in Chinatown through defaulting on mortgage payments and city taxes. No one purchased properties at tax sales and consequently the City of Victoria was in debt because it acquired too many properties which had become virtually valueless. CCBA was already in financial difficulty and did not have money to help indigent Chinese labourers. They were forced to seek aid from White agencies. Many unemployed Chinese workers in mines and sawmills were eligible for some employee benefits such as workers' compensation. They started to rely on their Chinese labour unions rather than exclusively on CCBA or clan, county, and other kinds of Chinese associations. Other destitute labourers had to use public services. In December 1931, for example, there were about 120 unemployed Chinese in Victoria. CCBA reported them to the City of Victoria and asked for relief.[125] On 24 December, the City informed CCBA that it would help 106 registered Chinese.[126] Those unemployed Chinese who had not registered would go to the soup kitchen organized by Mrs. Robert Brent Mosher, widow of former American consult in Victoria. She opened the Chinese Relief Mission at 1428 Government Street in December 1931.[127] She had a contract with the three levels of governments that specified that the mission would get a subsidy of $250 per month if it provided two meals a day for 60 men or more. For fewer than 60 men, 20 cents per day per person would be given. In reality, Mrs. Mosher provided meals for 75 hungry Chinese who, like many other White people, were unemployed.[128] Chinese merchants, organizations, and individuals donated vegetables, live pigs and cash to help the mission. After its grant ended in March 1932, the city took over the mission on 15 April.[129] Registration was taken and each individual given a card with a number to be presented at lunch and supper. Mrs. Mosher was assisted by Jack Keen, Wong King, and other Chinese volunteers and nicknamed "Chinatown's Angel" by the Chinese. For three years from December 1931 to December 1934, relief authorities in Victoria also provided 15 cents a day for poor elderly Chinese fed by the Chinese Anglican Mission run by Mrs. M. Field. Many Chinese were in very poor health before going to have meals in these soup kitchens, and an unknown number died from malnutrition.

In 1934 and 1935 the BC government also tried to deal with indigent Chinese on welfare rolls by paying them passage to China on the condition that they returned to Canada only after at least two years.[130] Poor but employed Chinese could not qualify for the repatriation offer and their needs could not be met by CCBA and other Chinese associations. As a result, Chinese began to learn the rules of the Canadian welfare system and their rights. For example, after soup kitchens in Chinatown were closed at the end of 1934, CCBA held a mass meeting and demanded that the City of Victoria put destitute Chinese on the same relief basis as White people. When the City declined to help, about 20 Chinese went to the legislature on 9 January 1935 and protested to relief authorities.[131] However, they were told to go back to the City of Victoria because the city was responsible for relief. Hence, one important aspect of the depression was that Chinese merchants, workers, and CCBA became more and more conversant with the rules of Canadian society, and Chinese people no longer looked to CCBA only for relief and other forms of assistance.

The depression aggravated CCBA's financial problem as well. On 18 May 1935, CCBA tried to establish a lottery committee to issue tickets to raise funds but had to stop the plan after it was told by the police that it was illegal to issue lottery tickets.[132] On 13 December, the old association building on Lot 458 and the new association building (the Chinese Public School) on Lots 606 and 607Wl/2 were sold in a tax sale.[133] CCBA invited Chinese merchants to set up a "Sustaining CCBA Property Committee" to solve the tax problem. With the merchants' help, the two properties were reclaimed in 1936 but there were still arrears of $1,800.[134] This amount did not include interest on the tax and the 1936 tax. By December 1937, tax in arrears amounted to $2,219.13.[135] The directors organized a drama and sold tickets to raise funds, but they raised only $1,338.[136] Accordingly, on 11 December 1937, CCBA decided to keep the old association building by paying all back taxes, and let the city to take over the Chinese Public School property, and then rent the school property from the government. The suggestion would be followed upon by the new board of directors.

On 17 February 1938, only 7 out of 11 associations sent representatives to serve on the board of directors. Few people were interested because they knew that they could not solve CCBA's financial problems. The 17 new directors met on 13 March. They thought that the Chinese Hospital was a financial burden to the association and decided to stop running it as of 1 April. After the City was informed of CCBA's decision, it increased the monthly subsidy to $40 a month, so CCBA continued to operate the Chinese Hospital.[137] The directors also decided to call the $2 departure fee "CCBA Charity Departure Fee" and appealed to large county associations for loans. For example, in July 1938, the Yee Hing Tong of Taishan Association lent $3,000 to CCBA and was told that the loan would be paid after CCBA overcame its financial difficulties.[138]

## Second Revision of the Constitution, 1932

Political conflicts often led to discord in CCBA in the 1920s and 1930s, which discouraged Chinese associations from sending representatives to serve as board directors. For example, annual election of directors between June 1925 and May 1930 were often postponed because a quorum could not be formed.[139] On 27 April 1929, for example, 24 representatives from 11 associations should be elected to serve on the board but only 13 representatives from 8 associations attended the election. As a result, the board for April 1929–May 1930 had only 13 members.

Since the 1930s, KMT had been controlling CCBA. For example, on 26 June 1930, the board had only 20 members from 9 associations because CKT and Nanhuashun Association did not send representatives.[140] Twelve board directors were KMT members. On 22 November 1930, Gao Yunshan, CCBA president, said that in many other societies, general elections were usually held at the beginning of the year instead of mid-year. He suggested that terms ended in December and the election for 1931 be held in January instead of in June. His suggestion was approved by the board. Nevertheless, the election had never been held in January because it was frequently postponed to February or even April because of there being insufficient representatives to attend meetings. Increasing lack of interest in the board was reflected by the resignation of both of the president and vice-president in 1932, and fewer than 10 directors attending meetings. On 15 July 1932, CCBA constitution was revised and approved.[141] The major changes were:

*3. Nominations*

*Names of nominees for the positions of president, vice-president, or other executive positions should be sent to the secretary at least ten days before the date for holding the annual meeting. In the event of no or insufficient nominees, the president, vice-president and other members of the board of directors shall continue to be in office until the next annual general meeting.*

*5. Quorum*

*At all general meetings the chair shall be taken by the president, or in his absence by the vice-president, or in the absence of both by an executive member, or in the absence of all executive members, then by a board director chosen at the meeting. Ten board directors will be a quorum.*

**8. Organization**

*The executive committee of the association consists of the president, vice-president, and 10 executive committee members.*

**9. Term of Office**

*The term of office for the executive committee is one year. Each executive committee member will continue to hold office until his successor is elected.*

**10. Executive Committee Meeting**

*The committee shall meet on the second Tuesday in every month. Seven members shall form a quorum.*

**15. Membership**

*An applicant for a member of the association must be nominated by a board director, and seconded by another board director. The application must be accompanied by a fee to be fixed and considered by the executive committee.*

**16. Membership Fee**

*The quarterly subscription shall be fixed by the executive committee and be payable in advance, on the first day of each and every quarter.*

Throughout the 1930s, few associations sent representatives to serve as directors. For example, the board election for 1934 was to be held in February but was postponed to 7 April because fewer than half of the 11 associations sent representatives. The election was held twice, and twice the elected presidents declined to take up office. Eventually, on 26 August 1934, it was decided that Wong Wah Yip, CCBA president in 1933, would continue to serve for another year. [142]

## Resisting Japan Campaigns, 1930s

On 18 September 1931, the Japanese invaded Manchuria. Chiang Kai Shek did not send troops to fight against the Japanese because he followed his policy of "pacifying internally first, fighting against invasion later." Instead he directed his army to fight against Chinese Communist Party members in South China. He said that the Japanese invasion was like a skin disease but that Communism was a heart disease in China. CCBA immediately held a meeting on 26 September 1931 and telegrammed to the Nationalist

Government to request it to stop the civil war and unite China to fight against the Japanese. On 4 October, CCBA held a mass meeting of all Chinese in Victoria at which *Yuduoli Huaqiao Juri Jiuguohui* (Victoria Overseas Chinese Resisting Japan and Saving the Nation Association) was formed. In English, it was known as the Chinese National Salvation Bureau (CNSB). It had an executive committee of 15 members, with Quan Yuen Yen as chairman. CNSB established several propaganda teams to do fund-raising. Four merchants generously donated $2,000 and sent the funds to General Ma Zhanshan in Heilongjiang Province.[143] CNSB also launched campaigns to urge Chinese Canadians not to buy and sell Japanese goods in Canada and to boycott commercial dealings with Japan. The wives of Liang Jiguang and Li Yugan, Nie Ruixing (later Mrs. Yu Chaoping), and a few other patriotic women established the Female Propaganda Committee to spread information about the boycott and fund-raising.[144] As CKT did not participate in the KMT-dominated CCBA, it established a separate organization known as Hongmen Juri Xiehui (Hongmen Resisting Japan Association) to carry out anti-Japan activities.

On 28 January 1932, Japan attacked Shanghai. Disregarding Chiang's order of not fighting, General Cai Tingkai, Commander of the 19th Route Army; General Jiang Guangnai, Chief of Staff of the 19th Route Army; and General Dai Ji, General Commandant of the Gendarmerie in Shanghai fought heroically. CNSB remitted $20,000 in Chinese currency to Shanghai for the army and $10,000 for the Nanjing government.[145] On 7 January 1933, CNSB received 200 commemorative badges, 500 copies of an appreciation certificate, and several copies of a group photo of the three generals to distribute to donors. (A donor of $10 was to be given a badge, a donor of $5 a certificate, and an association donor of $10 or more a group photo and a certificate.) The Chinese Public School, for example, received the group photo for its economic and moral support of the army (Plate 23). On 5 March 1932, CNSB sent a letter to Chiang Kai Shek and asked him why he did not send troops to support the army.[146] In China, KMT led by Hu Hanmin and other

Plate 23  Photo of three generals, 1938

senior KMT members set up KMT South-West Executive Headquarters (KSEH) in Guangzhou to oppose Chiang's policy of "pacifying internally first, fighting against invasion later." The political division in KMT in China led to a split in the party in Canada as well. Both KMT members in Victoria and CKT wanted to stop the civil war and supported KSEH in fighting against the Japanese. They had the support of You Yongzeng, chief editor, and Liang Jiguang, deputy editor, of *New Republic*, whereas the Chinese consulate and KMT members in Vancouver supported Chiang's policy of non-resistance. On 2 April 1932, CNSB requested the Nationalist Government not to make peace with Japan.

In 1933, Fang Zhengwu, commander of the 10th Route Army, set up the Resisting Japan Alliance Army with the Chahar Army in Inner Mongolia to fight the Japanese. When he lost the battle, he escaped to Hong Kong and then went to the United States and Canada to spread anti-Japanese propaganda. On 2 May 1936 You Yongzeng informed CNSB of Fang's arrival.[147] After the welcome party organized by CNSB on 27 May, You accompanied Commander Fang to other cities in Canada and the United States to advocate the fighting against the Japanese. Canada allowed You to enter the country because he came as an official of the Nationalist Government although he actually came to Victoria to take up the editorial job at *New Republic*. On 28 September, CCBA learned that Bo Qwun Ko, Chinese consul in Vancouver, who belonged to the Chiang clique, was suspected of reporting secretly to the Immigration Office that You had not come to Canada as a government officer but rather to work as a newspaper editor.[148] Such an affront infuriated both CCBA and Vancouver CBA. On 2 October, they sent out a circular denouncing Bo and offering $500 for evidence of the person or persons who had reported to the Immigration Office against You (Figure 45):

*As Vancouver CBA and Victoria CCBA want to stop vicious fellow countrymen from informing the Immigration Office secretly, we decided on four types of punishment. (1) A mass meeting will be held to deal with these informers. (2) Chinese across Canada will be informed of the malicious act and crime of the informers and asked to sever relations with them. (3) If a person has proof about an informer and reports to the two CBAs in Vancouver and Victoria, he/she will be rewarded $500. (4) We will report to the National Government about the informer so that the government can confiscate all his assets in China and punish him. We will*

▲訂定懲戒僑奸辦法四章

▲卽晚拍發控告保君嘻電

雲域兩埠中華會館爲制止僑奸向移民局告密事。昨一日開內會館聯席會議。當時議決各案。經誌前報。惟第二條懲戒辦法呈報。益補述如下一，開全僑大會實力對付。二，將其罪狀通告全加與其絕交。三。如有知某人向移民局告密。及有確實証據。先來報告雲域兩會館者。及有確實紅五百大元。四，將告密者呈報國民政府查封家產。及以法律懲戒。另將上述懲戒辦法呈報廣東政府收僑務委員會備案。同時擬定致外交部請撤保君嘻職之電稿。卽晚由內會館署名發電。茲錄電文如下。外交部鈞鑒。駐雲高華領事保君嘻。向移民局告密立法院專員尤永增任報館主筆。圖逐出境。辱國辱僑。致移民局對華僑壓迫加甚。有總搜查之處。人人自危。全僑痛憤。請卽將保領事撤辦。以息僑憤。雲高華中華會館暨域多利中華會館同叩冬。

Figure 45  Joint circular of CCBA and Vancouver CBA, 20 October 1936

*send a telegram to the Foreign Office in China and inform the Office that Consul Bo Qwun Ko in Vancouver told the Immigration Office secretly that You Yongzeng, the Legislative Officer, was in fact working as a newspaper editor and did not enter Canada as a government official, and advised the Immigration Office to drive him out of Canada. This is an insult to our country and overseas Chinese people. The Immigration Office will pressure us more and will carry out an overall investigation of Chinese immigrants. All of us are infuriated. Please fire Consul Bo to pacify the anger of our fellow countrymen.*

CCBA thought that centralization of efforts by the entire community was necessary in all protests and fund-raising campaigns. Hence, on 17 December 1936, it passed a resolution that the Victoria branch of KMT would lead all associations unifying fund-raising campaigns against Japan. These campaigns temporarily stopped power struggles in CCBA and strengthened KMT's leadership without open challenges in the Chinese community.

## Board of Directors, 1936

On 27 February 1936, Yu Chaoping and Zhao Anguo, two KMT members, suggested that CCBA should be headed by an executive committee of all board directors instead of by the president and vice-president mainly because few directors attended meetings. Their suggestion was accepted.

Hence, CCBA was headed by an executive committee of 18 members in 1936 and an executive committee of 14 members in 1937. It was found that too many board directors heading an association were unworkable. Hence, CCBA reverted in 1938 to having the president and vice-president to lead the association. The executive committee consisted of 11 members: the president, vice-president, supervisor, secretary, treasurer and deputy treasurer, social convener and deputy social convener, school director, school principal, and hospital director.

Study of CCBA minutes from 1938 to 1944 reveals that attendance of representatives from the member associations was poor. When two new societies, namely, Qiaosheng Shaonian Tuan (Overseas Student Youth Association) and Jinlong Drama Society applied to CCBA to send representatives to the association in 1938, CCBA immediately accepted their application without consideration. With few board directors, CCBA had to create specific committees for many special events such as fundraising for China relief, and anti-Japanese campaigns. For example, a special committee was formed in March 1939 to raise funds for wounded soldiers and refugees in Guangdong and Guangxi province.[149] In April 1939, Chinese communities in Duncan, Chemainus, Nanaimo, Cumberland and Port Alberni were invited to send representatives to a special committee for welcoming the British monarch. All these committees had separate accounts and were disbanded after they had completed their tasks.

With the prolonged economic depression, and an increasing number of Chinese working and living away from Chinatown, CCBA's control was confined to an ever-decreasing Chinatown population which primarily sought the security of Chinatown, or to people having business there.

## Sino-Japanese War, 1937–1945

On 27 May 1936, CNSB heard from China that the government led by Chiang Kai Shek was negotiating with Japan peace and immediately sent a telegram to protest the peace agreement.[150] Chiang went to Xian on 4 December 1936 and planned to launch a major offensive to destroy Chinese Communists in the northwest. However, he was kidnapped by Chang Hsueh-liang, the warlord of Manchuria, who had been ousted from his homeland by the Japanese. Chang did not want to fight the Chinese Communists. Instead he demanded that Chiang stopped the civil war and united with the Chinese Communists against the Japanese. Some of

Chang's officer wanted to execute Chiang, but a Communist delegation led by Zhou Enlai arrived in Xian on 15 December and said that the Chinese Communists would accept Chiang as leader on the condition that he united China to fight the Japanese. After he accepted the proposal, Chiang was released and flew back to Nanjing on 25 December. The Sino-Japanese War officially started on 7 July 1937 when the Nationalists and Communists joined to fight against the Japanese. KMT members in Victoria set up the Gongzhai Hui (Government Bond Sale Association) and encouraged Chinese to purchase the Liberty Bonds (Jiuguo Gongzhai) to help China. The Bonds were issued on 1 September 1937, bearing interest at 4% per annum (Figure 46). After Guangzhou was occupied by the Japanese in October 1938, Chinese communities across Canada organized fund-raising campaigns for purchasing planes for Guangdong Province. On 27 November, CCBA and other Chinese associations requested the Canadian government stop selling military equipments to Japan.[151] CCBA mobilized the "One Bowl of Rice" fund-raising campaign in 1939 and raised $17,000 for relief for Chinese refugees (Plate 24). A group of Chinese women also raised funds for the purchase of ambulances for China. The patriotic feeling to fight the Japanese helped CCBA unite the divided Chinese community and brought temporarily divergent points of views into accord.

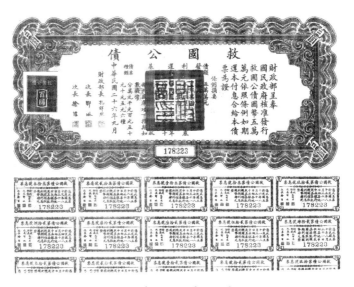

Figure 46  Liberty Bond, issued in 1937

Plate 24  One bowl of rice fund-raising campaign, 1939

During the eight years of war against the Japanese, overseas Chinese carried out fund drives for almost every conceivable military purpose. In Victoria, some individuals established musical and dramatic societies and did performances to raise funds for China. For example, a group of local-born Chinese youths established the Yang Yang Musical Club in 1939, and another group of youths established the Chinese Youth Association (Huaqiao Qingnian Lianhehui) a year later. Both associations were very active in fund-raising activities in Chinatown. The Victoria's Chinese Young Girls' Patriotic Society was established in 1940 and organized drama performances to raise funds for child refugees in China. The entire Chinese community in Victoria enthusiastically supported these organizations but it was not keen to support CCBA. Hence, CCBA had to join CNSB (Victoria Branch), Gongzhai Hui (Victoria Branch), and Hongmen Resisting Japan Association in the anti-Japanese activities. Discordance between CKT and CCBA still remained. For example, on 14 January 1939, CKT sent a letter to CCBA protesting that it had invited several associations on 11 January to discuss the remittance of relief money to China but not CKT's Hongmen Resisting Japan Association. CKT demanded to convene a new meeting for this affair.[152] Occasionally, people were displeased by CCBA directors' decision. For example, the Victoria Branch of the American Overseas Chinese Anti-Imperialism Union sent letters in September and November 1938, asking CCBA permission to fund-raise in Chinatown for the No. 8 Route Army led by Chinese communist commanders. The request was turned down twice by KMT-dominated CCBA on the ground that the union was not a "permanent organization."[153] On the other hand, CCBA mobilized Chinese communities to raise funds to help the No. 5 Route Army led by Li Zongren and Bai Chongxi, two KMT commanders.[154] They sent a thank-you letter to CCBA, Victoria CNSB, and Victoria Chinese Liberty Fund Association for raincoats and rubber shoes for their soldiers.[155] In 1939, there was an outcry in Chinatown that some CCBA leaders had mismanaged the Saving Nation funds although they refuted the allegation. For example, three members who had used CCBA's name to ask Western people for relief funds infuriated the Chinese community; they were fired by CCBA from the Government Bond Sale Association.[156] On 20 January 1940, CCBA established a United Saving Nation Headquarters in Victoria to coordinate fund-raising campaigns.[157] It failed to get CKT's cooperation mainly because of its conflict with KMT. For example, at CCBA meeting on 20 May 1940, discussion of fund-raising for China could not happen because most of the time was wasted by two political parties arguing over the reading of Dr. Sun's will. This dispute prompted the Chinese consulate to send a letter in August 1940 to CCBA and encouraged KMT and CKT to cooperate on helping China fight Japan (Figure 47):[158]

> *According to the instruction of the Overseas Chinese Bureau, CKT and KMT could not cooperate together because of their argument over the reading of Dr. Sun's will at meetings. Our instruction is that the will of Dr. Sun will be read only at formal mass meetings and it is unnecessary to read the will at ordinary meetings. We encouraged the two parties to unite to fight for China.*

To a certain degree, the war against Japan did help unite the divided Chinese community temporarily. For example, when CCBA received China's appeal in September 1940 for donations to buy planes, it set up the

Figure 47  Instruction of Chinese Consul-General in Vancouver, 29 August 1940

Overseas Chinese Aviation Rescue Nation Donation Committee.[159] Eleven fund-raising teams were formed to go to Chinese market-gardening, green houses, laundries, groceries; vegetable retailing, community associations, youth groups, female groups or *fangkou* and asked for a donation of at least five dollars a person. By November, 676 Chinese had donated US$10,590.[160]

# Endnotes

1 *Daily Colonist*, 27, 28 December 1899.
2 David T.H. Lee, *Overseas Chinese History in Canada* (Vancouver: Canadian Freedom Publisher, 1967), 298.
3 *Ibid.*, 299.
4 Wong Wah Yip, Kuomintang member, private interview, January 1978.
5 *The Chinese Freemasons contribution for 140 Years, 1863–2003* (Vancouver: Zhongguo Hongmen Minzhidang Headquarters in Canada, 2003), 142.
6 CCBA, 4 March 1915.
7 David Chuenyan Lai, "A Brief History the Hongmen in Victoria," in *the 34th National Convention of the Chinese Freemasons of Canada Special Issue* (Victoria: Zhongguo Hongmen Minzhidang, Victoria Branch, 2008), 62.
8 *A Brief Introduction to Party History* (Victoria: Kuo Ming Tang, Victoria Branch), August 1996, 28.
9 Edgar Wickberg. *From China to Canada* (Toronto: McClelland and Stewart, 1982), 106.
10 *Daily Colonist*, 10 February, 1903.
11 *Ibid.*, 6 April 1904.
12 *Ibid.*
13 David Chuenyan Lai, *Chinatowns: Towns Within Cities in Canada* (Vancouver: UBC Press, 1988), 190.
14 CCBA, 22 May 1908.
15 David T.H. Lee, *op. cit.*, 460.
16 AC, A Record the Income and Expense of National Subscription, 1914.
17 *Daily Colonist*, 30 September 1898.
18 *Ibid.*, 2 October 1898.
19 *Ibid.*, 30 September 1898.
20 *Ibid.*, 4 October 1898.
21 *Ibid.*, 8 November 1903.
22 *Ibid.*, 5 November 1903.
23 Commemorative Issue of the 70th Anniversary of Shon Yee Benevolent Association of Canada, 1914–1984, 16. The anonymous author did not want to disclose the surname of this clan.
24 Zheng Jinhou, *A Brief Account of Shon Yee Hui's Victims to an Assassin*, Commemorative Issue of the 90th Anniversary of Shon Yee Benevolent Association of Canada, 1914–2004, 35. The author did not want to disclose the name of the party.
25 *Daily Colonist*, 14 October 1909.
26 *Ibid.*, 12 October 1909.
27 *Ibid.*, 29 November 1909.
28 Compiled from annual reports of the Superintendent of Immigration, Department of the Interior, 1891–1910.
29 Letter, CCBA of Victoria to CBA of Montreal, 18th lunar day of the 5th lunar month, 1914 in *A Volume of CCBA Correspondence and Notices from 1914–1915*.
30 CCBA, 17 May 1920.
31 *Ibid.*, 23 April 1915.

32  Royal Commission on Chinese and Japanese Immigration Report, 1902, *Sessional Papers of the Dominion of Canada*, No. 54, Vol. 13, Ottawa, 1902.
33  AC, Circular to Fellow Countrymen for Donations to Fight Against Discriminatory Regulations, 20 March 1902.
34  Victoria School Board, Minutes, 1905–10, meeting, 29 August 1907, 77.
35  *Ibid.*, meeting, 11 September 1907, 78.
36  CCBA bought Lot 606 from Lim Dat on 24 August 1908 and W1/2 of Lot 607 from Lee Mong Kow on 8 March 1909 (LRO DD 505 and DD 10925).
37  *Daily Times*, 6 and 7 August 1909, and *Daily Colonist*, 7 August 1909.
38  After the downfall of the Manchu government and the establishment of the Republic of China in 1912, the school was renamed Chinese Public School (Huaqiao Gongli Xuexiao).
39  Zhitai was a respectful form of address to a high-ranking official such as the governor-general of a province (Zongdu). In this case, the letter might be addressed to the governor-general of Guangdong Province since nearly all Chinese had come from there.
40  CCBA, 23 July 1900.
41  AC, 11 March 1902.
42  CCBA, 30 November 1904.
43  *Ibid.*, 28 May 1900.
44  *Ibid.*, 13 May 1902.
45  *Ibid.*, 6 April 1907.
46  *Daily Colonist*, 10 May 1907.
47  AC, List of donors and amount of donations to help famine in Guangdong Province, 1907.
48  *Ibid.*, Receipt from Hong Kong, 21 November 1908.
49  CCBA, 24 July, 3 August and 7 September 1914.
50  AC, Receipt to CCBA, 21May 1900, and CCBA, 16 August 1906.
51  Statutes of the Province of Saskatchewan, 4th Session, 2nd Legislature, 1912: Chap. 17 An Act to Prevent the Employment of Female Labour in Certain Capacities (assent given 15 March 1912).
52  CCBA, 11 November 1914.
53  The board of directors in 1907 had 56 members.
54  CCBA, 15 August 1915.
55  *Ibid.*, 16 and 22 August 1916.
56  *Daily Times*, 17 January 1917.
57  *Ibid.*, 31 January 1917.
58  *Daily Colonist*, 31 October 1916 and *Chinese Times*, 30 October 1916.
59  *Chinese Times*, 1 November 1916.
60  *Daily Times*, 21, 22 and 23 November, 13 December 1916.
61  *Ibid.*, 17 January 1917.
62  *Chinese Times*, 1 February 1917.
63  CCBA, 24 June, 10 and 13 August 1920.
64  *Ibid.*, 22 January 1921.
65  *Ibid.*, 4 February 1922.
66  *Daily Colonist*, 29 November 1921.
67  Victoria School Board, Minutes, meeting, 11 January 1922.
68  *Ibid.*, 18, 24 January 1922; minutes, January 1920–December 1922, 1157, 1159.
69  On 2 November 1908, the Fisgard Street Chinese School in Chinatown, a segregated school, was opened for Chinese pupils from Grade One to Grade Four. After Grade Four, they were permitted to enter other graded schools and study with White children. (*Daily Times*, 2 November 1908).
70  *Daily Colonist*, 27, 29 August 1922.
71  *Daily Times*, 6 September 1922.
72  For details of the segregation, see David Chuenyan Lai, "The Issue of Discrimination in Education in Victoria, 1901–1923," *Canadian Ethnic Studies*, XIX, 3 (1987), 47–67.
73  CCBA, 9 April 1922.

74  *Ibid.*, 17 and 25 April 1922.
75  *Ibid.*, 13 November 1927. LRO, Series Roll 3748B Indefeasible Fees, 82499-82999.
76  Letter, City Treasurer to T.M. Miller, lawyer for CCBA, 15 December 1921.
77  CCBA, 8 May 1926.
78  *Ibid.*, 24 October 1926.
79  *Ibid.*, 6 June 1930.
80  LRO, Letter from Edwin Charles Smith, tax collector, City of Victoria to Registrar of Title, 22 October 1930 I Series Roll 3748B Indefeasible Fees, 82499-82999.
81  Census of Canada, 1931, 1941.
82  Minutes, Municipal Council of Victoria, 21 February, 14 March 1938.
83  *Ibid.*, 4, 11 April 1938; *Letter Book of the City of Victoria*, 4 January–30 December, 1938, 4032.
84  Canada, Department of Immigration and Colonization, Annual Reports, 1918, 1919.
85  Canada, House of Commons, *Debates*, 8 May 1922, 1509.
86  *Chinese Times*, 17 May 1923.
87  Canada, Statutes of Canada, 1923, 13–14 George V, Chap. 38, *An    Act    Respecting    Chinese Immigration*, 301–15.
88  *Chinese Times*, 2, 4 July 1924 and AC: Circular of CCBA, 6 May 1924.
89  CCBA, 11 September 1923.
90  *Ibid.*, 24 September 1923.
91  *Ibid.*, 10, 17 June 1925.
92  *Ibid.*, 5, 15 July 1925.
93  *Ibid.*, 14 August 1925.
94  *Ibid.*, 22 August 1925.
95  *Ibid.*, 23 December 1925.
96  *Daily Colonist*, 14 April 1925.
97  Sam Lum, President, Dart Coon Club, private interview, February 1984.
98  *Daily Times*, 7 February 1928.
99  *Ibid.*, 19 January 1928, *Chinese Times*, 6 February 1928.
100  *Daily Colonist*, 7 February 1928.
101  *Daily Times*, 23 January 1928.
102  *Daily Colonist*, 7 February 1928, *Chinese Times*, 6, 9, 21 February 1928.
103  *Daily Times*, 10 February 1928.
104  *Ibid.*, 10, 13 February 1928, *Daily Colonist*, 10 February 1928. *Chinese Times*, 10 February 1928.
105  Sam Lum, President, Dart Coon Club, private interview, February 1984.
106  *Daily Times*, 16 February 1928.
107  *Chinese Times*, 21 February 1928.
108  *Edmonton Journal*, 17 January 1929.
109  *Chinese Times*, 8 August 1927.
110  *Daily Times*, 16 November 1928.
111  CCBA, 16 September 1928
112  *Ibid.*, 9 December 1928
113  *Ibid.*, 18 February 1925, *New Republic*, Victoria, 19 February 1925
114  CCBA, 8 March 1925.
115  *Ibid.*, 14 March 1925.
116  *Ibid.*, 4 April 1925.
117  *Ibid.*, 30 January 1926.
118  *Ibid.*, 24 October 1927.
119  *Ibid.*, 8 September 1928.
120  *Ibid.*, 15 September 1928.
121  Letters, from T.M. Miller, CCBA solicitor, to Walter Lee, CCBA President, 27 January and 3 February 1930.
122  CCBA, 5 February 1930.

123 *Ibid.*, 9 August 1932; 22 May, 17 December 1933; 18 May, 6 July 1935; 9 December 1936; 19 February 1937.
124 *Ibid.*, 27 July 1930.
125 *Ibid.*, 8 December 1931.
126 *Ibid.*, 24 December 1931.
127 *Daily Colonist*, 20 May 1932.
128 *Ibid.*, 18 June 1934.
129 *Ibid.*, 24 December 1932.
130 *Ibid.*, 3 May 1935 and *Chinese Times*, 27 April and 8 July 1935.
131 *Province*, Vancouver, 9 January 1935.
132 CCBA, 11 August, 1935.
133 LRO, Documents Filed Roll 329: 36073, 36573, and 36574.
134 *Ibid.*, Documents Filed Roll 334, 394642; CCBA, 9 December 1936.
135 CCBA, 11 December 1937.
136 *Ibid.*
137 *Ibid.*, 9 April 1938.
138 *Ibid.*, 23 July 1938.
139 *Ibid.*, 29 January, 8 February 1927 and 26 May 1928.
140 AC, "List of Association Representatives to CCBA, May 1930–1931." Record of Names of Executive Members of CCBA, 1930.
141 Certificate No. 6421 (Soc) Extraordinary Resolution of the Chinese Consolidated Benevolent Association, submitted by Lee Hok Ming, Secretary, 15 July 1932.
142 CCBA, 26 August 1934.
143 *Ibid.*, 12 December1931.
144 *Ibid.*, 31 October 1931.
145 *Ibid.*, 6 February, 5 March 1932.
146 *Ibid.*
147 *Ibid.*, 2 May 1936.
148 *Ibid.*, 28 September 1936.
149 *Ibid.*, 8 March 1939.
150 AC, Minutes of Chinese National Salvation Bureau Meeting, Victoria, 27 May 1936.
151 *Ibid.*, Letter from Chinese Liberty Fund Association, Victoria to CCBA, 27 November 1938.
152 *Ibid.*, Letter from Chee Kung Tong to CCBA, 14 January 1939.
153 CCBA, 10 September and 19 November 1938.
154 *Ibid.*, 25 January 1939.
155 AC, Letter from Li Zongren and Bai Chongxi to CCBA, 1 November 1938.
156 *Ibid.*, 20 January 1940.
157 *Ibid.*
158 AC, Letter from Chinese Consulate in Vancouver to CCBA, 24 July 1940.
159 CCBA, 26 September 1940.
160 *Ibid.*, 2 November 1940.

**7**

# Political Dominance, 1940s–1960s

# Political Dominance,
# 1940s–1960s

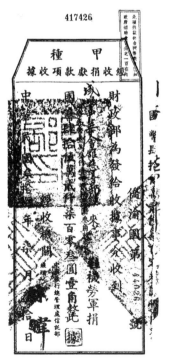

Figure 48  Receipt for donation for Purchase of shoes and socks, 30 July 1945

The 1941 census reveals that Metropolitan Vancouver had 7,880 Chinese residents and the City of Vancouver 7,174. Metropolitan Victoria had 3,435 Chinese residents and the City of Victoria 3,037; Metropolitan Toronto had 2,559, and the City of Toronto 2,326.[1] With a larger Chinese population and a stronger Chinatown economy, Vancouver CBA became leader of Chinese communities in western Canada; the Chinese Community Centre of Ontario (CCCO) was the leader in eastern Canada. Both associations led other CBAs in fundraising campaigns to support China's fight against the Japanese and to appeal to the Canadian government for abolition of discriminatory laws against Chinese. For example, Vancouver CBA initiated the Committee to Send Relief for the Wounded Soldiers and Refugees in Guangdong and Guangxi provinces and told Victoria CCBA to set up a branch committee.[2] In July 1944, CCBA succeeded in raising can $13,128.39 ($452,703.10 in Chinese currency) and sent the money to China for purchase of shoes and socks for Chinese soldiers (Figure 48). At the end of the Second World War, both Vancouver CBA and CCCO requested repeal of the 1923 Chinese Immigration Act. Vancouver CBA renamed itself CBA (National Headquarters) in 1949, and tried to take the lead for all of Canada, and represented Chinese in fighting against discriminatory.[3] However, CCCO also wanted to take the lead and organized on 8 May 1952 a national convention of Chinese representatives across Canada to discuss a trip to Ottawa to lobby MPs for the elimination of restrictive regulations on Chinese immigration.[4]

After the 1940s, CCBA lost its leading position in Canada and was considered by Vancouver CBA (NH) as a coordinator of Chinese communities on Vancouver Island only. For example, when CBA (NH) wanted to raise $600 for a trip to Ottawa to fight for human rights, it sent a letter to CCBA on 4 June 1973 instructing CCBA to be responsible for raising $150 from Chinese communities on Vancouver Island.[5] The CCBA did so.

## World War II

The seeds of KMT leadership were planted in Canada in the late 1920s, germinated when the war against Japan began in 1937, and blossomed after 1941. Canada's alliance with China enhanced KMT's prestige in Canada. After the fall of Nanjing to the Japanese, the Nationalist Government retreated to Chongqing in Sichuan Province and re-established the wartime capital there. Meanwhile, Wang Ching-wei, the left wing leader of KMT, and opponent of Chiang Kai-shek, was convinced of China's inability to resist Japan. He established a puppet Government in Nanjing in March 1940, signed a peace treaty with Japan and appealed to overseas Chinese for support. In October, 1941, the National Government immediately instructed the consuls in Canada and other countries to register all overseas Chinese organizations in order to strengthen its tied with them. On 15 January 1942, Herbert Lee, CCBA president, completed the Overseas Chinese Organization Survey Form and stated in it that the objectives of CCBA were to "support the good and remove the bad in Chinatown, and support the Nationalist Government of China."[6] He also reported that Victoria had about 2,500 Chinese, CCBA's income relied on rents, and its

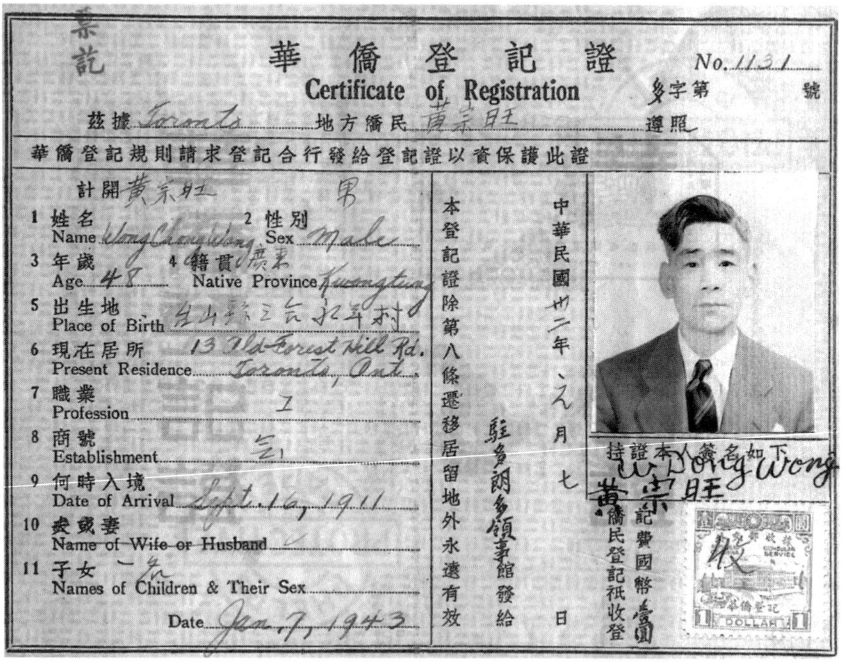
華僑登記證 No. 1131

Certificate of Registration 字第 號

茲據 Toronto 地方僑民 黃宗旺 遵照

華僑登記規則請求登記合行發給登記證以資保護此證

計開 黃宗旺 男

1 姓名 Name Wong Chong Wong 2 性別 Sex Male

3 年歲 Age 48 4 籍貫 廣東 Native Province Kwangtung

5 出生地 Place of Birth

6 現在居所 Present Residence 13 Old Forest Hill Rd. Toronto, Ont.

7 職業 Profession 工

8 商號 Establishment

9 何時入境 Date of Arrival Sept. 16, 1911

10 夫或妻 Name of Wife or Husband

11 子女 Names of Children & Their Sex

Date Jan. 7, 1943

本登記證除第八條遷移居留地外永遠有效

駐多朗多領事館發給

中華民國卅二年一月七日

持證本人簽名如下 W. Dong Wong 黃宗旺

僑民登記費國幣壹圓

Plate 25 A certificate of Registration of an overseas Chinese in Toronto, 1943

expenses in 1940 were $2,242.78. Later, the Nationalist Government sent letters to overseas Chinese associations, telling them not to support Wang's puppet government. It also started the registration of overseas Chinese. (Plate 25)

In Canada, KMT Central Committee sent representatives to Chinatowns to reorganize their factionalized KMT parties according to a clear hierarchy of authority. In Victoria, for example, KMT members united all the Chinese with CCBA as a leader to organize campaigns to help China. Meanwhile, merchants in Chinatowns across Canada organized numerous Kangri Houyuan Hui (Anti-Japan Supporting Societies) along trade, industrial, professional and educational lines. For example, a group of young local-born Chinese merchants including Wah Quon, Lee Kim, Harry Lou Poy, and Dick Chu formed the Chinese Youth Association (Huaqiao Qingnian Lianhehui) in 1940. They boycotted Japanese products in Canada and organized fund-raising campaigns to provide aid for war victims in China.

Chinese girls and housewives had never had an important role in

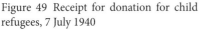

Figure 49  Receipt for donation for child refugees, 7 July 1940

Figure 50  Coins sold by Chinese Women Committee Resisting Japan

community affairs until the war against Japan began. CCBA, for example, enlisted the help of board directors' wives and young Chinese girls in many wartime projects such as fund-raising for Chinese children who had lost their families. In the summer of 1940, the Women's Team of Chinese Liberty Fund Association of Victoria (Jiuguo Gongzhai) sent US$525 ($7,000 in Chinese currency) to China for child relief (Figure 49). Young girls established Victoria's Chinese Young Girls' Patriotic Society and organized fashion parades of authentic Chinese garments to raise funds for over seven Guangdong Children Housing Centres which provided food and lodging for over 7,000 Chinese children.[7] The Chinese Women's Committee Resisting Japan organized several fund-raising campaigns to do such things as selling coins for relief of war victims (Figure 50). Chinese merchants mobilized Chinese communities on Vancouver Island to purchase Victory Bonds to help China (Plate 26).

The Second World War promoted cooperation between Chinese and non-Chinese communities in Canada. For example, CCBA helped fund-raise for and made donations to the Community Chest of Greater Victoria,

Plate 26  Chinese merchants promoting sale of Victory Bonds, 1940

the Greek War Relief Fund Organization, Queen Alexandra Solarium for Crippled Children, and the Canadian Red Cross Society.[8] On 30 September 1940, the Chinese Vegetable Peddlers Association received a letter of thanks from Andrew McGavin, mayor of Victoria, for donating $138 to aid victims of air raids in Britain.[9] When the BC government sold War Savings Certificates in December 1940, Chinese in Victoria participated in the purchase.[10] When BC suffered from severe flooding in the summer of 1948, CCBA raised funds to help flood victims.[11] The association also fund-raised in June 1955 when asked by the Handicapped Children Centre for donations from the Chinese community.[12]

On the other hand, the host society was equally enthusiastic in support of China relief. For example, the Committee for Medical Aid for China in Victoria, chaired by Ruth T. Kipling, obtained surplus wheat and shipped it to China as a gift from the Canadian government to the people of China.[13] Both CCBA and Chinese Youth Association in Victoria raised funds to ship a boat-load of 7,500 tons of wheat to Guangdong Province.

## Organizational Changes, 1940s

Clan and county associations had maintained the patriarchal and hierarchical structures during their long histories. However, some of them were less effective than they should have been. There had frequently been dissolution and subsequent reorganization. In September 1940, for example, CCBA sent letters to 36 Chinese associations asking for donations to purchase aircrafts for Guangdong Province (Table 9). A few

Table 9  Chinese Associations in Victoria, September 1940

| Group | Number | Name |
|---|---|---|
| (A) Political | 1 | Kuomintang (Chinese Nationalist League) |
| | 2 | Chee Kung Tong |
| | 3 | Dart Coon Club |
| (B) County | 4 | Ning Yung Yee Hing Tong (Taishan County) |
| | 5 | Kong Chow Association (Xinhui County) |
| | 6 | Tiecheng Chongyi Hui (Zhongshan County) |
| | 7 | Hook Sin Tong Society (Zhongshan County) |
| | 8 | Hong Fook Tong (Enping County) |
| | 9 | Kwong Fook Tong (Kaiping County) |
| | 10 | Ying On Tong (Zengcheng County) |
| | 11 | Chong How Tong (Panyu County) |
| | 12 | Nanhuashun Huiguan (Nanhai, Huaxian, Shunde counties) |
| (C) Clan | 13 | Oylin Kung Shaw (Zhou) |
| | 14 | Lee's Benevolent Association (Li) |
| | 15 | Lung Kong Tin Yee Association (Liu, Guan, Zhang, or Zhao) |
| | 16 | Wong Kong Har Tong (Huang) |
| | 17 | Chan Wing Chun Tong (Chen) |
| | 18 | Lum Sai Hor Tong (Lin) |
| | 19 | Gim Doo Tong (Ma) |
| | 20 | Yee Fung Toy Society (Yu) |
| | 21 | Gee Tuck Tong (Wu, Cai, Zhou, Weng or Cao) |
| | 22 | Suoy Yuen Tong (Lei, Kuang, Fang) |
| | 23 | Nan Yang Tong (Ye, Deng, Yuan) |
| (D) Dialect | 24 | Yen Wo Society (Hakka natives) |
| (E) Religion | 25 | United Chinese Christian Society |
| (F)Youth/Recreation | 26 | Victoria Chinese Canadian Club |
| | 27 | Chinese Youth Association |
| | 28 | Dong Yuen |
| | 29 | Han Yuen |
| | 30 | Yinlu |
| | 31 | Sailors' Recreation Club |
| (G) Business/Trade | 32 | Chinese Trade Association |
| | 33 | Chinese Agricultural Cooperative |
| | 34 | Greenhouse United Association |
| | 35 | Chinese Vegetable Peddlers Association |
| | 36 | Melon and Vegetable United Association |

associations were essentially inactive but they still had money. Some were later reorganized and changed their names. For example, Chong How Tong was renamed Yushan Society in December 1940, Hong Fook Tong was renamed Yen Ping Association in 1947, and Nanhuashun Society was renamed Sam Yap Society in 1948. CKT was renamed Zhongguo Hongmen Zhigongdang (Hongmen Chee Kung Party of China) in March 1944 and again renamed in September 1946 as Zhongguo Hongmen Minzhidang.[14] To Western public, it was known as the Chinese Freemasons. Throughout the 1940s, fewer than 23 out of the 36 associations sent representatives to CCBA because some associations existed in name only. However, the Chinese Youth Association was very active. It bought the two empty lots behind the Chinese Public School in 1945 and used them as a tennis court for members.[15]

Many new overseas Chinese associations in the world were created during the war against Japan. To learn more about them, the Chinese government instructed Chinese consulates in June 1944 to survey overseas Chinese organizations. The survey form asked not only the name, address, history, membership, date of establishment, sources of income, and other details of the organization but also the name of the association's leader, his/her profession, and whether he/she was a KMT member.[16] The objective of the survey was probably to help KMT strengthen its tie and communication with overseas Chinese associations.

## Board Of Directors, 1945

The old CCBA building and the new one (Chinese Public School) had become so dilapidated by the early 1940s that both buildings needed

extensive repair. The upper floors of the old CCBA building were unsuitable for habitation and left vacant, with windows board up (Plate 27). The cost to make the repairs of the two buildings was estimated at $3,900.[17] CCBA board directors appealed to their member associations for help but found it difficult to get them to meet to discuss the issue. According to the

Plate 27  CCBA old association building, 1971

1921 constitution, only 11 member associations were qualified to send a total of 24 representatives to serve on the board of directors. However, in the late 1930s and the early 1940s, fewer than half sent representatives to CCBA. In 1940 and 1941, for example, no one interested in the president post, and CCBA was headed again by a group of board directors. The system seemed not to be working, so CCBA tried hard to go back to electing the president and vice-president in 1942 but few representatives attended meetings. On 3 May, 1944 only 6 out of 11 associations sent a total of 13 representatives to attend the board meeting. Over half of the representatives were KMT members or supporters. In view of the poor attendance and lack of interest, Wong Wah Yip, a KMT member, suggested on 8 March 1945 that although there were 18 Chinese associations or clubs in Chinatown which had not paid the $100 donation to support the CCBA as a "member association," they should be invited to send one representative each to serve on the board of directors. The 18 organizations were Oylin Kung Shaw, Lee Association, Lung Kong Tin Yee Association, Wong Kong Har Tong, Chan Wing Chun Tong, Lum Sai Ho Tong, Gim Doo Tong, Yee Fung Toy Society, Suoy Yuen Tong, Nan Yang Tong, Tiecheng Chongyi Hui, Yen Wo Society, Tong Yuen Club, Chinese Youth Association, Chinese Trade Association, Chinese Agricultural Cooperative, Chinese Vegetable Peddlers Association, and Yang Yang Musical Club.[18] With representatives from these organizations, CCBA would have more board members and could create a charity committee and a publicity committee to do fundraising. On 27 August 1945, CCBA appealed to 31 Chinese organizations for contributions to repair both association buildings, and suggested that each association to donate from $30 to $300 (Figure 51).[19]

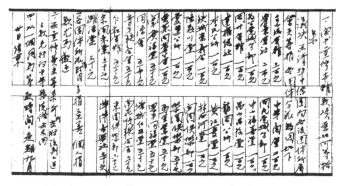

Figure 51  CCBA's appeal to Chinese organizations for donation, August 1945

In March 1946, letters were sent to 34 Chinese organizations in Chinatown, inviting them to send representatives to CCBA for the board of directors for April 1946 to March 1947. When the general election was held on 7 April 1946, only 23 associations sent representatives to attend because some organizations had lost their old members and were defunct. One of the main reasons was that BC post-war economic difficulties forced the provincial government to encourage Chinese residents to return to their home countries for at least two years. It would pay them the passage from Vancouver to Hong Kong and US$10 for the trip from Hong Kong to China. Many Chinese seniors therefore left Canada for China.[20] With the loss of old members and without new ones, many clan or county associations became inactive or defunct. Moribund organizations included Ying On Tong (Zengcheng County), Chan Wing Chun Tong, Yee Fung Toy Society, Nan Yang Tong and Tsang Sam Sheng Tong. The three inactive association were Suoy Yuen Tong, Gim Doo Tong, and Yen Wo Society. After the war, Yang Yang Musical Club, Chinese Vegetable Peddlers Association, and Gee Tuck Tong closed.

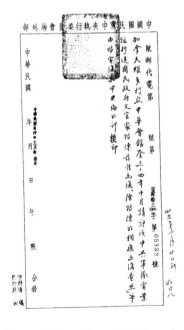

Figure 52  Letter from KMT Central Executive Committee to CCBA, 23 November 1945

## People's Republic, 1949

The civil war between the Nationalist government and the Chinese Communist Party broke out soon after the end of the Second World War. In October 1945, the KMT-dominated CCBA sent a letter to KMT's Central Committee, asking it to fight against the Chinese Communists (Figure 52). Meanwhile, working through the CBAs across Canada, the Nationalist government encouraged over 1,000 Chinese on 21 November 1947 to select two representatives to the Chinese National Assembly, scheduled to open on 25 December 1947 in Nanjing.[21] All Chinese over the age of 20 were eligible to vote because of dual-citizenship. Six candidates from Chinatowns in Vancouver, Toronto, and Victoria, three largest

Chinatowns in Canada, competed for the two assembly seats. The Nationalist government used this method to enlist the support of overseas Chinese, but it did not have the support of the Hongmen people. From 1945 to 1953, the two Hongmen organizations, namely CKT and Dart Coon Club, refused to send representatives to the KMT-dominant CCBA. Not until 1954 did these two organizations send representatives.

On 1 October 1949, the People's Republic of China was established on the mainland whereas the Nationalist government retreated to Taiwan and set up the Republic of China there. Chinese communities across Canada became fragmented into pro-Taiwan, pro-China, and neutral groups. CBAs in Canada were still strongly under the control of KMT members and merchants or workers who were still loyal to the exiled government in Taiwan. CCBA, for example, still had a "built-in" election procedure which ensured KMT control of the association. On 27 March 1953, Leung Mui Fong, a board director, proposed the organization of an Overseas Chinese Anti-Communist and Saving the Country Association (Huaqiao Fangong Jiuguohui). CCBA called a meeting on 8 April to discuss the proposal but it was cancelled because of an insufficient number of representatives being present. When the so-called Anti-Communist Righteous People (Fangong Yishi) came to Victoria on 7 October 1954, CCBA raised $700 to welcome them.[22] Some Chinese youths in Victoria who had escaped Communist China, established Zhonghua Qingnian Hui (China Youth People Society) in 1948, and were soon invited by CCBA to send a representative to its board. This additional member strengthened the KMT's position in CCBA. Many young local-born representatives believed that CCBA was merely an agent for Taiwan and began losing interest in working for the association.

CCBA presidents usually have little help from other directors and had to perform all tasks such as dealing with the financial problems of the Chinese Cemetery, Chinese Public School, and Chinese Hospital, and organizing fund-raising campaigns. As a result, it was difficult to get someone to be president. Li Yesen, a restaurant merchant, served as president for six years from 1952 to 1957. In March 1958, only 16 associations sent 23 representatives to attend the election of the board of directors.[23] As Li did not wish to continue his post and no one wanted to be president, CCBA was headed again by an executive committee of three board directors in 1958. In the following year, the committee expanded to 13 board directors. CCBA had to go back to the system of electing a president and a vice-president since it could not make decisions with so many committee members without a leader.

## Organizational Changes, 1950s–1960s

In the late 1950s and early 1960s, regulations on Chinese immigration were relaxed. In 1957, Chinese residents were permitted to apply for their families to come to Canada before they acquired Canadian citizenship. In following years, admissible classes to Canada were widened to include unmarried children, fathers, and mothers. With the arrival of family members, more Chinatown residents moved to the suburbs. With the slow fading of virulent anti-Chinese prejudice, the invisible wall of suspicion which separated Chinatown from the rest of the city was removed. The number of students at the Chinese Public School steadily dropped from 130 in 1947 to 76 in 1951.[24] Both the Canadian-born generation of Chinese and immigrants from China entered white and blue collar occupations and were integrated into the host society. These changes accounted for the depopulation and decline of Chinatown, and the decreasing influence of CCBA as a community leader.

Many clan and county associations in Chinatown became defunct mainly because their membership continued to decline. Meetings were still conducted in Chinese which was not understood by young local-born representatives. As they could not actively participate in meetings, they lost interest and eventually left the associations. To interest these young people, CCBA formed some youth teams in the 1950s, such as the Chinese Girls' Drill Team formed in 1950 (Plate 28),[25] and the cub pack of Chinese

Plate 28  Chinese Girls' Drill Team, 1950

pupils established in 1952 at Chinese Public School.[26] In February 1955, a few young KMT members established the Chinese Nationalist League Youth Association and recruited young men and boys who had escaped Communist China and come to Canada.[27] This association last less than two years because it was difficult to increase membership since many people feared reprisals against their relatives still living in China if they became members.

As more and more Chinese integrated into the host society, new community societies were formed. For example, a group of young local-born Chinese merchants established the Victoria Chinatown Lions Club in April 1956, and their Western friends later joined the club as well. The same year, some Western people established the Victoria Canada-China Friendship Association. Its objective was to develop and further the ideals of friendship and understanding between the peoples of Canada and the People's Republic of China. As many members of the Chinese Student Athletic Club were assimilated into school sports, the club became defunct by the late 1960s.[28] However, in 1960, a group of young Chinese immigrants from China established Zhonghua Qingnian Hui (China Youth Society) and in the same year a group of local-born Chinese youths established Huasheng Tiyuhui (Chinese Students Gymnastic Club). Another group in 1967 established a musical club known as Shengyun Yinyueshe (Shengyun Musical Society). Three new clubs sent representatives to the CCBA board.

Board directors had always been male until 1959, when a Women's Committee was set up and wives of three board directors were invited to serve on it. That same year, CCBA established the Women's Athletic Team and the Boy Scout Group, marking the beginning of CCBA board's having female directors.

## Financial Problems, 1950s–1960s

After the Second World War, the major functions of CCBA were to run the Chinese Cemetery, Chinese Hospital, and Chinese School. It had three separate financial accounts: the CCBA account, the Chinese Hospital account and the Chinese School account. When there was a special event, a committee was set up to fund-raise for the event. For example, in March 1958, CCBA participated in BC's centennial celebration and set up the Victoria Chinese Community Centennial Celebration Committee chaired by Jack Lee; a separate account was established.[29] When the City of Victoria celebrated its centennial, a special committee chaired by Fan Lee raised funds for decorating cars and performing the dragon dance in the parade on 21 May 1962.[30]

CCBA account was always deficient. Income for it came only from rents of the old association building and from occasional renting of the assembly hall in the Chinese Public School. When renters of the old association building were late in paying, they aggravated the association's financial problem. Furthermore, rent income was insufficient to cover the taxes on the association buildings, maintenance of the Chinese Cemetery, salaries of the secretary and janitor, and other expenses. In April 1961, for example, CCBA owed $3,700 tax.[31] The Chinese School and Chinese Hospital had separate budgets. When they were short of funds, CCBA was responsible for providing subsidies. In addition, the small Chinese communities on Vancouver Island still looked to CCBA as leader and asked for its help and advice. For example, when Nanaimo's Chinatown was burnt to the ground on 30 September 1960, the community asked CCBA for financial help. CCBA raised $2,000 to help the fire victims.[32]

In the late 1950s, about 850 crates of bones were still stored in the Chinese Cemetery. Before the war, it had been a common practice to open graves in the cemetery and dig up bones seven years after burial. The bones were cleaned, dried, and packed into wooden crates. Crates were also sent from Chinese communities across Canada to Victoria and stored in a wooden "bone house" in the Chinese Cemetery until there was enough to warrant a bulk shipment. The last shipping to Hong Kong was in 1930. The next shipment was scheduled for 1937 but it prevented by outbreak of the Sino-Japanese War. CCBA also stopped exhuming remains in the Chinese Cemetery, and available tomb sites were soon occupied. By the late 1940s, the cemetery had more than a thousand graves. Many were dug between existing tombs and only a few inches apart. There was a rumour that some graves were only two or three feet deep and above other graves. Finally, CCBA stopped exhuming the remains and closed the cemetery in the early 1950s. Meanwhile, Chinese communities in other cities continued to send crates of bones to Victoria, awaiting delivery to China when the war ended.

After the People's Republic of China was established in 1949, shipping bones to China became impossible. From time to time, hooligans broke the wooden door of the "bone house" and took out the bones and threw them at each another, so CCBA replaced the door with an iron gate. But some mischievous teenagers threw fire-crackers into the "bone house" one Hallowe'en night, forcing CCBA to cover the house with a cement wall. Finally in April 1961, CCBA decided to rebury the bones.[33] As it did not have funds for reburial, it started a fund-raising campaign in the Chinese community and raised $18,230.15. It then reburied the 820 unclaimed crates of bones in 13 mass graves on 15 October 1961.[34]

In April 1965, the Dart Coon Club moved out from the top floor of the old association where the Palace of Sages was located. [35] Without a renter, the top floor would be empty and the temple shrine unprotected, so CCBA set up a Palace of Sages Management Committee headed by Jack Lee to look after the shrine. The committee borrowed $4,000 from the bank and removed the shrine and other artifacts in the temple to the assembly hall of the Chinese Public School in order to preserve the shrine and temple artifacts as a showcase of the association's rich heritage (Plate 29). The shrine was rededicated on 22 May 1966.[36] However, CCBA could not pay off the loan and owed the interest on it for seven years.

Plate 29  Installation of the Palace of Sages, 1966

## Chinese Hospital

During the Second World War, Victoria became more committed to help administer the Chinese Hospital. It was re-licensed in November 1941 as a private hospital instead of as a convalescent home; Dr. Richard Felton, City Medical Officer, became the first superintendent. [37] In 1943, the hospital was converted into the 7th First Aid Post to be an auxiliary hospital for Chinese casualties during emergencies. [38] After the war, the hospital became a nursing home. In January 1945, Dr. Felton informed the city's Health Committee that the hospital which had 20 beds, needed an additional 16 to 20 beds. The expansion plan was shelved because CCBA lacked the funds to share expansion costs with the city. However, the expansion proposal led to the discovery that the hospital building on Lot 461 was built on the property of the old CCBA building on Lot 458. [39] Accordingly, in 1951, the city purchased 25 feet of land in Lot 458 from CCBA for $300. [40]

In the late 1940s and early 1950s, neither CCBA nor the city was sure which was responsible for the hospital administration. Eventually, on 15 June 1953, the city asked CCBA to take over administration and charged a monthly rent of only 60 dollars. In September 1958, Lum Doy (Lum Tak Kui) was picked up by the police a few yards from the Chinese Hospital and died a few hours later. [41] He weighed less than sixty pounds and had suffered from malnutrition and hunger while he was sick. An investigation into his death revealed that the Chinese Hospital had no bed for him and he refused to enter a Western hospital. His tragic death aroused public concern and prompted CCBA to consider adding a new one-storey wing to the hospital. [42] Initially, provincial and city governments were enthusiastic in support of the expansion project. However, CCBA found later that it did not own the hospital and so was ineligible for a provincial hospital grant. In 1959, Victoria City Manager C.C. Wyatt proposed a way around this difficulty by suggesting transfer of the property to CCBA on condition that the building would revert to the city if CCBA failed to obtain government grants or the building ceased to be used as a hospital. [43] Since it was necessary to have a separate organization to run a community hospital, the Chinese Community Hospital Society of Victoria was incorporated in 1961, and licensed the Chinese Hospital as a community hospital instead as a nursing home. [44] The society asked the provincial government for a grant to build the new wing and on 11 February 1963 the government approved $18,333 on condition that the society owned the hospital property. [45] On 21 February, Victoria City Council rejected the recommendation to convey the hospital property to CCBA for the nominal sum of one dollar. Instead it suggested CCBA buy the property for $12,000. [46] CCBA directors debated this suggestion extensively. Some thought that unlike the pre-war situation, many elderly Chinese people had families in Canada and did not rely on the Chinese Hospital when sick. A few directors thought that the clamour for a new wing addition might be an emotional reaction to Lum Doy's death rather than a rational decision based on demand. While CCBA was debating, it was informed that Dong Gong (Dang Kang Shun), a former labourer, who had died in the Chinese Hospital, had bequeathed his life savings to the hospital.[47] This unexpected good fortune ended discussion. In June 1964, CCBA decided to renovate instead of adding a new wing.[48] The total cost of renovation amounted to $30,000, of which 80% came from Dong Gong's bequest.

## Chinese Public School

In August 1944, the CCBA appealed to reputable community leaders to be directors and formed a Redeeming and Repairing CCBA Properties Fund-raising Committee.[49] Ten teams of fund-raisers sought for donations in Victoria and 1 team went to small Chinese communities outside Victoria for support. The teams received a good response. For example, the Port Alice Chinese Club, an association in a small Chinese community, succeeded in raising $95.50 for CCBA.[50] With enough funds, CCBA redeemed the school property from the City and started to work on the repair of the old association building.[51]

Although the school had a separate committee to manage its finances, CCBA was still responsible for its expenses and do fund-raising campaigns for it. When the committee could not pay teachers' salaries for several months, CCBA took $1,500 from the Chinese Cemetery Fund on 29 April 1953 to pay them. To support the school, the Chinese Youth Association donated the tennis court to CCBA on 17 May 1956. The tennis court was converted to a car-park for rental and the rents helped finance the school (Plate 30).[52] To cut down expenses, CCBA also decided at the 29 November 1966 meeting that the president would also be the school principal without salary.

Plate 30  Parking lot behind Chinese Public School, 1982

## Addition of Directors, 1966

In the 1960s, only about 20 out of about 30 associations sent representatives to CCBA. As over half of its representatives were KMT members, CCBA still celebrated National Day on October 10, and did not participate in the National Day celebration of the People's Republic of China on 1 October. At board meetings, few people spoke out; their silence was taken by KMT members as approval of their suggestion and decisions.

It became more and more difficult for CCBA to operate as few representatives attended meetings. Accordingly, Wong Wah Yip, a KMT member, moved on 29 November 1966 that each association be invited to send an additional representative to sit on the board. His motion was unanimously approved. On 16 February 1967, the board members increased to 57. In June 1968 Consul General Pang Qiping told Ambassador Xue Yuqi of the Republic of China that CBAs in Canada would call for a nation-wide Overseas Chinese Convention in July or August, and discuss the protest to the Canadian government's recognition of the People's Republic of China; CCBA was one of the eight CBAs. On 11 June 1968 it held a special board meeting to discuss the proposed convention, but few directors attended because they did not know the purpose of the meeting. At it, 12 board members supported the motion to openly oppose Canada's recognition of the Republic of China whereas only one board member opposed the motion.[53] When the CCBA's decision was learned, Dart Coon Club and Chinese Freemasons were against it and withdrew their representatives from the board. The Victoria Chinatown Lions Club followed suit whereas representatives of Lum Sai Ho Tong and Kong Chow Association resigned from the board.[54] On 26 July, the Chinese Community Centre of Ontario sent a telegram to all CBAs inviting them to send representatives to the nation-wide Overseas Chinese Convention at which it would discuss sending a delegation to Ottawa and requesting the prime minister not to recognize the People's Republic of China.[55] CCBA met on 4 August to discuss the invitation but representatives were so divided that no decision was made. Another meeting was called on 16 October but cancelled because few representatives attended. Hence, no representatives were sent by CCBA to the convention in Toronto.

Sam Lum, secretary of Dart Coon Club, was elected president of CCBA in 1968. When Dart Coon Club withdrew its representatives, Sam Lum could not represent it. Then he was invited by Kong Chow Association to be its representative so that he could continue to serve as president. He found it difficult to run the association as the board was controlled by a majority of KMT members, especially after the board increased its membership in 1966. He worked on a revision of the constitution. On 20 March 1968 the board of directors decided that the 1969 election was postponed until the revised constitution had been discussed and approved. They also decided that the board for the year of 1968 would continue to serve for another term.[56]

At the board meeting on 25 May 1969, Sam Lum reported that the constitution had been revised and would be presented to the board for consideration. It was also decided to hold a community-wide meeting in Victoria on 6 July to discuss the revision. However, the meeting was cancelled because less than one-third of the Chinese community in Victoria attended. A meeting of the board was to be held on 5 October to discuss the constitution revision, but also had to be cancelled as there was no quorum. Probably the board directors were not enthusiastic about revising the constitution.

## Endnotes

1  Census of Canada, 1941, Table 33, Table 43, 508–17.
2  CCBA, 8 March 1939.
3  David H.T. Lee, *Overseas Chinese History in Canada* (Vancouver: Canadian Freedom Publisher, 1967), 196.
4  CCBA, 17 October 1951, 25 April and 4 June 1952.
5  *Ibid.*, 7 June 1947. CCBA decided to raise $75, and asked Chinese community in Nanaimo to raise $25, Duncan, $20, Port Alberni, $20 and Chemainus, $10.
6  AC, Overseas Chinese Organization Survey Form, 15 January 1942.
7  *Ibid.*, Letter from the overseas Cantonese information office of Kwong Tung Government to CCBA, 2 April 1941.
8  *Ibid.*, Letters to CCBA from W.W. Martin of Community Chest of Greater Victoria, 22 October, 1940; T. Pappas of the Greek War Relief Fund, 21 December 1940; Cobble Hill of Queen Alexandra Solarium, 15 February 1941; A.H. Pease of the Canadian Red Cross Society, 26 September 1941; Frank Synes of Vancouver Island Dog Fanciers' Association, 2 April 1941.
9  *Ibid.*, Letter to Chinese Vegetable Peddlers Association from Andrew McGavin, Mayor of Victoria, 30 September 1940.
10  *Ibid.*, Letter to CCBA from G.N. Stacey, War Savings Committee of the Province of British Columbia, 9 December 1940.
11  CCBA, 7 June 1948.
12  *Ibid.*, 13 June 1955.
13  AC, letter to CCBA from May H. Tripp, Committee for Medical Aid for China, 24 January 1940.
14  Chuenyan Lai, "A Brief History of Hongmen in Victoria," *The 34th National Convention of the Chinese Freemasons in Canada, 2007*," Victoria, 2008, 60–64.
15  LRO, Lot 615 was bought on 11 August 1945 for $890 (DD11945 and Lot 616 bought on 13 August 1945 for $800 (154429-I).

16  AC, Overseas Chinese Organization Survey Form, 1944.

17  CCBA, 27 August 1945.

18  *Ibid.*, 8 March 1945.

19  *Ibid.*, 27 August, 15 October 1945.

20  *Ibid.*, 22 May 1946.

21  *Daily Colonist*, 22 November 1947.

22  CCBA, 1 October 1954.

23  *Ibid.*, 30 April 1958.

24  *To Commemorate Victoria's Chinese Consolidated Benevolent Association, 1884-1959 and Chinese Public School, 1899-1959* (Victoria: Chinese Consolidated Benevolent Association, 1959), 26.

25  *Daily Colonist*, 21 May 1950.

26  *Ibid.*, 13 November 1952.

27  *Daily Times*, Victoria, 28 February 1955.

28  *Victoria Chinese Student Athletic Club Alumni Reunion, 19-20, May 1990*, pages unnumbered.

29  CCBA, 10 March 1958.

30  *Ibid.*, 15 March 1962.

31  *Ibid.*, 6 April 1961.

32  *Ibid.*, 20 February 1964.

33  *Ibid.*, 6 April 1961.

34  *Ibid.*, 15 January 1962 and *The Times*, 16 October 1961, and *Daily Colonist*, 17 October 1961.

35  CCBA, 22 March 1965.

36  *Daily Colonist*, 21 May 1966 and *The Times*, Victoria, 24 May 1966.

37  Minutes of Municipal Council of Victoria, 3 November 1941, and letter book of the City of Victoria, 15 December 1941, 3127.

38  *Daily Times*, Victoria, 10 June 1943.

39  David Chuenyan Lai, "From Self-Segregation to Integration: The Vicissitudes of Victoria's Chinese Hospital," *BC Studies*, (Winter 1988–89), 80, 62.

40  LRO, by-law, no. 3686 and indenture between CCBA and Corporation of the City of Victoria, 29 August 1951, ref. no. 221252; IFB, Vol. 1 February 28, No. 99-1 221252-I; CCBA, 13 May 1952.

41  *Daily Colonist*, 13 September 1958.

42  CCBA, 27 October 1958.

43  *Daily Times*, Victoria, 16 January 1959.

44  Dr. Andrew Rose, Inspector of Hospitals, private interview, November 1976.

45  BC news release from Department of Health Services and Hospital Insurance, 11 February 1963.

46  Minutes of Municipal Council of Victoria, 21 February and 25 April 1963.

47  BC Court Registry, Law Courts, Victoria. Dong Gong's will. The gross value of the estate of Dong Gong amounted to $26,190.43, of which he bequeathed $1,000 to Carl Peter Lambert, executor of his will, and the residue to the Chinese Hospital.

48  *Daily Colonist*, 11 June 1964.

49  CCBA, 1 August 1944.

50  AC, Letter from Port Alice Chinese Club to CCBA, 25 September 1944.

51  Receipt No. 9807, sent by B.L. Hewartson, Acting City Lands Commissioner, City of Victoria, to CCBA, 25 July 1944.

52  CCBA, 20 September, 4 October and 1 November 1970.

53  *Ibid.*, 11 June 1968.

54  *Ibid.*, 4 July 1968.

55  *Ibid.*, 30 July 1968.

56  *Ibid.*, 20 March 1968.

# 8

# Nominal Leadership,
# 1970s–2000s

# ⊹8⊹

# Nominal Leadership,
# 1970s–2000s

The Canadian government introduced a new immigration policy on 1 October 1967 based on nondiscrimination and universality. Immigrants were to be chosen according to a "point system" based on education and training, occupational skill, knowledge of Canada's two official languages, and other qualifications. The policy gave people all over the world an equal opportunity to be admitted to Canada. As a result, since 1967 Chinese immigrants have come from many lands and cultures: Hong Kong, Taiwan, China, Southeast Asia, Latin America, the United States, and other places. Many were professional people such as doctors, engineers, architects, and teachers. On 13 October 1970, Canada established diplomatic relations with the People's Republic of China. Three years later Prime Minister Pierre Elliott Trudeau and Premier Zhou Enlai reached an agreement whereby Chinese were permitted to leave China to join their families in Canada, and Canadian immigration officials would be sent to China to process applications directly. As a result, the number of immigrants from China increased from only 47 in 1971 to 903 in 1975, and has continued to increase rapidly since.[1]

After the 1950s, Victoria's Chinatown, like many other old Chinatowns, struggled to survive depopulation caused by death, departure, and decentralization. In 1962, the City of Victoria purchased Chinatown's dilapidated buildings on Cormorant Street and demolished them for development of Centennial Square.[2] The Hongmen people sold their association building and moved to the building at 557–59 Fisgard Street (Plate 31). I conducted a field survey of Victoria's Chinatown in 1971 and found that its areal extent had dwindled to about two city blocks, and its residents decreased to 143.[3] About a quarter was elderly men and three-quarters were low-income young couples with children who were taking advantage of cheaper rents and proximity to work. In 1966, several dilapidated tenement buildings were condemned by the city and tenants evicted.[4] Upper floors were left vacant, windows boarded

Plate 31  Dart Coon Club and Chinese Freemasons Building on Fisgard Street, 1990

up, and only ground floors used as retail spaces. Some old buildings were demolished and the space converted to parking lots. Chinatown became a blighted neighbourhood, seen by many Westerners as well as Chinese as an undesirable slum and eyesore. In the 1970s, not only the city government but also CCBA was undecided whether Chinatown should be preserved or demolished. Town planners, councillors, and the Chinese community differed among themselves. Although Victoria's Chinatown has lost much of its former lustre and mystery, its remaining fragment has a nineteenth-century townscape. It is one of the few Chinatowns in North America to retain cohesive groupings of nineteenth century buildings (Figure 53). Behind them are narrow passageways, covered alleys, and interior courtyards. These labyrinthine features define the special heritage character of the once "Forbidden Town" where Westerners dared not enter. I recommended to CCBA that Victoria's Chinatown should be preserved.

In 1986, the Canadian government introduced an Immigrant Investor Program under which many Chinese entrepreneurs and investors with large amounts of capital left Hong Kong and Taiwan for Canada. Most went to large metropolitan cities such as Toronto, Vancouver, Montreal, and Calgary, and invested heavily in Canadian business and industry. All resided in the suburbs and suburban Asian-themed shopping malls and plazas were developed.[5] New immigrants to Victoria were very small in number

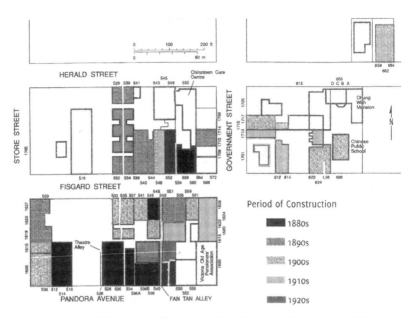

Figure 53  Heritage buildings and alleys, Victoria's Chinatown, 2009

compared to larger cities and did not bring in investment capital to develop suburban malls. However, most settled in suburban municipalities such as Saanich and Oak Bay. The movement of former Chinatown residents to the suburbs hastened Chinatown's decline. Many suburban Chinese residents had no ties to Chinatown because they did not depend on its traditional institutions and did not know or care about CCBA's authority. In fact, many new immigrants saw traditional institutions as an evidence of the social backwardness of Chinatown. In the 1970s and 1980s, a few Chinese Vietnamese boat-people or relative-sponsored Chinese immigrants, who could not speak English, lived and worked in Chinatown. They relied on it as a training base where they learned to master English, and acquired a trade, such as cooking, from their fellow countrymen. They usually joined one or two clan, county, or other social associations for companionship.

Today, CCBA has ceased to be the formal mechanism of access to either the Canadian or Chinese government. Many new immigrants and native-born youths are better educated and trained. They can communicate with government officials without CCBA's help. As well, CCBA has lost many traditional functions, such as shipment of bones to China, co-ordination of protests against discrimination, and mediation of inter-association disputes.

In spite of its decline in influence, CCBA is still symbolically above other Chinese associations in Chinatown and represents the Chinese community there. However, its leadership, although nominal, is not unchallenged.

## Constitution Revision Proposal, 1970s

On 22 February 1970, 15 out of 24 associations sent representatives to the CCBA general election. Sam Lum was re-elected president. In June, he proposed again that CCBA constitution be revised since Canada was going to recognize the People's Republic of China.[6] At the board meeting, the directors decided that every association should send an additional representative to CCBA for revision of the constitution. On 1 November, Sam Lum completed the draft of a revised constitution and submitted it to the board directors and association representatives for review.[7] The draft included re-organization of the board of directors by which the number of KMT members would be reduced. A board director was selected to revise the draft but did not do so because of being too busy. So, the urge for the constitutional revision gradually petered out.

At the end of 1971, there were 22 Chinese organizations in Victoria (Table 10). On election day of 12 February 1972, only 15 associations sent a total of 33 representatives to the meeting. Dart Coon Club, Chinese Freemasons (Minzhidang), Victoria Chinatown Lions Club, and Lum Sai Ho Tong had withdrawn from CCBA. Kwong Fook Tong, Lock Yuen and the Chinese Students Association were virtually defunct and did not send representatives. The constitutional revision request was brought up again in the summer of 1972. Board directors decided to meet on 16 October to discuss the matter but the meeting was cancelled because only a few directors attended and there was no quorum. Many CCBA directors hesitated to consider the revision. Some were traditionalists, and did not want to subvert the established order of things by a new constitution. Some directors were still nationalists in politics or ambivalent about Canada's recognition of the People's Republic of China. So, the proposal to revise the constitution eventually died.

## Lack of Interest

In the 1970s, 14 to 15 out of about 22 associations sent representatives to CCBA for the annual election. Few wanted to sit on the board mainly

Table 10  Chinese Associations in Victoria, December, 1971

| Group | | Name |
|---|---|---|
| (A) Political | 1 | Kuomintang (Chinese Nationalist League) |
| | 2 | Chinese Freemasons (Minzhidang) |
| | 3 | Dart Coon Club |
| (B) County | 4 | Hoy Sun Ning Yung Yee Hing Tong (Taishan County) |
| | 5 | Kong Chow Association (Xinhui County) |
| | 6 | Tiecheng Chongyi Hui (Zhongshan County) |
| | 7 | Hook Sin Tong Society (Zhongshan County) |
| | 8 | Enping Tongxian Hui |
| | 9 | Sam Yap Society (Panyu, Nanhai and Shunde) |
| | 10 | Yushan Fensuo (Panyu County) |
| | 11 | Kwong Fook Tong (Kaiping County) |
| (C) Clan | 12 | Lee's Benevolent Association (Li) |
| | 13 | Lung Kong Tin Yee Association (Liu, Guan, Zhang or Zhao) |
| | 14 | Wong Kong Har Tong (Huang) |
| | 15 | Lum Sai Hor Tong (Lin) |
| (D) Dialect | 16 | Yen Wo Society |
| (E) Recreation | 17 | Han Yuen |
| | 18 | Lock Yuen |
| | 19 | Shengyun Musical Club |
| | 20 | Liu Lang Club |
| (F) Others | 21 | Victoria (Chinatown) Lions Club |
| | 22 | Chinese Students Association |

because CCBA was still crippled by debts and tax. In November 1970, the directors had spent a lot of time organizing a lottery and bingo in order to raise funds for the payment of $2,700 city tax by July 1971.[8] To resolve the immediate problem, they temporarily transferred $1,000 from the Chinese School budget to pay the taxes. CCBA had a bank loan in 1965 for removal of the Palace of Sages and still could not pay off the debt; it still owed the bank $400 in October 1971. As the Chinese Public School had deteriorated badly, the cost of required repair was estimated at $20,000.[9] Hence, in October 1976, board directors formulated a system of rewards or public recognition; thereby donors of $500 or more to the restoration of the school building would have their photographs on a plaque which would be hung in the school (Plate 32). Names of donors who contributed between $60 and

$500 would be engraved on small copper plaques (Plate 33). The continual fund-raising tasks scared off people to serve on the board of directors. Although many people wanted to do community services, they did not want to spend all their time in looking for money to maintain CCBA. Furthermore many Chinese thought that CCBA was dominated by KMT and leaned politically to the government in Taiwan. It was no longer an apolitical community organization and many association representatives did not want to get involved in the conflicts between KMT and the Hongmen people at board meetings. Hence, few people wanted to be board directors. In addition, an increasing number of Canadian-born Chinese rejected the CCBA's authority and tended to affiliate themselves more with Western organizations. For example, Victoria Chinatown Lions Club attracted a greater public attention outside Chinatown and overshadowed the image of CCBA as the "sole spokesman" of the Chinese community. On 6 November 1971, the Club proposed to CCBA the building of a Chinese Activity Centre or Cultural Centre; its operation to be independent of CCBA. The centre proposal was discussed several times in the 1970s in the Chinese community but

Plate 32  Plaque to recognize donors of $500 or more, 1976

Plate 33  Plaque to recognize donors of less than $500, 1976

eventually it did not materialize because the project would involve a large investment and much manpower.[10]

As its prestige decreased in the Chinese community, CCBA began to lose its power and influence in Chinatown. Recognition of the People's Republic of China by Canada made some directors vacillate between supporting and rejecting the Beijing government. Many directors tried to stay away from the politics and wanted CCBA to be apolitical and remain as a traditional charity organization. For example, BC Provincial Celebration Committee invited every ethnic group in the province to send two representatives to the opening ceremony of the Centennial Celebration on 6 January 1971: the female representative would carry the Canadian flag and the male representative would carry the national flag of their native country. CCBA had been debating which flag it would take: the flag of the Republic of China with which Canada no longer had diplomatic relationship, or the Five Stars flag of the People's Republic of China which was recognized by Canada. Since directors' attitudes towards Beijing and Taiwan were ambivalent, no decision could be reached even after several meetings. Ultimately no representatives were sent to the opening ceremony.[11] In September 1972, the Chinese Canadian Friendship Association invited CCBA to send a representative to its banquet to celebrate the National Day of the People's Republic of China on 1 October, but CCBA declined the invitation.[12] When the KMT-dominated CBA in Vancouver called for the Fourth National Convention of CBAs across Canada in 1977, CCBA sent three representatives and instructed them not to participate in any Chinese political activities at the convention.[13]

## Organizational Growth, 1970s–1980s

In the 1970s, several new Chinese associations emerged. In August 1970, a group of local-born Chinese youths formed the Victoria Chinese Youth Association.[14] A group of about 12 youths such as Fred Chow, Tommy Mar, Dick Quon, Tommy Sum, and Yuen Fan Fei started planning the Chinese Canadian Friendship Association (CCFA) in December 1970. It was officially opened in May 1971 and hoisted the Five Stars Flag on the national day of the People's Republic of China on 1 October. A few other nascent youth clubs were also formed but most were short-lived. For example, in 1971 a group of students from China set up the Chinese Students Association, which lasted for only one or two years. That same year, another group of Chinese youths such as Henry Low established the Vagabond Club (Liulang Hui) to learn kung fu from a kung fu master, but it lasted for only two or three years and was replaced in 1975 by the Chinatown Recreation Club (Huabu Kanglehui). In 1974, a group of young Chinese ladies established the Victoria Chinese Ladies Club, and in the same year, Wong Sheung, a kung fu master, set up Wong Shueng Kung Fu

Club. Wong Kong Har Tong had been led by a prominent KMT member until he passed away in the early 1970s. Master Wong Sheung took over leadership of the tong, renaming it Wong's Association in 1979.

In the 1980s, a few new Chinese organizations appeared. Shengyun Musical Club was virtually defunct by the end of 1980 because its members were getting old, but in the same year, some young Chinese musicians established a new musical club known as the Gum Sing Chinese Musical Club. In December 1981, a group of University of Victoria students established the Chinese Canadian Mutual Help (Tongji She) in Chinatown. It lasted for only a few years and became defunct after its founding members left Victoria. The Chinese Canadian Friendship Association (CCFA) had always been confused by many people as the Canada China Friendship Association (CCFA) organized by Westerners. Hence, in 1982, the Chinese organization changed its name to the Chinese Canadian Cultural Association (CCCA) so that it would have a different acronym. In February 1983, the Victoria Branch of the Chinese Canadian Veterans Association was established.[15] In 1988, the Victoria Chinese Cultural Centre Society and Victoria Hong Kong Overseas Chinese Association were set up.[16] The same year, University of Victoria undergraduate students and graduate students formed the UVic Chinese Students and Scholars Association.

Many of these new organizations recognized the People's Republic of China, especially after the US established diplomatic relations with the People's Republic on 1 January 1979. The US affirmed that there was only one China and that Taiwan was part of China. Beijing acknowledged that the American people could carry on commercial, cultural and other unofficial contacts with the people of Taiwan. KMT's power in CCBA began to fade and many directors switched allegiance to the People's Republic of China. Before 1979, for example, CCBA turned down an invitation of CCFA for three times to join its 1 October National Day celebration.[17] But on 14 September 1980, CCBA directors unanimously approved to sending the president to participate in the October celebration. In 1984, CCBA even accepted CCCA (formerly known as CCFA) representative to sit on the board. In 2000, the Democratic Progressive Party in Taiwan, traditionally associated with the Taiwan independence movement, won the Taiwan presidency with Chen Shuibian as president, ending KMT rule in Taiwan. Many Victoria KMT members dissociated themselves from the Taiwan government and its independent policy. These were the last vestiges of KMT's political influence in Chinatown. With the increase of new immigrants and local-born youths, many Chinese traditional associations had fewer functions to perform and became defunct.

## Third Revision of the Constitution, 1982

CCBA tried to project an image as a charity organization and not a political agent of Taiwan. Hence, on 14 February 1980, it altered the association's objectives and sent an English copy of its constitution to the BC government for registration as a charity organization.[18] The constitution stipulated that the purposes of CCBA were to operate and maintain the Chinese Public School, the Chinese Hospital, and the Chinese Cemetery in Victoria; to organize Chinese language and Chinese painting courses to promote preservation and sharing of the ethnic cultural heritages and further group understanding among all Canadians; to help newly landed Chinese immigrants to solve housing and employment problems; and to donate to charitable institutions such as the Easter Seal Society, Heart Fund Society, and Cancer Society as well as the Red Cross.

CCBA also held several meetings to revise the Chinese version of the constitution. The first draft was completed on 12 July 1981 and mailed to 29 Chinese associations in Victoria. When CCBA held its general election in January 1982, only 14 out of 29 associations sent 33 representatives to attend the meeting. The new board worked on the revision.[19] After several changes, the third revision of the constitution was approved by the board on 19 December 1982 and implemented the following year.[20] The major changes were:

### 1. Name

Chinese Consolidate Benevolent Association of Victoria is also known as Chinese Community Centre of Victoria, B.C. It has been registered with the Province of British Columbia as a charity organization.

### 2. Objective

CCBA is the headquarters for the welfare of Chinese living in Victoria. Its objective is to enhance Chinese cooperative spirit for the welfare of both Chinese and non-Chinese people.

### 3. Organization

a) All Chinese organizations in Victoria are association members of CCBA.

b) Each association member is now considered as a CCBA charter member and will send three representatives to sit on the Board of Directors for a term of two years.

c) In the future, any organization which wishes to be an association member of CCBA needs the recommendation of two CCBA charter members. If two-thirds of the Board of Directors approve the application, the applicant will have to pay a foundation membership fee.

d) Any Chinese individual living in Victoria who does not belong to any association member of CCBA, can apply to be a board director upon the recommendation of five Chinese residents in Victoria. The Board of Directors will consider the application. The total number of applicants should not exceed six persons.

e) The Board of Directors will elect 22 members of the Executive Committee:

1) President and Vice-President
2) Secretary (an employee)
3) Two Supervisors
4) Association Affairs Chairman and deputy Chairman
5) Treasurer and deputy Treasurer
6) External Affairs Chairman and deputy Chairman
7) Welfare Chairman and deputy Chairman
8) Property Chairman and deputy Chairman
9) Publication Chairman and deputy Chairman
10) Recreation Chairman and deputy chairman
11) Education Chairman and deputy chairman
12) Auditor and deputy auditor

f) The term of office for an Executive Committee member is two years. The President and Treasurer are not permitted to serve more than two terms of office continuously.

g) A quorum for an Executive Committee meeting is formed by at least seven members.

h) The Board of Directors can invite previous CCBA Presidents and/or reputable community leaders as Advisors of the Association.

From 1967 to 1982, KMT could send five representatives to be board directors whereas other associations were entitled to send only two or three representatives. The revised constitution permitted every member association to send three representatives to sit on the board and thus reduced the KMT's control. In 1983, for example, out of 41 board directors, 10 were KMT members, whereas at least 9 others were CKT members or supporters of the People's Republic of China, the remaining 22 directors was apparently apolitical.

### Chinatown Beautification, 1979–1986

Before the Second World War, many Chinese residents treated Chinatown as a temporary residential and working place rather than as a permanent home. They had no sense of commitment to Chinatown and no incentive to maintain it. Such an indifferent attitude changed after the 1970s as new immigrants came to work and reside in Chinatown. In September 1978, I was asked by Victoria's Heritage Advisory Committee to survey the views and opinions of the Chinese community about the future of Chinatown. I knew that such a survey would not be possible without the help of CCBA and other Chinatown associations. Hence, before I accepted the task, I informed CCBA on 11 March 1979 of the council's intention to rehabilitate Chinatown. CCBA directors elected me to coordinate the community-wide survey and promised me their help and cooperation.[21]

Plate 34  Beautification of Victoria's Chinatown, 1981

The survey was completed in June 1979 and the report on *The Future of Victoria's Chinatown: A Survey of Views and Opinions* presented to the city council on 17 July.[22] The report's recommendations for Chinatown rehabilitation were approved on 4 September.[23] This move marked the beginning of cooperation between the City of Victoria and the Chinese community led by CCBA to preserve and rehabilitate Chinatown. I was unanimously elected by 20 CCBA board directors to be chairman of the Chinatown Redevelopment Committee.[24] The first phase of rehabilitation (1979–81) included repainting and cleaning of heritage buildings, street beautification, erection of the Gate of Harmonious Interest (Plate 34), construction of a Care Facility, and re-

vival of social activities.[25] The second
phase (1982–86) included construction
of Chung Wah Mansion, Fan Tan Alley Rehabilitation, and installation of
directional signs to Chinatown.[26] The
CCBA re-emerged as the unquestioned
voice and leader in Chinatown.

On 8 March 1983, Her Majesty
the Queen and His Royal Highness the
Duke of Edinburgh visited Victoria,
and viewed Chinatown (Plate 35).
So far, Victoria's Chinatown is the
only Canadian Chinatown visited
by a British monarch.[27] Victoria has
several times been the location for
TV and movie productions. In May
1989, for example, John Badham, a

Plate 35  Visit to Chinatown by
Queen Elizabeth II, 8 March 1983

British filmmaker, used Victoria and Chinatown in *Bird on a Wire,* a big-
budget romantic/adventure film staring Mel Gibson and Goldie Hawn.
In December 1995, the Historic Sites and Monuments Board of Canada
designated Victoria's Chinatown a National Historical District. Recent
influxes of tourists and curious visitors to Chinatown reflect its growing
economic and historic significance to the City of Victoria.

## Care Facility Centre

The Chinese Hospital had never been run as a hospital according to
regulations. In December 1976, the Department of Health informed Peter
Wong, CCBA hospital administrator, that if the Chinese Hospital did not
have a resident superintendent, it should have four graduate nurses on
duty 24 hours a day, 7 days a week, and several orderlies on both day and
evening shifts.[28] Unable to meet these requirements for a hospital licence,
Wong applied for a community care facility licence on 31 May 1977, ending
the institution's operation as a hospital as of 30 June.[29] However, the new
regulations governing community care facilities were equally demanding
and strict.[30] For example, each resident in a care home had to be provided
with a single room, an en-suite toilet and a hand-basin.[31] The city, still
owner of the property, was unwilling to spend money on the old building,

but CCBA did not have funds for its complete conversion. It was, therefore, not qualified to be licensed either as a hospital or as a community care facility. Accordingly, CCBA decided in December 1977 to register the Chinese Hospital as a private boarding home for elderly people and ended its connection with the Long Term Care Program.[32]

Without a government subsidy, Wong reduced the staff to only one graduate nurse, four orderlies, and a cook, and cut down the home's capacity from 22 to 20 beds. By February 1979, all 12 residents were Chinese male and over 80 years of age. As operation of the home still ran a deficit, CCBA decided on 3 June 1979 to close it.[33] The residents were transferred to James Bay Lodge.

As chairperson of the Chinatown Rehabilitation Project, I saw the need for a care facility in Chinatown. Supported by a research grant from the University of Victoria, I did a questionnaire survey of 277 seniors in the summer of 1979 and completed the report on *A Care Home in Victoria's Chinatown: A Survey of the Need*. With the help of Councillor Bob Wright and Mel Cooper, the construction of an intermediate care facility was approved by the provincial Ministry of Health on 21 May 1980.[34] The facility was built on the former site of the Chinese Hospital with funding from the Canada Mortgage and Housing Corporation (CMHC) and operation costs were subsidized by the provincial Ministry of Health (Plate 36). The facility officially opened on 25 February 1982 and is run by the Victoria Chinatown Care Society. The city gave the society a 99-year lease at $1 a year. Unlike the previous Chinese Hospital, the Chinatown

Plate 36  Chinatown care facility, 1982

Care Centre admits females as well as non-Chinese patients; in the first few months following the opening, two-thirds of the centre's 30 residents were Caucasians as many Chinese seniors still thought that the centre was poorly managed.[35]

## Chung Wah Mansion

In June 1982, I was appointed by the City of Victoria as chairman of Chinatown Housing Sub-Committee and in that capacity surveyed the need for subsidized housing in downtown Victoria in July. The survey revealed that 54 out of 91 respondents preferred living in Chinatown.[36] The 54 respondents consisted of 37 Chinese or Vietnamese, 22 Caucasian and 2 unidentified. In November, CCBA created the CCBA Victoria Housing Society and sold the school's parking lot to the society for a million dollars.[37] The society then applied to CMHC to fund a housing project. In April 1984, CMHC approved funding of four million dollars to construct a five-storey apartment building known as Chung Wah Mansion (Plate 37). The Mansion officially opened on 20 October 1985.

Plate 37   Chung Wah Mansion, built on former site of parking lot, 1991

## Charity Work After 1979

CCBA did not have the burden of the Chinese Hospital after 1979 and did not run the Chinatown Care Facility. Furthermore, on 26 November 1981, the City of Victoria exempted the Chinese Public School from taxation under Section 273 (a), (b), and (c) of the Municipal Act.[38] CCBA's financial situation became stronger after it sold the parking lot to CCBA Victoria Housing Society. It was concerned more the welfare of not only Chinese community but communities of other ethnic groups. In 1979, for example, it donated $4,645 for Vietnamese relief and sponsored a Vietnamese refugee family of six to come to Victoria.[39] In 1982, it donated $2,000 to the University of Victoria to set up a scholarship to promote China and Chinatown studies.[40] In 1988 and 1989, it contributed about $3,000 to the Handicapped Children's Clinic, Cancer Society, United Way, Royal Theatre Expansion Project, and Kaleidoscope Theatre.[41] CCBA also continued to raise funds to support relief in China. For example, it raised $8,700 for China flood relief in December 1978; $2,000 for Taiwan earthquake victims in October 1999; and $9,800 for victims of the Sichuan earthquake in June 2008.[42] It is impossible to list all CCBA's donations to the Victoria Hospice, Heart and Stroke Foundation, Chinatown Care Centre, and other organizations, and to a few individuals such as a post-doctorate student from China whose family was seriously hurt in a car accident, and a Chinese woman who had financial difficulties after her husband died of cancer. On 14 November 1993, CCBA donated to the political campaigns of three Chinese politicians. Later, some directors thought that CCBA should not be involved in politics, and the board of directors decided in May 1995 that CCBA would not make contributions to fund-raising campaigns of any political candidate or party in future.[43]

## Chinese Public School

CCBA continued to promote Chinese culture by increasing support of the Chinese Public School. Its annual subsidy was increased from $20,000 in 2004 to $40,000 in 2007.[44] Grades 1 to 7 gather daily from 4 to 6 pm Monday through Friday. On Saturday, Grades 1 to 6, and Mandarin and painting classes for children are held. Mandarin classes for adults run from 7 to 9 pm on Monday and Thursday. The school is open not only to Chinese children but also to children of other ethnic groups. The total number of students was 140 in October 2009, including about ten non-Chinese children or children of mixed marriages.

Today the school building is multi-functional, housing the school, a century-old decorative shrine, and CCBA headquarters. The assembly hall is frequently used by the school for its activities; by CCBA for committee and public meetings, festival celebrations, and other social functions; and by other organizations for seminars, exhibitions, and other activities. The building is not only a significant landmark in Chinatown but also one of the most unique heritage structures in Victoria. The pagoda-like building is an outstanding example of a combination of Chinese and Western decorative elements (Plate 38). The tile roofing, upturned eaves and roof corners, and ornate wooden balcony, together with Italianate cornices, Gothic trefoils, and Moorish windows contribute to this effect.[45] It is a tourist destination and a heritage building designated by the City of Victoria.

Plate 38  Chinese Public School, 1991

## Chinese Cemetery

CCBA always has a financial burden maintaining the Chinese Cemetery, which had been closed for burials since 1950. Its condition deteriorated for decades. Many headstones were broken, tilted at odd angles, or pulled out of the ground, and caved-in grave sites left a hazardous surface. The fence around the cemetery was broken and the entire site was strewed with litter, plastic bags, and dog waste. In March 1990, Randy Wilson, representing a group of development companies, proposed to purchase the eastern rocky platform of the Chinese Cemetery for one million dollars.[46] Half the sum was to go to CCBA and the other half was to be used for construction of a pagoda, landscaping, and beautification of the cemetery as a memorial park. The developer, consisting of four companies, would subdivide the rocky platform for housing. CCBA signed the agreement for the sale in September, and authorized it to apply to Oak Bay Municipality to rezone the cemetery.[47] Rezoning would permit the developer to build a seven-lot subdivision on the rocky platform. At Oak Bay council meetings in October and November, a large group of Western residents near the Chinese Cemetery crowded into the council chamber to protest against the housing development.[48]

In view of their protests, Oak Bay adopted Bylaw 3675 (16th Zoning Bylaw Amending Bylaw) on 8 April 1991, which placed the entire CCBA property into a cemetery-use zone and ensured that any development or subdivision of the property could only occur after a public consultation process.[49] CCBA petitioned the Supreme Court of British Columbia to declare Bylaw 3675 invalid. Justice J.E. Hall heard the case in December and decided on 4 February 1992 that Oak Bay was within its power to rezone the Chinese Cemetery, including the rocky portion, as cemetery use only.[50] On 2 September, CCBA submitted documents to the Court of Appeal and appealed the decision of the Supreme Court. The same day, Western residents near the Chinese Cemetery formed the Friends of the Chinese Cemetery with the objective of promoting preservation of the Chinese Cemetery's historical and natural values.[51] CCBA felt that the objective of these "Friends" was not to preserve the cemetery but to prevent housing development in front of their properties. On 3 February 1994, the Court of Appeal upheld the Supreme Court's decision.[52] In April, CCBA submitted a rezoning application to Oak Bay which called for five water-front lots on the rocky platform.[53] In exchange for subdivision approval, CCBA offered to build a public waterfront walkway around the entire property and donate the remainder of the cemetery land to Oak Bay as a park. This suggestion addressed residents' concern. Nevertheless, the application was turned down by Oak Bay Council on 13 June 1994.[54]

In December 1995, the National Historic Sites and Monuments Board designed the Chinese Cemetery a national historic site because of its being a significant cemetery landscape which "expresses the values and beliefs of an important and distinct cultural community in Canada." The cemetery was chosen according to the principles of *fengshui* (meaning literally wind and water) (Plate 39). It is flanked by the "Azure Dragon" (a higher rocky elevation) on its left and by the "White Tiger" (a lower platform) on its

Plate 39  Chinese Cemetery at Harling Point, 1980s

right. It is backed with a "Pillow Mountain" (Gonzales Hill), where the two cosmic forces of Dragon (the yang or male element) and Tiger (the yin or female element) converse. The site, embraced by the "Living Water"' (symbol of wealth) of McNeil Bay, Juan de Fuca Strait, and Gonzales Bay, commands a "Grand Hall" (Juan de Fuca Strait) in the front, and faces a distant "Worshipping Mountain Range" (Olympic Mountains). The altar, formed by a wide platform and two tall incinerators, is a typical Chinese structural style not found in any other Chinese cemetery in Canada. This cemetery is the first one in Canada chosen according to the principles of *fengshui*. Furthermore, the cemetery site is home to several rare species of wild flowers such as the White Fawn Lily, the Early Camas, and Macoun's Meadowform.[55] A number of significant geological and geomorphologic features are visible along the waterfront: cherty argillite and metamorphic ribbon chert of the Leech River Formation bedrock, prominent glacial striations and flutes, large glacial grooves, and Saanich granodiorite erratics.[56] One such glacial erratic, known as "harpoon rock," is associated with local Songhees oral tradition. The story tells of a harpooner hunting seals, and Hayls, "the Transformer," turns him into stone and makes him boss over the seals.[57] The National Historic Sites and Monuments Board of Canada decided that the wilderness, elegant antiquity, cultural features, and natural landscape of the Chinese Cemetery deserved preservation.

On 8 September 1998, David Hurford, Special Assistant to Hon. David Anderson, Victoria MP, asked me to chair the Harling Point Chinese

Cemetery Committee, which included Ida Chong, Oak Bay Gordon Head MLA; John Pallett, Oak Bay councilor; two Harling Point neighbours; and CCBA representatives.[58] I submitted the cemetery beautification plan at the Chinese Cemetery Beautification Committee meeting on 13 October.[59] My proposal included a survey of the condition of the graves, a study of the geological features and wild flowers, restoration of the wooden fence, and construction of a Chinese arch as an entrance. The Greenway Project of the District of Oak Bay would also be part of the beautification project. Total cost of the beautification was estimated at $180,000.

The beautification project was approved by CCBA and launched in December 1998.[60] I was appointed chairman of the Beautification Project and designed the Gate of Peaceful Repose (An Xi Men) as a gateway (Plate 40).[61] The gate consists of two Chinese Characters, An Xi (Peaceful Repose) on top of two maple leaves, symbolizing that those buried in the cemetery will rest peacefully in Canada and will not dream of returning to China.

Throughout 1999 and 2000, CCBA and the Beautification Committee worked hard on fund-raising and succeeded in applications for funding from the Canada Millennium Partnership Program, the Province of British Columbia BC 2000 Community Spirit Program, the Provincial Capital Commission, and District of Oak Bay. To match government funding, CCBA and Western residents near the cemetery launched fund-raising campaigns in the Chinese and non-Chinese communities. On 18 November 1999, Governor-General Adrienne Clarkson, a Chinese descendant, toured the cemetery during a visit to Victoria.[62] So far, the cemetery is the only Chinese cemetery in Canada visited by a governor-general

Plate 40  The Gate of Peaceful Repose, 2001

of Canada (Plate 41). The Cemetery
Beautification Project was completed
in March 2001. The ribbon-cutting ceremony by Senator Vivienne Poy, David Anderson, Ida Chong, Mayor Alan
Lowe and other dignitaries took place
on 8 April.[63]

## Fourth Revision of the Constitution, 1988

According to the 1982 constitution,
the Executive Committee of the CCBA
Board of Directors consisted of 22
members. In 1985, the Board added
four official positions to the Executive
Committee, namely, treasurer and
deputy treasurer of the Chinese Public

Plate 41  Visit to Chinese Cemetery by
Governor-General Adrienne Clarkson,
18 November 1999

School and the chair and vice-chair of the Women Team. A committee of
five board directors was formed on 10 April 1988 to carry out the fourth
revision of the constitution.[64] The committee recommended that all board
directors would first elect the 26 Executive Committee members and
then elect the president, vice-president, supervisor and vice-supervisor.
Presidents and supervisors would in turn appoint the 22 executive
committee members to various official posts. The recommendation was
debated at the 4 December 1988 meeting. Some directors thought that
the two presidents and two supervisors should not have the power to
elect other executive committee members to various official posts. It was
decided that directors would elect the 26 executive committee members
and also elect them to various official positions in the committee.[65] The
draft of the revised constitution was approved at a board meeting but it has
never been published.[66]

On the election day, most directors left soon after election of the two
presidents, two supervisors and the 22 executive members; and only a few
stayed behind to elect the 22 executive members to various positions. As
a result, John Yuen, the president in 1991, decided that the two presidents
and two supervisors would appoint the executive committee members to
various official positions.[67]

## Fifth Revision of the Constitution, 1998

In January 1997, Paul Chan was elected CCBA President and proposed a revision of the constitution. On 9 February, a committee of seven board directors revised the constitution for the fifth time. The draft was completed in May and copies given to all Chinese member associations for review. The revised constitution was approved on 19 April 1998. Central to the amendments were the following changes:

a)    The Association had an additional objective: "It is also the objective of the association not to participate in any political activities."
b)    The four new positions in the Executive Committee created in 1985 were officially recorded in the constitution.
c)    The foundation membership fee of a new association member was to be decided on $300.
d)    Application by an individual to sit on the Board of Directors was abolished.
e)    The quorum for a board meeting would be at least 26 board directors.

## Organizational Growth, 1990s–2000s

Some traditional associations in Chinatown have officially ceased to function although they are still carried on informally by elderly members. In 1991, only 18 Chinese traditional associations had an office in Chinatown (Figure 54). New associations were formed by educated new immigrants or local-born and local-educated professional young people. For example, they established the Victoria Chinatown Lioness Club and the Victoria Chinese Commerce Association in 1991. Both organizations have non-Chinese professionals as members and dilute to a certain extent the influence of CCBA. With their professional background, these new leaders can exert more socio-economic and educational influence than Chinese traditional leaders in the non-Chinese community. In 1993, CCBA accepted these two organizations as well as the Victoria Chinatown Care Centre as members and permitted them to send representatives to sit on the board of directors.[68] In 2004, a group of Chinese seniors from People's Republic of China established the Victoria Chinese Seniors Association with Qu Degui as the chairman. It has not applied to the CCBA for admission as a member association. Hence it does not have representatives to sit on the CCBA board.

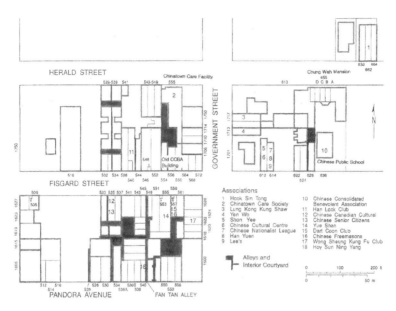

Figure 54  Chinese associations, Victoria's Chinatown, 1991

In February 1994, a few people with the surname Chan planned to organize a clan association known as the Gee How Oak Tin Association, but it failed as few people came after the first meeting.[69] In May 2005, Kaiping people in Victoria welcomed the visit of Zhao Ruizhang, Secretary of Kaiping County government, to the city. He encouraged local Kaiping natives to reactivate the Hoy Ping Huiguan.[70] The Huiguan was subsequently re-organized under the leadership of a group of Kaiping natives including Ho Nan Hing, Fred Chow, Harry Wong, Ken Quan, and William Woo. The association was officially opened to membership on 30 October 2005.

## Sixth Revision of the Constitution, 2007

The major functions of the Women's Team were organization of the Chinese New Year party, school summer picnics, and other social activities. In recent years, many male directors have also participated in these activities. Hence on 11 February 2001, CCBA renamed the Women's Team the Special Affairs Team. To get support and advice from reputable community leaders, CCBA increased the number of its honorary advisors from five to ten persons, including two female members. In the past, the candidate receiving the largest number of votes would become president, and the candidate receiving the second largest number of votes would be vice-president. Cooperation between president and vice-president was usually hard to achieve. Hence, on 14 January 2007, there was a request for revision of the constitution.[71] On 14 December 2008, the board decided that in the forthcoming election, the president and vice-president would be a team

Table 11  Chinese Associations in Victoria, January 2009

| Group | | Name |
|---|---|---|
| (A) Political | 1 | Kuomintang (Chinese Nationalist League) |
| | 2 | Chinese Freemasons (Minzhidang) |
| | 3 | Dart Coon Club |
| (B) County | 4 | Hoy Sun Ning Yung Yee Hing Tong (Taishan County) |
| | 5 | Kong Chow Association (Xinhui County) |
| | 6 | Tiecheng Chongyi Hui (Zhongshan County) |
| | 7 | Hook Sin Tong Society (Zhongshan County) |
| | 8 | Enping Tongxian Hui (Enping County) |
| | 9 | SamYap Society (Panyu, Nanhai and Shunde) |
| | 10 | Yushan Fensuo (Panyu County) |
| | 11 | Kaiping Huiguan (Kaiping County) |
| (C) Clan | 12 | Lee's Benevolent Association (Li) |
| | 13 | Lung Kong Tin Yee Association (Liu, Guan, Zhang, or Zhao) |
| | 15 | Wong's Association (Huang) |
| (D) Dialect | 16 | Yen Wo Society (Hakka natives) |
| (E)Recreation | 15 | Han Yuen |
| | 17 | Gum Sing Chinese Musical Club |
| | 18 | Wong Sheung Kung Fu Club |
| (F) Business | 19 | Victoria Chinese Commerce Association |
| (G) Social | 20 | Chinese Canadian Cultural Association |
| | 21 | Victoria Chinese Ladies Club |
| | 22 | Zhonghua Wenhua Zhongxin |
| | 23 | Victoria Hong Kong Overseas Chinese Association |
| | 24 | Victoria Junior Lion Club |
| (H) Religion | 25 | Chinese Pentecostal Church |
| (I) Others | 26 | Victoria (Chinatown) Lions Club |
| | 27 | Victoria Chinatown Lioness Club |
| | 28 | Victoria Chinese Canadian Veterans Association |
| | 29 | Victoria Chinatown Care Centre |

and be elected as "one" candidate. This change would be incorporated in the revision of the constitution. In January 2009, CCBA board of directors had 87 members from 29 Chinese associations (Table 11).

## Functions in 2009

Today, CCBA directors involve the host society in their social activities. They invite politicians, government officials and leaders of other racial groups to social and cultural parties in Chinatown where the Chinese community and the non-Chinese community exchange views. These interactions promote racial harmony and help bring about a more harmonious multicultural society. Several CCBA presidents were awarded honorary citizenships for their contributions to the City of Victoria. And CCBA directors are consulted whenever the Chinese community is called on to participate in civic affairs, parades, or receptions. Western organizations often invite CCBA to send representatives to their meetings whenever they ask for Chinese support.

CCBA will continue to expand its charity commitments on the one hand, and revitalize Chinese culture and traditions in the face of Westernization on the other hand. As an increasing number of immigrants come from China and establish their own associations, CCBA will have an uphill task to integrate both Cantonese and Mandarin Chinese in the Chinese community. It will also face a formidable task in building up cultural ballast among the growing younger generations of Chinese who cannot speak Chinese languages or dialects.

## Endnotes

1  Canada, Department of Manpower and Immigration, *Immigration Statistics*, 1971–76.
2  Chuenyan Lai, "A Brief History of Hongmen in Victoria," *The 34th National Convention of the Chinese Freemasons in Canada, 2007* (Victoria, 2008), 63.
3  Chuen-yan David Lai, "Socio-Economic Structures and Viability of China," in *Residential and Neighbourhood Studies in Victoria*. ed. C.N. Forward, Western Geographical Series (Victoria, University of Victoria, Department of Geography, 1973), 120.
4  *Daily Times*, 14 July 1966.
5  David Chuenyan Lai, "The Impact of New Immigration Policies on the Development of New Chinatowns and New Chinese Shopping Plazas in Canada," *Asian Profile*, 28, 3 (2000), 110.
6  CCBA, 7 June, 5 July 1970.
7  *Ibid.*, 20 September, 4 October, 1 November 1970.
8  *Ibid.*, 16 November 1970, 26 March 1971.
9  *Ibid.*, 11 April 1976.
10  *Ibid.*, 21 November 1971, 7 December 1975, and Letter from Peter Lou-Poy, CCBA president to Mayor Michael Young, 11 March 1979.

11   *Ibid.*, 3 January 1971.
12   *Ibid.*, 28 September 1972.
13   *Ibid.*, 31 July 1977.
14   *Daily Colonist*, 27 August 1970.
15   *Chinatown News*, Vancouver, June 1955, No. 14, 27. The Chinese Canadian Veterans Association is also known as the Army, Navy and Air Force Pacific Unit 280 Chinese Canadian Veterans Association and was established in Vancouver in 1947.
16   CCBA, 25 June 1988.
17   *Ibid.*, 13 October 1970, 28 September 1972, 6 May 1976.
18   AC, Certificate no. S-642, signed by L.G. Huck, Deputy Registrar of Companies, 14 February 1980.
19   CCBA, 10 May, 14 June, 12 July, 16 August, 21 November 1981, 22 September 1982.
20   *Ibid.*, 19 December 1982.
21   *Ibid.*, 11 March, 8 April 1979. CA, Letter of Peter Lou-Poy, CCBA, president to Mayor Michael Young, 11 March 1979.
22   Chuenyan David Lai, *The Future of Victoria's Chinatown: A Survey of Views and Opinions*, Vol. 1, Recommendations; and Vol. 2, Tabulation of Data (Victoria: City of Victoria, 1979).
23   City of Victoria, Group B Committee's report to mayor and board of aldermen in council, 4 September 1979.
24   CCBA, 8 June 1980.
25   David Chuenyan Lai, *Chinatowns: Towns within Cities in Canada* (Vancouver: UBC Press), 261–65.
26   *Ibid.*, 265–7.
27   Betty Campbell, ed., *Royal Visit to Victoria, British Columbia, Canada* (Victoria: Campbell's Publishing, 1983), 10.
28   AC, Letter from Dr. Andrew Rose, Inspector of Hospitals, to Peter Wong, Administrator of the Chinese Hospital, 2 December 1976.
29   *Ibid.*, Application to Community Health Service, Capital Regional District, 31 May 1977.
30   *Ibid.*, Letter dated 7 January1997 from Dr. A.B. Allen, Deputy Regional Health Office, and letter of 10 January 1977 from Andrew Rose, Inspector of Hospitals, to Peter Wong.
31   *Ibid.*, BC Community Care Facilities Licensing Act, Chap. 4, 1969, 6.
32   *Ibid.*, Letter from Peter Wong, administrator of Chinese Hospital to K. Wilkens, Land Commissioner, City of Victoria, 5 December 1977.
33   CCBA, 3 June 1979.
34   AC, Letter from Jeremy Tate, Ministry of Health to CCBA, 21 May 1980.
35   Laura Meyer, Administrator, Victoria Chinatown Care Centre, private interview, held in June 1988.
36   David Chuenyan Lai, *Final Report on the Survey of the Need for Low-Rental Housing in Chinatown and Elsewhere in Downtown Victoria* (City of Victoria: Chinatown Housing Sub-Committee, Housing Advisory Committee, 29 July 1982), 1–4.
37   *Chinese Canadian Bulletin*, Vancouver, Vol. 25 No. 153, December 1985, 15.
38   Letter from Mark Johnston, Administrative Assistant, City of Victoria to CCBA, 28 January 1982.
39   CCBA, 3 October 1979, 13 July 1980.
40   *Ibid.*, 17 January 1982.
41   *Ibid.*, 13 March, 8 May, 1988, 10 December 1989.
42   *Ibid.*, 13 December 1998, 10 October1999, 8 June 2008.
43   *Ibid.*, 14 May 1995.
44   *Ibid.*, 12 September 2004 and 11 November 2007.
45   David Chuenyan Lai, *The Forbidden City Within Victoria: Myth, Symbol, and Streetscape of Canada's Earliest Chinatown* (Victoria: Orca Book Publishers, 1991), 126.
46   AC, Letter to CCBA from Executive Production Ltd., 21 March 1990; CCBA, 22 April 1990.

47  *Ibid.*, Agreement signed 7 September 1990 between CCBA and developers (Harling Point Estates Ltd., Pablo's Dining Lounge Ltd., Sylvia J. Arsens, and Pablo Hernandez).

48  *Times-Colonist*, 24 October, 7, 8 November 1990.

49  CCBA, 22 April 1990.

50  Friends of Chinese Cemetery Newsletter, No. 1, February 1993, 4.

51  *Oak Bay Star*, 2 September 1992.

52  *Times-Colonist*, 4 February 1994.

53  *Ibid.*, 19 April 1994.

54  *Ibid.*, 15 June 1994.

55  AC, Consultant report on wild flowers in the Chinese Cemetery by Dr. Adolf Ceska and Mrs. Oluna Ceska, May 2000.

56  *Ibid.*, Consultant report on the geology of the coastal area of the Chinese Cemetery by Dr. Dan Smith, March 2000.

57  Grant Keddie, historian, Royal BC Museum, private interview, March 2000.

58  *Ibid.*, Letter from David Hurford to Paul Chan, CCBA, 8 September 1998.

59  Minutes, Chinese Cemetery Beautification Committee, Oak Bay Municipality, 13 October 1998.

60  *Chinatown Newsletter*, CCBA, December 1998, No. 35, 26–27.

61  Minutes, Chinese Cemetery Beautification Committee, 14 November 2000.

62  *Sing Tao Daily*, Vancouver, 19 November 1999.

63  *Chinatown Newsletter*, CCBA, April/May, 2001, No. 49, 3, 27.

64  CCBA, 10 April 1988.

65  *Ibid.*, 4 December 1988.

66  Paul Chan, former CCBA president, private interview, January 2009.

67  John Yuen, CCBA president, private interview, December 1991.

68  CCBA, 11 September 1993.

69  Paul Chan, CCBA board director, private interview, June 1994.

70  *Ming Pao Daily*, Vancouver, 7 July 2005.

71  CCBA, 9 September 2007.

# 9

# Retrospect and Prospect

# Retrospect and Prospect

Chinese in Canada were excluded from Canadian society before the Second World War. They were confined to Chinatowns which became their home, sanctuary, training base for learning Western way of life, and springboard for assimilation to host society. Chinatown had developed a government to resolve both its internal and external problems. This book uses Victoria's Chinatown as a case study which provides a more nuanced operation of a Chinatown government within a municipal government, and details the evolution of Chinatown community leadership. It is an example of voluntary communalism, a political system in which a racially or culturally defined group governs itself, makes its own laws, lives according to its own traditions and is ruled by its own elites. In the past, although city mayors did not recognize Chinese jurisdictional rights in Chinatown, they considered the Chinese Consolidated Benevolent Association (CCBA) in Victoria as the legitimate spokesman for all the Chinese, and city police recognized the right of CCBA to regulate criminal matters within Chinatown.

CCBA, created in 1884 by gentry-merchants, had also the support of the Manchu government. It worked for Chinese communities across Canada before a Chinese consulate general was established in Ottawa in 1909. After that year, CCBA continued to run Chinatown as a *de facto* Chinese government in Victoria. It was a structure of defensive adaptation to discrimination and ostracism. The measures of its defending strategies included an authoritarian control over members by gentry-merchants, and an intensive sense of group identification through language, consanguinity, endogamy, and the like. The wealthy merchants provided employment for Chinese labourers or recruited them for work in British Columbia. Hence, the merchant leadership as CCBA directors was a boss-subordinate relationship. The mass of poor Chinese labourers followed the leaders partially because of socio-economic force. In addition, the leaders established the relationship with the group around some common interest, such as protection against discrimination and foreign abuses. They had a magnetism which acted as a cohesive force in social organization of the Chinese community.

CCBA directors set up rules and regulations in Chinatown and acted as a liaison with Western governments. Their charity to Chinese people extended from Canada to China and other parts of the world. Unlike the Six Companies in San Francisco, CCBA had never been accused of usurping the Canadian judicial processes and was tolerated by the host society as an *imperium in imperio*. With the downfall of the Manchu government, CCBA began to lose its oligarchic rule. After the 1910s, clan, county, and other community organizations became important components of Chinatown's social system and their leaders gradually replaced the gentry-merchants as CCBA's board directors. During the Second World War, KMT members relied on the support of the Nationalist government in China and held the reins of control over the Chinese populace. Their centralized authority in Chinatown was legitimized by the need to fight Japan but began to weaken after the war ended and the People's Republic of China was established. The recognition of the People's Republic by Canada in 1970 and by the US in 1979 heralded the demise of KMT influence in CCBA.

Today, CCBA no longer has absolute power over member associations but rather functions as a general policy-making body and coordinator of social and cultural activities in Chinatown. It is still at the top of a loosely structured hierarchy of Chinese associations because its board of directors comprises community leaders from 29 organizations in Chinatown who are most involved in its affairs. Directors still command respect, but they no longer can turn respect into power. However, Chinese Public School Board and Chinatown Housing Society are still their influential bases. They sit on their boards and are virtually an interlocking directorate of these two important institutions.

## The Future

Since 1899, revolutions and political dissension in China have been factors in creating disunity in Chinese communities in Canada: the Chinese Reform Association vs Tong Meng Hui and CKT (1899–1911); right-wing KMT vs left-wing KMT (1926–1927); Resisting Japan KMT and non-resisting KMT (1932–1936); KMT vs CKT (1912–1950s); and the pro-Taiwan vs pro-Beijing supporters (1950–1970s). In addition, Chinese communities today are no longer a unified cultural group in Canada but rather a medley of culturally diversified people: Chinese old-timers, local-born Chinese, Chinese from Hong Kong, Taiwan, and China, Vietnamese Chinese, Malaysian Chinese, and Chinese from other countries.

Chinatown has also changed and ceased to be an isolated enclave of Chinese residents. In Victoria, for example, many Westerners live in and do business in Chinatown. CCBA is not the bulwark for the Chinese community but it will continue to be a primary acculturating agent. It provides a cultural bridge to local-born Chinese children who have grown up in Canada but look Chinese. It also promotes strong social ties and sustains traditional Chinese culture, which emphasizes important collectives such as the family, clan, county or community. The Chinese Public School continues to promote strong adherence to Chinese culture, respect for legal norms and parental supervision, all of which will help lower delinquency among Chinese Canadian youth. CCBA still acts as a soliciting and collecting organization in Chinatown: raising funds for disaster relief in Canada as well as China and other parts of the world. Its supremacy is still based on tradition, although it has no power to dictate policy or issue orders to other Chinese associations. It will maintain its cultural and social activities as a *raison d'etre* of its existence.

Most CCBA board directors have not only established rapport in Chinatown but also belong to the Chinatown populace whom they are expected to guide and serve. Their influence is felt in all kinds of practical matters of daily life. They have the biggest voice and stake in Chinatown affairs. Although CCBA directors are not true representatives of the Chinese populace in Victoria, they are still acknowledged by Chinatown stores and institutions as the official voice. As such they are in a strong position to mobilize the support of Chinatown to events in the host society. The practical importance of this research is that a better understanding of the leadership patterns of CCBA in the past and at present will help improve the interaction between city government and Chinatown populace, and the relationship between the Western and Chinese communities.

Appendices

# Appendices

## A  Glossary of English and Chinese Names

### 1. Personal Names

| | |
|---|---|
| Albert Mar | 馬呈瑞 |
| Bai Chongxi | 白崇禧 |
| Bill Lowe | 劉鴻源 |
| Bill Yee | 余宏榮 |
| Bo Qwun Ko | 保君皥 |
| Cai Tingkai | 蔡廷鍇 |
| Chan Cai | 陳才 |
| Chan Sang Kai | 陳陞階 |
| Chan Tong Ork | 陳棠岳 |
| Chan Yu Tan | 陳耀壇 |
| Chang Hsueh-Liang | 張學良 |
| Chang Tsoo | 張祖 |
| Charles Bo | 劉子達 |
| (alias Loo Gee Guia) | |
| Chen Fengchang | 陳鳳昌 |
| Chen Shuibian | 陳水扁 |
| Chen Yunxu | 陳雲綉 |
| Chiang Kai-shek | 蔣介石 |
| Chow Quong | 周廣 |
| Chue Chuen Lai | 徐全禮 |

| | |
|---|---|
| (alias Chue Lai) | 徐禮 |
| (alias Chue Wai San) | 徐畏三 |
| Chue Lum Fook | 徐林福 |
| Clarence Lee | 李麟祥 |
| Dick Quon | 關發勳 |
| Fan Lee | 李毓芬 |
| Fang Ganqian | 方幹謙 |
| Fang Zhengwu | 方振武 |
| Feng Ziyou | 馮自由 |
| Foon Sien | 黃文甫 |
| (alias Wong Mun Po) | 黃文甫 |
| Fred Chow | 周朝公 |
| Fung Kum Shoong | 馮錦淳 |
| (alias Kum Shoong) | 馮錦淳 |
| Gao Yunshan | 高雲山 |
| Guan Guonuan | 關國煖 |
| Guan Yiunan | 關耀南 |
| Guangxu | 光緒 |
| Guo Songtao | 郭嵩燾 |
| Harry Wong | 黃光大 |
| He Tiehun | 何鐵魂 |
| Ho Nan Hing | 何南興 |
| Hu Hanmin | 胡漢民 |
| Huang Chang | 黃昌 |
| Huang Sic Chen | 黃錫銓 |
| Huang Tsim Hsim | 黃遵憲 |
| Huang Yulin | 黃裕麟 |
| Huang Zhenwei | 黃湊爲 |
| Jiang Guangnai | 蔣光鼐 |
| Kang Yuwei | 康有爲 |
| Ken Quan | 關文堅 |
| Lai Wing Yiu | 黎榮耀 |
| Lee Chong | 李祥 |
| Lee Folk Gay | 李福基 |
| (alias Lee Man Wai) | 李文惠 |
| Lee Hong Yuen | 李鴻元 |
| (alias Lee Hoon Yuen) | |
| Lee Min Sun | 李勉辰 |
| Lee Mong Kow | 李夢九 |
| Lee Sai Fan | 李世播 |

| | |
|---|---|
| Lee Tin Poy | 李天沛 |
| (alias Chuck Lee) | |
| Lee Yick Tack | 李奕德 |
| Lee Yick Wei | 李奕衛 |
| (alias Lee Sui Ting) | 李瑞廷 |
| Lee Ying Chang | 李英燦 |
| Lee Yow Young | 李容佑 |
| Leung Mar | 馬啓亮 |
| Leung Mui Fong | 梁梅舫 |
| Li Gongwu | 李公武 |
| Li Hongqia | 李雄洽 |
| (alias Li Runhua) | 李潤華 |
| Li Hung Chang | 李鴻章 |
| Li Jiguo | 李濟國 |
| Li Mingwan | 李名皖 |
| Li Shifan | 李世瑹 |
| Li Tianshi | 李天實 |
| Li Youyao | 李祐耀 |
| Li Yuen Hung | 李源雄 |
| Li Yugan | 李毓幹 |
| Li Zijing | 李子敬 |
| Li Zongren | 李宗仁 |
| Liang Jiguang | 梁緝光 |
| Liang Qichao | 梁啓超 |
| Lim Bang | 林彬 |
| (alias Lim Lai Bang) | 林禮彬 |
| Lim Fat | 林發 |
| Lim George Yuen | 林佐然 |
| Lin Pao Heng | 林葆恆 |
| Lin Dagu | 林大谷 |
| Lin Zanqing | 林贊卿 |
| Liu Tongchun | 劉同春 |
| Loo Chew Fan | 盧超几 |
| Loo Chock Fan | 盧卓几 |
| Loo Yang Kiu | 盧仰喬 |
| Louie Ming Ha | 雷鳴夏 |
| Lu Yangqiao | 盧仰喬 |
| Lum Doy | 林德鉅 |
| (alias Lum Tak Kui) | |
| Lum Lop Fong | 林立滉 |

| | |
|---|---|
| Luo Chang | 羅昌 |
| Luo Fenglu | 羅豐祿 |
| Luo Yuehu | 駱月湖 |
| Ma Zhanshan | 馬占山 |
| Mar Sau | 馬秀 |
| (alias Mar Sum Ming) | 馬心銘 |
| Mar Yick | 馬奕 |
| Mar Yin Yuen | 馬延遠 |
| Mei Boxian | 梅伯顯 |
| Nelson Lee | 李以業 |
| Nie Ruixing | 聶瑞杏 |
| Owyang King | 歐陽賡 |
| Peng Qiping | 彭啓平 |
| Peter Quan | 關祝唐 |
| Qu Degui | 曲德貴 |
| Quan Yiu Nan | 關耀南 |
| Quong Yuen | 關源 |
| (alias Quong Cum Yuen) | 關錦源 |
| Quan Yuen Yen | 關元恩 |
| Seto Ying Shek | 司徒英石 |
| (alias Seto Mao) | 司徒旄 |
| Shum Moon | 沈滿 |
| Sun Yat Sen | 孫逸仙 |
| Tang Hualong | 湯化龍 |
| Tommy Mar | 馬金衛 |
| Tommy Sum | 沈劍光 |
| Victor Li | 李仁 |
| Wang Bodu | 黃伯度 |
| Wang Chang | 王昌 |
| Wang Ching-wei | 汪精衛 |
| William Woo | 胡翰章 |
| Won Alexander Cumyow | 溫金有 |
| (alias Cum Yow) | |
| Wong Soon Lum | 黃宣琳 |
| Wong Tien Lui | 黃天侶 |
| Wong Wah | 黃華 |
| Wong Yuk Shan | 黃玉珊 |
| Wu Hop Yat | 吳俠一 |
| Wu Minghe | 吳銘賀 |
| Wu Shangying | 吳尙鷹 |

Wu Ziyuan 吳紫垣
Xu Bingzhen 許秉榛
Xu Gongbao 徐公寶
Xue Yuqi 薛毓麟
Ye Huibo 葉惠伯
  (alias Yip On) 葉恩
  (alias Charley Yip Yen)
Yip Sang 葉生
  (alias Yip Chun Tin) 葉春田
You Yongzeng 尤永增
Yu Chaoping 余超平
Yuan Shih Kai 袁世凱
Yuen Fan Fei 阮鵬飛
Zhang Yinhuan 張蔭桓
Zhao Liu 趙六
Zhao Ruizhang 趙瑞彰
Zhao Shan 趙善
Zhao Xi 趙喜
Zhou Guoxian 周國賢
Zhou Jiachao 周家超

## 2. Companies or Stores

Bow Chee Tong 寶芝堂
Boon Yune 寶源
Fook On Wing 福安榮
Fook Yuen 福源
Hip Lung 協隆
Hoon Yuen 鴻元
  (alias Hong Yuan)
Hop Gut 合吉
Hop Wo 合和
  (alias Yang Woo Sang) 人和生
  (alias Yuen Chong) 源昌
Kam Yuen 錦源
King Tyre 乾泰
Kwong Chong 廣昌
Kwong Lee 廣利
Kwong On Lung 廣安隆
Kwong On Tai 廣安泰
Kwong Sang Tai 廣生泰

| | |
|---|---|
| Kwong Tai Chong | 廣泰昌 |
| Kwong Tai Lung | 廣泰隆 |
| Lee Chuck | 聯昌 |
| Quong Man Fung | 廣萬豐 |
| Sam Kee | 森記 |
| Sang Yuen | 生源 |
| Seun Yuen | 信源 |
| Shing Lee | 生利 |
| Sing Lee | 成利 |
| Siu Chong | 兆昌 |
| Tai Chong | 泰昌 |
| Tai Chong Yuen | 泰昌源 |
| Tai Chuen | 泰全 |
| Tai Soong | 泰巽 |
| Tai Yuen | 泰源 |
| Wah Yuen | 華源 |
| Wing Cheong | 永祥 |
| Wing Chong Loong | 永昌隆 |
| Yang Wo Sang | 人和生 |
| Yee Chong Tai | 怡昌泰 |
| Yick Yuen | 益源 |
| Ying Chong Lung | 益昌隆 |
| Yueh Chong Lau | 悅昌樓 |
| Yuen Chong | 源昌 |

## 3. Associations, Societies or Political Parties

| | |
|---|---|
| American Overseas Chinese Anti-Imperialism Union | 美洲華僑反帝國大同盟 |
| Baohuanghui (Chinese Empire Reform Association) | 保皇會 |
| Bing Kung Tong | 秉公堂 |
| Chan Wing Chun Tong | 陳穎川堂 |
| Chau Luen Kon Sol | 昭倫公所 |
| Chee Kung Tong (Chinese Freemasons) | 致公堂 |
| China Defence League | 保衛中國同盟 |
| Chinatown Recreation Club Huabu Kanglehui | 華埠康樂會 |
| Chinese Agricultural Cooperative | 華人農業合作社 |
| Chinese Anglican Church | 華人聖公會 |

| | |
|---|---|
| Chinese Association for Promotion of Aviation | 中國航空建設協會 |
| Chinese Benevolent Association (National Headquarter) | 全加中華總會館 |
| Chinese Canadian Cultural Association (formerly Chinese Canadian Friendship Association) | 華僑聯誼會 |
| Chinese Canadian Mutual Help | 同濟社 |
| Chinese Canadian Veteran Association | 華裔加拿大退伍軍人會 |
| Chinese Cultural Centre | 中國文化中心 |
| Chinese Liberty Fund Association | 華僑勸募救國公債友會 |
| Chinese Methodist Church | 華人美以美會 |
| Chinese Pentecostal Church | 華人神召會 |
| Chinese Presbyterian Church | 華人長老會 |
| Chinese Seniors Activity Centre | 華人耆英會 |
| Chinese Students Athletic Club Huasheng Tiyuhui | 華生體育會 |
| (alias Huaqing Tiyuhui) | 華青體育會 |
| Chinese Trade Association | 中華商會 |
| Chinese Vegetable Peddlers Association | 賣菜同業公會 |
| Chinese United Church | 華人協和會 |
| Chong How Tong (Panyu County) | 昌後堂 |
| Chow Oylin Kung Shaw | 周愛蓮公所 |
| Dart Coon Club | 達權社 |
| Democratic Progressive Party | 民進黨 |
| Diguo Xianzhengdang (Constitution Party) | 帝國憲政黨 |
| (alias Xianzhengdang ) | 憲政黨 |
| Ding On Fang | 定安房 |
| Dong Yuen | 東園 |
| Enping Tongxianhui | 恩平同鄉會 |
| Fook Hing Tong (Xinhui County) | 福慶堂 |
| Fook Yum Tong (Nanhai County) | 福蔭堂 |
| Gee How Oak Tin Association | 至孝篤親會 |
| Gee Tuck Tong | 至德堂 |
| Gongyi Gongsuo | 公一公所 |
| Gongzhai Hui | 公債會 |
| Greenhouse United Association | 玻璃屋聯合會 |

| | |
|---|---|
| Guacai Lianhehui | 瓜菜聯合會 |
| Gum Sing Chinese Musical Club | 金聲音樂社 |
| Guomin Gonghui | 國民公會 |
| Guomin Jiuji Ju | 國民救濟局 |
| Guomin Juanju | 國民捐局 |
| Han Yuen Club | 閒園俱樂部 |
| Hang On Tong (Shunde County) | 行安堂 |
| Hip Sing Tong | 協勝堂 |
| Hip Yee Tong | 協義堂 |
| Ho Lo Kong Tong | 何盧江堂 |
| Hong Fook Tong Charity Association | 恩平同福堂 |
| Hongmen Chouxiang Ju | 洪門籌餉局 |
| Hongmen Juri Xiehui (Hongmen Resisting Japan Association) | 洪門抗日社協會 |
| Hook Sin Tong (Zhongshan County) | 福善堂 |
| Hop Yin Fang | 合英房 |
| Hoy Ping Huiguan | 開平會館 |
| Hoy Sun Ning Yung Benevolent Association | 台山寧陽總會館 |
| Huaqiao Gongsuo | 華僑公所 |
| Huaqiao Juri Jiuguohui (Chinese National Salvation Bureau) | 華僑拒日救國會 |
| Huaqiao Qingnian Lianhehui (Chinese Youth Association) | 華僑青年聯合會 |
| Huaqiao Zonghui | 華僑總會 |
| Jijishe (Sworn Oath Society) | 擊楫社 |
| Jinbiquan | 金幣券 |
| Jinlong Drama Society | 金龍劇社 |
| Jiuguo Gongzhai (Liberty Bonds) | 救國公債 |
| Kacheng Zhonghua Xiehui | 卡城中華協會 |
| Kangri Jiuguohui | 抗日救國軍會 |
| Kong Chow Association | 岡州會館 |
| Kun Ying Fang | 羣奕房 |
| Kuomintang (Chinese Nationalist League) | 國民黨 |
| Kwong Duck Tong | 廣德堂 |
| Kwong Fook Tong (Kaiping) | 廣福堂 |
| Lee's Benevolent Long Sai Tong | 李隴西堂 |

| | |
|---|---|
| Lee Association | 李氏公所 |
| Li Dunzong Gongsuo | 李敦宗公所 |
| Liberty Bond Association | 勝利公債會 |
| Liulong Club (Vagabond Club) | 流浪會 |
| Lok Yuen | 樂園 |
| Lum Sai Hor Tong | 林西河堂 |
| Lung Kong Tin Yee Association | 龍岡親義公所 |
| Maicai Tongye Gonghui (Chinese Vegetable Peddlers Associaiton) | 賣菜同業公會 |
| Mar Gim Doo Tong | 馬紫金堂 |
| Minsheng Reading Room | 民聲閱書報社 |
| Minzhidang (Chinese Freemasons) | 民治黨 |
| Ming Yee Tong | 名義堂 |
| Nan Yang Tong | 南陽堂 |
| Nanhuashun United Association | 南花順聯會 |
| Ning Yung Benevolent Association | 寧陽總會館 |
| On Leung Tong | 安良堂 |
| On Sun Tong | 安順堂 |
| On Yick Tong | 安益堂 |
| Po On Tong (Dongguan County) | 寶安堂 |
| Qiaosheng Shaonian Tuan | 僑生少年團 |
| Sam Yap Society | 三邑同鄉會 |
| Seto Kou Lun Tong | 司徒教倫堂 |
| Shangmen Xiaofan Lianhehui | 上門小販聯誼會 |
| Shengyun Musical Club | 聲韻音樂社 |
| Shi Shi Xuan | 適適軒 |
| Shon Yee Benevolent Association | 鐵城崇義會 |
| Suey Sing Tong | 萃勝堂 |
| Suoy Yuen Tong | 遡源堂 |
| Tong Yan Chung Shan Tong | 湯甄中山堂 |
| Tongyuanhui (Chinese Canadian Club) | 同源會 |
| Tongmenghui | 同盟會 |
| Tsang Sam Sheng Tong | 曾三省堂 |
| Tung Fook Tong (Enping) | 恩平同福堂 |
| United Chinese Merchant Association | 中華商會 |
| Victoria Canada China Friendship Association | 域多利加中友好協會 |

| | |
|---|---|
| Victoria Chinatown Care Centre | 域多利華埠療養院 |
| Victoria Chinatown Lioness Club | 域多利華埠女獅子會 |
| Victoria Chinatown Lions Club | 域多利華埠獅子會 |
| Victoria Chinese Canadian Veterans Association | 域多利華人退伍軍人會 |
| Victoria Chinese Commerce Association | 域多利中華商會 |
| Victoria Chinese Ladies Club | 華人婦女會 |
| Victoria Hong Kong Overseas Chinese Association | 香港旅加華人會 |
| Victoria Junior Lion Club | 幼童醒獅團 |
| Victoria's Chinese Young Girls' Patriotic Society | 華僑少女互助會 |
| UVic Chinese Students Association | 維多利大學中華同學會 |
| UVic Chinese Students and Scholars Association | 維多利亞大學學生學者聯誼會 |
| UVic Chinese Youth Connection | 維多利亞大學華青聯會 |
| Wah Kiu Hong Hoong Gow Gock Woy | 華僑航空救國運動募捐委員會 |
| Wong Kong Har Tong | 黃江夏堂 |
| Wong Sheung Kung Fu Club | 黃相健身會 |
| Wong's Association | 黃氏宗親會 |
| Xieyushu Tang | 謝玉樹堂 |
| Xinning Yee Hing Tong | 新寧餘慶堂 |
| Yang Yang Musical Club | 洋洋音樂社 |
| Yee Fung Toy Tong | 余風采堂 |
| Yee Hing Tong (Taishan County) | 餘慶堂 |
| Yee Hop Fang | 義合房 |
| Yen Wo Company (Hakka natives) | 人和堂 |
| Yesujiao Lianhui (alias Christ Church United Society) | 耶穌教聯會 |
| Yih Lu | 隱廬 |
| Ying On Tong (Zengcheng County) | 仁安堂 |
| Yushan  Fensuo | 禺山分所 |
| Zhaoyi Gongsuo | 昭一公所 |
| Zhonghua Gongdang | 中華工黨 |
| Zhonghua Gongsuo | 中華公所 |
| Zhonghua Huiguan | 中華會館 |
| Zhonghua Qingnianhui | 中華青年會 |
| Zhonghua Zonghuiguan | 中華總會館 |

## 4. Place Names

| | |
|---|---|
| Baoan | 寶安 |
| Beicun | 北村 |
| Bengbu | 蚌埠 |
| Dongguan | 東莞 |
| Enping | 恩平 |
| Guangdong | 廣東 |
| Guangxi | 廣西 |
| Heshan | 鶴山 |
| Huaxian | 花縣 |
| Huang Hua Gang | 黃花岡 |
| Kaiping | 開平 |
| Nancun | 南村 |
| Nanhai | 南海 |
| Panyu | 番禺 |
| Sanyi | 三邑 |
| Shunde | 順德 |
| Siyi | 四邑 |
| Taishan | 台山 |
| Xiangshan | 香山 |
| Xinhui | 新會 |
| Yahu | 鴉湖 |
| Yangjiang | 陽江 |
| Zengcheng | 增城 |
| Zhongshan | 中山 |

## 5. Official Titles and Ranks

| | |
|---|---|
| Collegian of the Imperial Academy of Learning | 例貢生 |
| Imperial-Awarded First Class Sub-Prefect | 欽加同知銜 |
| Imperial-Awarded First Class Sub-Prefect of the First Rank of the Privilege of Wearing Peacock Feather | 欽加一品同知銜賞戴花翎銜 |
| Imperial-Awarded First Class Sub-Prefect of the Fifth Rank | 欽加五品同知銜 |
| Imperial Student of the Expectant of Assistant District Magistrate of Blue Feather of the Fifth Rank | 藍翎五品銜候選縣丞國學生 |
| Lieutenant | 千總銜 |
| Military Merit Award of the White Crystal Button of the Fifth Rank worn on Head Dress | 軍功賞給五品頂戴 |

| | |
|---|---|
| Milky White Crystal Button of the Sixth Rank worn on Head Dress | 六品頂戴 |
| Qinchai Dachen (Imperial Commissioner) | 欽差大臣 |
| Single-eyed Peacock Feather Intendant | 花翎道銜 |
| Sub-District Magistrate of Guangxi | 廣西巡檢 |
| Transparent White Crystal Button of the Fifth Rank worn on Head Dress | 五品頂戴 |
| Zhitai | 制台 |
| Zhushi (Second Class Secretary) | 主事 |

## 6. Other Terms

| | |
|---|---|
| Aiguo Xuetang | 愛國學堂 |
| Commission on Overseas Affairs | 僑務委員會 |
| Fangkou | 房口 |
| Qinge Xiaoxue | 菁莪小學 |
| Lequn Yishu | 樂羣義塾 |
| Liberty Bond | 勝利公債 |
| Lie Sheng Gong (Palace of Sages) | 列聖宮 |
| National Subscription Bureau | 國民捐局 |
| Rixin Bao (alias Sun Bo or Chinese Reform Gazette) | 日新報 |
| Sangquan Ruguo | 喪權辱國 |
| Shantang | 善堂 |
| Shen Shang | 紳商 |
| Tai Hon Kong Bo (Chinese Times ) | 大漢公報 |
| Taipingfang | 太平房 |
| Wa Ying Yat Po | 華英日報 |
| Xinminguo Bao (New Republic) | 新民國報 |
| Yushan Xiaoxue | 禺山小學 |

# B  Presidents of CCBA, 1884–2010

**(1884–1920)    正董事 Zheng Dongshi**

| | |
|---|---|
| 1884 | 李祐芹 (Lee Yau Kain) (alias 李泮池 Lee Poon Chee) |
| | 黃彥豪 (Wong Yin Ho) (alias 黃瑞朝 Wong Soy Chew) |
| 1885 | 李祐芹 (Lee Yau Kain) |
| | 黃彥豪 (Wong Yin Ho) |

| 1886 | 陳鳳昌 (Chen Fengchang) |
|---|---|
| 1887 | 李泮池 (Lee Poon Chee) (alias 李祐芹 Lee Yau Kain) |
| 1888 | 董謙泰 (Tong Him Tai) (alias 董基 Tong Kee) |
| 1889 | 黃玉珊 (Huang Yushan) |
| 1890 | 徐日亭 (Xu Riting) |
| 1891 | 李英三 (Lee Ying San) |
| 1892 | 徐爲經 (Xu Weijing ) |
| 1893 | 黃德臣 (Wong Tuck Son) |
| 1894 | 黃德臣 (Wong Tuck Son) |
| 1895 | 盧仁山 (Lo Yan Shan ) |
| 1896 | 麥乾初 (Mai Qianchu) |
| 1897 | 翟幹臣 (Zhai Ganchen) |
| 1898 | 黃福康 (Huang Fukang) |
| 1899 | 董謙泰 (Tong Him Tai) |
| 1900 | 李瑞庭 (Lee Sui Ting) (alias 李奕衛 Lee Yick Wei) |
| 1901 | 黃錦峯 (Huang Jinfeng) |
| 1902 | 黃錦峯 (Huang Jinfeng) |
| 1903 | 黃錦峯 (Huang Jinfeng) |
| 1904 | 陳雨田 (ChenYutian) |
| 1905 | 翟幹臣 (Zhai Ganchen) |
| 1906 | 黃臻爲 (Huang Zhenwei) |
| 1907 | 李錦周 (Lee Kum Chow) (alias 李棣 Lee Dye) |
| 1908 | 李錦周 (Lee Garm Chau) or (Lee Kam Tao) 李鑑濤 |
| 1909 | 關崇德 (Guan Chongde) |
| 1910 | 周瑞祺 (Zhou Ruiqi) |
| 1911 | 張錫亮 (Zhang Xiliang) |
| 1912 | 張錫亮 (Zhang Xiliang) |
| 1913 | 馬傑端 (Ma Jieduan) |
| 1914 | 周家超 (ZhouJiachao) |
| 1915 | 周家超 (ZhouJiachao) |
| 1916 | 劉子達 (Loo Chee Guia) (alias Charles Bo) |
| 1917 | 鄭慶仰 (Zheng Qingyang) |
| 1918 | 鄭慶仰 (Zheng Qingyang) |
| 1919 | 鄭慶仰 (Zheng Qingyang) |
| 1920 | 鄭慶仰 (Zheng Qingyang) |

**(1921–1937)**　　**正總理 Zheng Zongli**

| 1921 | 張錫 (Zhang Xi) |
|---|---|
| 1922 | 馬谷如 (Ma Guru ) |
| 1923 | 劉光祖 (Lau Kwong Joo) (alias Joseph Hope) |

| 1924 | 羅超然 (Luo Chaoran) |
| 1925 | 趙安國 (Zhao Anguo) |
| 1926 | 李枝 (Li Zhi) |
| 1927 | 林煥有 (Lin Wanyou) |
| 1928 | 張惠滔 (Zhang Huitao) |
| 1929 | 黃耀華 (Huang Yaohua) |
| 1930 | 高雲山 (Gao Yunshan) |
| 1931 | 鍾玉樓 (Zhong Yulou) |
| 1932 | 梁緝光 (Liang Jiguang) resigned |
|      | 李子平 (Li Ziping) |
| 1933 | 黃華挹 (Wong Wah Yip) |
| 1934 | 張惠滔 (Zhang Huitao) |
| 1935 | 李豪伯 (Herbert Lee) |
| 1936 | 執行委員 (Executive Members) |
| 1937 | 執行委員 (Executive Members) |

## (1938–2010)  正主席 / 主席 Zheng Zhuxi / Zhuxi

| 1938 | 鍾玉樓 (Zhong Yulou) |
| 1939 | 鍾玉樓 (Zhong Yulou) |
| 1940 | 執行委員 (Executive Members) |
| 1941 | 執行委員 (Executive Members) |
| 1942 | 李豪伯 (Herbert Lee) |
| 1943 | 李豪伯 (Herbert Lee) |
| 1944 | 李樂天 (Li Letian) |
| 1945 | 周家超 (Zhou Jiachao) |
| 1946 | 關祝華 (Wah Quon) |
| 1947 | 執行委員 (Executive Members) |
| 1948 | 執行委員 (Executive Members) |
| 1949 | 李昌發 (Li Changfa) |
| 1950 | 關祝華 (Wah Quon) |
| 1951 | 余超平 (Yu Chaoping) |
| 1952 | 李業森 (Li Yesen) alias Lee Gan |
| 1953 | 李業森 (Li Yesen) |
| 1954 | 李業森 (Li Yesen) |
| 1955 | 李業森 (Li Yesen) |
| 1956 | 李業森 (Li Yesen) |
| 1957 | 李業森 (Li Yesen) |
| 1958 | 常務委員 (Standing Committee Members) |
| 1959 | 常務委員 (Standing Committee Members) |
| 1960 | 關祝華 (Wah Quon ) |

| 1961 | 關祝華 (Wah Quon) |
| 1962 | 李毓芬 (Fan Lee) |
| 1963 | 李毓芬 (Fan Lee) |
| 1964 | 李惠賢 (Jack Lee) |
| 1965 | 李惠賢 (Jack Lee) |
| 1966 | 李惠賢 (Jack Lee) |
| 1967 | 李惠賢 (Jack Lee) |
| 1968 | 林樹森 (Sam Lam) |
| 1969 | 林樹森 (Sam Lam) (no election) |
| 1970 | 林樹森 (Sam Lam) |
| 1971 | 劉述堯 (Augustine Lowe) |
| 1972 | 劉述堯 (Augustine Lowe) |
| 1973 | 劉述堯 (Augustine Lowe) |
| 1974 | 徐鈞 (Ken Chee) |
| 1975 | 劉炳輝 (Ben Lowe) |
| 1976 | 雷裕騰 (Peter Lou Poy) |
| 1977 | 雷裕騰 (Peter Lou Poy) |
| 1978 | 雷裕騰 (Peter Lou Poy) |
| 1979 | 雷裕騰 (Peter Lou Poy) |
| 1980 | 陳新民 (Philip Chan) |
| 1981 | 雷裕騰 (Peter Lou Poy) |
| 1982 | 劉述堯 (Augustine Lowe) |
| 1983–84 | 劉述堯 (Augustine Lowe) |
| 1985–86 | 劉述堯 (Augustine Lowe) |
| 1987–88 | 周伯昌 (John Joe) |
| 1989–90 | 袁臻榮 (John Yuen) |
| 1991–92 | 袁臻榮 (John Yuen) |
| 1993–94 | 梁肇成 (Joe Leung) |
| 1995–96 | 梁肇成 (Joe Leung) |
| 1997–98 | 陳振沛 (Paul Chan) |
| 1999–00 | 陳振沛 (Paul Chan) |
| 2001–02 | 周步發 (Paul Chow) |
| 2003–04 | 梁肇成 (Joe Leung) |
| 2005–06 | 梁肇成 (Joe Leung) |
| 2007–08 | 黃杰 (Kit Wong) |
| 2009–10 | 黃杰 (Kit Wong) |

# Endnote Abbreviations

AC      Archives of Chinese Consolidated Benevolent Association (Meeting minutes, correspondences, notices etc.) stored in the Archival Library, University of Victoria

AFB      Absolute Fees Book

CCBA      Chinese Consolidated Benevolent Association's Minutes of Monthly Meetings, Annual Report, stored in CCBA's office, Victoria

JLABC      Journal of Legislative Assembly of British Columbia

LRO      Land Registry Office, British Columbia

BCARS      British Columbia Archives and Records Service (formerly Provincial Archives of British Columbia)

SBC      Statutes of British Columbia

SPLABC      Sessional Papers of the Legislative Assembly of British Columbia

# Bibliography

# Bibliography

## Government Documents

British Columbia. Court Registry, Law Courts, Victoria
British Columbia. Land Registry Office, *Absolute Fees Book*
British Columbia. Legislative Assembly, Sessional Papers
British Columbia. Statutes of the Province of British Columbia
Canada. Statutes of Canada
Canada. Censuses of Canada
Canada. Department of Manpower and Immigration. *Immigration Statistics*
Canada. House of Commons. Sessional Papers
Canada. Royal Commission on Chinese Immigration: Report and Evidence, Ottawa, 1885
Canada. Royal Commission on Chinese and Japanese Immigration Report, 1902, *Sessional Papers of the Dominion of Canada*, No. 54, vol. 13, Ottawa, 1902

## City Directories

Henderson's British Columbia Directory and Street Index
Mallandaine's Victoria Directory

## English and Chinese Newspapers

*British Colonist*, Victoria, British Columbia (11 December 1858–28 July 1860), renamed

*Daily British Colonist* (31 July 1860–23 June 1866)
*Daily British Colonist and Victoria Daily Chronicle* (25 June 1866–6 August 1872)
*Daily British Colonist* (7 August 1872–31 December 1886)
*Daily Colonist* (1 January 1887–31 October 1980)
*Daily Times*, Victoria, British Columbia (1884–6 November 1971), renamed
*The Times* (8 November 1971–30 October 1980)
*Times-Colonist*, Victoria, British Columbia (4 Sept. 1980–present)
*Chinatown News*, Vancouver
*Ming Pao Daily*, Vancouver
*Sing Tao Daily*, Vancouver
*Wah Ying Yat Bao* (*Chinese Times*), Vancouver, 1907–September 1910, renamed
*Tai Hon Yat Bo* (*Chinese Times*), Vancouver, October 1910–5 November 1915,
    renamed
*Tai Hon Kong Bo* (*Chinese Times*), 6 November 1915–3 October 1992
*Xinminguo Bao* (*New Republic*), Victoria

## Published or Unpublished Materials in English

Adams, John. *Historic Guide to Ross Bay Cemetery*. Victoria: Heritage Architectural
    Guides, 1983
Brunnert, H.S. and V.V. Hagelstrom. *Present Day Political Organization of China,
    1911*. Taipei: Book World Co., 1911
Burgess, John Stewart. "Community Organization in the Orient," *The Survey*,
    XLVI (1921), 434–6
Cameron, M.E. *The Reform Movement in China, 1898–1912*. New York: Octagon
    Books, 1963
Ceska, Adolf and Oluna. Consultant Report on Wild Flowers in the Chinese
    Cemetery, May 2000
Chen, H.K. "History of Chinese Scouting in Victoria, BC," Vancouver: *Chinatown
    News*, 18 January 1990
Etzioni, Amitai. *Modern Organizations*. New Delhi: Prentice-Hall of India, 1986
Fairbank, John K., Edwin O. Reischauer, and Albert M. Craig. *East Asia: Tradition
    and Transformation*. Boston: Houghton Mifflin Co., 1978
Fallers, L.A., ed. *Immigrant and Associations*. The Hague: Mouton, 1967
Freedman, Maurice. "The Chinese in South-east Asia: A Longer View," *Asian
    Horizon*, 1 (1948), 13–4
Freedman, Maurice. "Immigrants and Associations: Chinese in Nineteenth-
    Century Singapore," *Comparative Study in Society and History*, III (1960), 25–48
Green, James W. and Selz C. Mayo. "A Framework for Research in the Actions of
    Community Groups," *Social Forces*, 31 (1953), 320–7

Hoy, Willliam Edwin. *The Chinese Six Company*. San Francisco: Chinese Consolidated Benevolent Association, 1941

Hillery, George A. Jr. "Definitions of Community: Areas of Agreement," *Rural Sociology*, 20 (1955), 111–23

Huang, Ten-ming. *The Legal Status of the Chinese Abroad*. Taipei: China Cultural Service, 1954

Johnson, Graham E. "Voluntary Associations and Social Change: Some Theoretical Issues," *International Journal of Comparative Sociology*, 16 (1975), 51–63

Lai, Chuen-yan. "The Chinese Consolidated Benevolent Association in Victoria: Its Origins and Functions," *BC Studies*, 15 (1972), 53–67

Lai, Chuen-yan David. "Socio-Economic Structures and Viability of China," in *Residential and Neighbourhood Studies in Victoria*. Ed. C.N. Forward, Western Geographical Series. Victoria, University of Victoria, Department of Geography, 1973, 101–129

Lai, Chuenyan David. "Home County and Clan Origins of Overseas Chinese in Canada in the early 1880's," *BC Studies*, 27 (1975), 3–29

Lai, Chuen-Yan David. "The Demographic Structure of a Canadian Chinatown in the Mid-Twentieth Century," *Canadian Ethnic Studies*, XI, 2 (1979), 49–62

Lai, Chuenyan David. *The Future of Victoria's Chinatown: A Survey of Views and Opinions*, Vol. 1, Recommendations; and Vol. 2, Tabulation of Data, Victoria: City of Victoria, 1979

Lai, David Chuenyan. "The Issue of discrimination in Education in Victoria, 1901–1923," *Canadian Ethnic Studies*, XIX, 3 (1987), 47–67

Lai, David Chuenyan. *Chinatowns: Towns Within Cities in Canada*. Vancouver: University of British Columbia Press, 1988

Lai, David Chuenyan. "From Self-Segregation to Integration: The Vicissitudes of Victoria's Chinese Hospital," *BC Studies*, 80 (winter 1988–89), 52–68

Lai, David Chuenyan. "Shipment of Bones to China," *Likely Cemetery Society's Annual Newsletter*, July 1991, pages unnumbered

Lai, David Chuenyan. *The Forbidden City Within Victoria: Myth, Symbol, and Streetscape of Canada's Earliest Chinatown*. Victoria: Orca Book Publishers, 1991

Lai, David Chuenyan. "The Impact of New Immigration Policies on the Development of New Chinatowns and New Chinese Shopping Plazas in Canada," *Asian Profile*, 28, 3 (2000), 99–116

Lai, H.M. "A Historical Survey of Organizations of the Left Among the Chinese in America," *Bulletin of Concerned Asian Scholars*, Fall (1972), 10–20

Lee, Jack Wai Yen. *The Legacy of Lee Mong Kow Prefecture*. Manuscript, Victoria, 2008

Lewin, Kurt. *Resolving Social Conflicts. Selected Papers on Group Dynamics*. New York: 1948

Li, Peter S. "Chinese Immigrants on the Canadian Prairie, 1910–1947," *Canadian Review of Sociology and Anthropology*, 19 (1982), 527–40

Lockard, Craig A. "Leadership and Power within the Chinese Community of Sawawak: A Historical Survey," *Journal of S.E. Asia Studies*, II, 2 (1971), 195–217

Lyman, Stanford M. "Contrasts in the Community Organization of Chinese and Japanese in North America," *Canadian Review of Sociology and Anthropology*, 5 (1968), 51–67

Macnab, Francis. *British Columbia for Settlers*. London: Chapman and Hall, 1898.

Meade, R.D. "Leadership Studies of Chinese and Chinese Americans," *Journal of Cross-Cultural Psychology*, 1 (1970), 325–32

Meade, R.D. and Whittaker, J.O. "A Cross-Cultural Study of Authoritarianism," *Journal of Social Psychology*, 72 (1967), 3–7

"The Ross Bay Cemetery: Rules and Regulations," *BC Gazette*, 9 August 1873

Price, Charles. "The Study of Assimilation." In *Migration*. Ed. J.A. Jackson. Cambridge: Cambridge University Press, 1969

C.N. Reynolds. "The Chinese Tongs," *American Journal of Sociology*, 40 (1935), 612–623

*Rules and By Laws of the Chinese Consolidated Benevolent Association*. Approved and Filed on 18 August 1884 by Chas. Leggatt, Acting Registrar General

Sanders, Irwin T. "Theories of Community Development," *Rural Sociology*, 23, 1 (1958), 1–12

Schulze, Robert O. "The Role of Economic Dominants in Community Power Structure," *American Sociological Review*, 23 (1958), 3–9

Siegel, Bernard J. "Defensive Structuring and Environmental Stress," *American Journal of Sociology*, 76 (1976), 11–31

Sennett, Richard. *Authority*. New York: Alfred A. Knopf, 1980

Smith, Dan. Consultant report on the geology of the coastal area of the Chinese Cemetery, March 2000

Souvenir program on Chinese Students Athletic Club 20th Anniversary Celebration and Re-Union, 1931–1950, Victoria, 1950, pages unnumbered

Sower, Christopher and Walter Freeman. "Community Involvement in Community Development Programs," *Rural Sociology*, 23, 1 (1958), 24–33

*Victoria Chinese Student Athletic Club Alumni Reunion, 19–20, May 1990*, pages unnumbered

Wickberg, E. *From China to Canada*. Toronto: McClelland and Stewart, 1982

Wickberg, Edgar. "Some Problems in Chinese Organizational Development in Canada, 1923–1937," *Canadian Ethnic Studies*, XI, 1 (1979), 88–98

Willmott, W.E. "The Chinese Clan Associations in Vancouver," *Man*, 64, 49 (1964), 33–7

Willmott, W.E. "Congregations and Associations: the Political Structure of the Chinese Community in Phnom-Penh, Cambodia," *Comparative Studies in Society and History*, 11 (1969), 282–301

Wang, Gungwu. *China and the Chinese Overseas*. Singapore: Times Academic Press, 1991

Wong, Foon Sien. *A Brief for Presentation to the Prime 24, 1950*, 1 (unpublished mimeograph)

Woon, Yuen-fong. "The Non-localized Descent Group in Traditional China," *Ethnology*, 25 (1979), 17–29

Wrong, Dennis H. *Power: Its Forms, Bases and Uses*. New York: Harper and Row, 1979

Wu, Monica. "History of the Chinese Canadian Association of P.E.I.," *Cultures PEI*, 5, 1 (Spring 1990), pages unnumbered

Yen, Ching-hwang. *Coolies and Mandarins Chinese Protection during Late Ch'ing Period*. Singapore: Singapore University Press, 1985

Yen, Ching-hwang. "Ch'ing's Sale of Honours and the Chinese Leadership in Singapore and Malta 1877–1912," *Journal of Southeast Asian Studies*, 1, 2 (September 1970), 20–32

## Published or Unpublished Materials in Chinese

Archives, Chinese Consolidated Benevolent Associations (correspond-ences, circulars, notices etc.), stored in the Archival Library, University of Victoria

Archives, Chinese Consolidated Benevolent Association (Minutes of Monthly Meetings, Annual Reports), stored in the Association's office

*Brief Introduction to Party History*. Victoria: Kuomintang, Victoria Branch, August 1996

Cao, Jianwu. *History of Chee Kung Tong's Revolution to Re-establish the Nation* (Unpublished, 1930), Archives of the Chinese Freemason, Victoria

*Chinese Freemasons Contribution for 140 years, 1863–2003*. Vancouver: Zhongguo Hongmen Minzhidang Headquarters in Canada, 2003

*Chinese Community Handbook*. Toronto: Sing Tao Newspapers (Canada) Ltd., 1987

Lai, Chuenyan. "Origin of the Chinese Benevolent Association (National Headquarters)" *Sing Tao Daily, Vancouver*, 8 November 2003

Circular, An Announcement of a Fund-Raising Campaign for the dual purposes of fighting against the head tax and establishing Zhonghua Huiguan as decided by all the Chinatowns' people, 15th lunar day of 3rd lunar month of the 10th Year of the Reign of Emperor Guangxu (9 April 1884)

*Commemorative Issue of the Grand Opening of the Yue Shan Society Building in Vancouver.* Vancouver: the Yue Shan Society, 1949

*Commemorative Issue of the Golden Anniversary of the Union of Lum Sai Hor Zongtang and Lin Jiumu Gongsuo*, 1980

*Commemorative Issue of the Establishment of the Chinese Consolidated Benevolent Association (1884–1959) and Chinese Public School (1899–1959)*, Victoria: Chinese Consolidated Benevolent Association, 1959

Commemorative Issue of the 70th Anniversary of Shon Yee Benevolent Association of Canada, 1914–1984

Committee to Democratize the CBA, *CBA Issue*, Vancouver, 1978

*Constitution of the Chinese Canadian Association of Kingston and District*, adopted on 30 October 1977 and amended on 5 November 1978

*Huaxie Shizhounian Jiniankan (Embarking on a New Milestone: A Commemorative Issue of the 10th Anniversary of Huaxie), 1977–1987.* Fredericton: The Chinese Cultural Association of New Brunswick, 1988

*Inside the Chinese Benevolent Association: A Report of Some Activities of the Highest Governing Body of the Chinese in Canada.* Vancouver: CBA(NH), 1969

Lai, David Chuenyan. "A Brief History of the Hongmen in Victoria," in *the 34th National Convention of the Chinese Freemasons of Canada Special Issue.* Victoria: Zhongguo Hongmen Minzhidang, Victoria Branch, 2008

Letter, Huang Sic Chen, Second Class Secretary of Consulate General in San Francisco, to Victoria merchants, 4th lunar day of 4th lunar month of the 10th Year of the Reign of Emperor Guangxu (27 April 1884)

Letter, Victoria's merchants to Huang Tsun Hsien, Consul General in San Francisco, requesting for the establishment of a consulate in Canada and Zhonghua Huiguan in Victoria, 2nd lunar month of the 10th Year of the Reign of Emperor Guangxu (March 1884)

Letter, CCBA of Victoria to CBA of Montreal, 18th lunar day of the 5th lunar month, 1914 in *A Volume of CCBA Correspondences and Notices from 1914–1915*

Lee, David T.H. *Overseas Chinese History in Canada.* Vancouver: Canadian Freedom Publisher, 1967

Lee, Hung Yuan. *A Brief Report of the History of the CBA of Manitoba in Canada,* 1989 (unpublished report)

*Special Issue to Commemorate the 75th Anniversary of Victoria's Chinese Consolidated Benevolent Association (1884–1959) and the 60th Anniversary of Victoria's Chinese Public School (1899–1959).* Victoria: Chinese Consolidated Benevolent Association, 1960

*Reminiscence and Expectation of Hongmen History.* Toronto: A Com-memoration of 100th Anniversary of the Establishment of Hongmen Minzhidang, 1894–1994

*Special Issue of the Annual Meeting of Pan-American CBAs.* Vancouver, June 1994, pages unnumbered

*Special Issue of the Third Pan-Canadian National Convention of the Lee Clan, Calgary, 3–5 August 1985.* Calgary: Special Issue Editorial Committee, 1986

*Special Issue of the Chinese Benevolent Association and Edmonton Chinatown Multi-cultural Centre, 1986.* Edmonton: Chinese Benevolent Association of Edmonton, 1986

*Special Issue of Edmonton Chinese Benevolent Association, 1991.* Edmonton: Chinese Benevolent Association of Edmonton, 1991

*Special Issue on the Second National Convention of Taishan People in Canada.* Victoria. May 1975

Suen, Jack. *Financial Statement of Xiacheng Zhonghua Gongsuo, 7 May 1989.* 10 May 1989

Yun, Dai. "Investigation of the Date of the Establishment of CBA in Vancouver," *Special Issue to Commemorate Victoria's Chinese Consolidated Benevolent Association, 1884–1859 and Chinese Public School, 1899–1959* (Victoria: Chinese Consolidated Benevolent Association, 1959) V, pages unnumbered

Zhang, Xinghui. "A Brief History of the Establishment of Canada's Chinese Community Center of Ontario." *The Annual Issue of Canada's Chinese Community Center of Ontario* (Toronto: Canada's Chinese Community Center of Ontario, 1972), 2–4

*Zhongguo Jindaishi Zhishi Shouce* (A Handbook for China's Recent History). Beijing: Zhonghua Bookstore, 1980

# Index

# Index